The Gospel of Matthew Through New Eyes

Volume One:
Jesus as Israel

Peter J. Leithart

ATHANASIUS PRESS
MONROE, LOUISIANA

The Gospel of Matthew Through New Eyes
VOLUME ONE: *Jesus as Israel*
Copyright © 2017 by Athanasius Press
205 Roselawn
Monroe, Louisiana 71201
www.athanasiuspress.org

ISBN: 978-0-9862924-5-3 (softcover)

All rights reserved. No part of this publication may be reproduced, stored in a retrieval system, or transmitted in any form or by any means—electronic, mechanical, photocopy, recording, or any other—except for brief quotations in printed reviews, without the prior permission of the publisher.

This publication contains The Holy Bible, English Standard Version®, copyright © 2001 by Crossway Bibles, a publishing ministry of Good News Publishers. The ESV® text appearing in this publication is reproduced and published by cooperation between Good News Publishers and Athanasius Press and by permission of Good News Publishers. Unauthorized reproduction of this publication is prohibited.

The Holy Bible, English Standard Version (ESV) is adapted from the Revised Standard Version of the Bible, copyright Division of Christian Education of the National Council of the Churches of Christ in the U.S.A. All rights reserved.

English Standard Version®, ESV®, and the ESV® logo are trademarks of Good News Publishers located in Wheaton, Illinois. Used by permission.

Contents

1	INTRODUCTION	5
2	**NEW ISRAEL	MATTHEW 1-4**	43
	Israel and Israel's God - 1:1; 28:18-20	43
	Son of David, Son of Abraham - 1:1-17	50
	Conceived of Mary by the Spirit - 1:18-25	58
	Magi from the East - 2:1-12	66
	God's Plan Unfolding - 2:13-23	73
	John the Baptist - 3:1-17	78
	In the Wilderness - 4:1-11	86
	The Kingdom of Heaven Comes Near - 4:12-25	94
3	**ON THE MOUNTAIN	MATTHEW 5-7**	103
	Sitting to Teach - 5:1-2	103
	Blessings of the Kingdom - 5:1-16	111
	Salt, Light, and the Law - 5:13-20	118
	Anger and Lust - 5:21-30	125
	Marriage and Speech - 5:30-37	133
	Resisting Evil - 5:38-48	141
	Righteousness Before God - 6:1-18	148
	Do Not Be Anxious - 6:19-34	155
	Logs, Dogs, and Pigs - 7:1-12	163
	Standing and Falling - 7:13-29	171
4	**TO THE LOST SHEEP	MATTHEW 8-12**	179
	Bearing our Infirmities - 8:1-2	179
	What Manner of Man? - 8:23-9:17	187
	News - 9:18-38	195
	The Lost Sheep of Israel - 10:1-15	203
	Hated by All - 10:16-33	210
	Not Peace but a Sword - 10:34-11:1	217
	The Greatest Prophet - 11:1-19	224
	The Yoke of Jesus - 11:20-30	232
	The Sabbath - 12:1-21	239
	The Spirit and Satan's Kingdom - 12:22-37	248
	Sign of Jonah - 12:38-50	257

1

INTRODUCTION
The Typological Structure of Matthew's Gospel

Discussions of the structure of Matthew typically begin with a lament that scholars have reached no consensus concerning the structure of Matthew. My analysis is no exception. Chiastic outlines have been proposed,[1] and there are clear hints of *inclusio*.[2] M. D. Goulder's intricate liturgical-midrashic treatment

---

1. For a survey of chiastic approaches, see David R. Bauer, *The Structure of Matthew's Gospel: A Study in Literary Design* (JSNT Supplement #31; Sheffield: Almond Press, 1989), pp. 36-40. See Charles Lohr, "Oral techniques in the Gospel of Matthew," *CBQ* (1961), pp. 403-435, esp. pp. 427-431. The most elaborately defended chiastic outline is that of James B. Jordan, *The End of the World: A Commentary on Matthew 23-25* (Niceville, FL: Biblical Horizons), pp. 7-13. Other studies have discovered chiasms in smaller portions of the gospel: Daniel Boerman, "The Chiastic Structure of Matthew 11-12," *CTJ* 40 (2005), pp. 313-25; David McClister, "Literary Structure as a Key to Meaning in Matt 17:22-20:19," *JETS* (1996), pp. 549-58; John Paul Heil, "The Narrative Structure of Matthew 27:55-29:20," *JBL* 110 (1991), pp. 419-438.

2. For instance: The name "Mary," used twelve times in the gospel, appears only once (13:55) between chapters 2 and 27. The gift of a rich tomb recalls the gifts of the magi at Jesus' birth. Herod's efforts to eliminate Jesus as a rival

fascinates but does not persuade.³ Recently, several scholars have applied narratological analysis to sketch the plot structure of Matthew,⁴ but narrative analyses suffer, as Christopher Smith has pointed out, from the fact that *nothing much happens* during long stretches of Matthew's gospel.⁵ Among the most popular schemes is that of B. W. Bacon, who proposed that the gospel was organized around five books, each of which consists of narrative and an extended discourse.⁶ Bacon's theory has its defenders,⁷ and some, building on Bacon, have seen a typological re-writing of the Hexateuch in Matthew's five-book pattern.⁸ Bacon's

---

king are matched by Pilate's willingness to impede the spread of the message of resurrection, and the death of the innocents at the beginning of the book finds a striking analogy in the death of innocent Jesus. Many have noted the contrasting parallelism between the "blessings" of the Beatitudes and the "woes" of Matthew 23.

3. M. D. Goulder, *Midrash and Lection in Matthew* (Eugene: Wipf & Stock, 1974).

4. Frank J Matera, "The Plot of Matthew's Gospel," *CBQ* 49 (1987), pp. 233-53; Warren Carter, "Kernels and Narrative Blocks: The Structure of Matthew's Gospel," *CBQ* 54 (1992), pp. 463-81; Dale Allison, "Structure, Biographical Impulse, and the *Imitatio Christi*," in Allison, *Studies in Matthew: Interpretation Past and Present* (Grand Rapids: Baker, 2005), ch. 7; Ulrich Luz, *Studies in Matthew* (Grand Rapids: Eerdmans, 2005), ch. 11; Mark Allan Powell, "Toward a Narrative-Critical Understanding of Matthew," *Interpretation* (1992), pp. 341-346.

5. Christopher R. Smith, "Literary Evidences of a Fivefold Structure in the Gospel of Matthew," *NTS* 43 (1997), p. 541.

6. Bacon elaborated his theory in *Studies in Matthew* (London: Constable and Company, 1930), esp. pp. 145-261.

7. Allison, "Structure, Biographical Impulse, and the *Imitatio Christi*," pp. 136-138; George Wesley Buchanan, *Typology and the Gospel* (Lanham, MD: University Press of America, 1987), p. 40; Christopher R. Smith, "Literary Evidences," pp. 540-51; N. T. Wright, *The New Testament and the People of God* (London: SPCK, 1992), pp. 384-390.

8. See Austin Farrer, *St. Matthew and St. Mark* (2d. ed.; Westminster: Dacre Press, 1966), ch. XI; Buchanan, *Typology*, pp. 40-57; Buchanan, *The Gospel of Matthew* (2 vols; Mellen Biblical Commentary; Watson E. Mills, gen ed.; Lewiston, NY: Mellen Biblical Press, 1996), *passim*.

proposal has been criticized on a number of points,[9] but neither Jack Kingsbury's minimalist structure[10] nor any alternative has won general acceptance.

In this introduction, I offer yet another analysis of Matthew's structure that combines some of Bacon's insights with Dale Allison's more recent work on the Mosaic typology of Matthew. I first offer a brief defense of some of Bacon's suggestions, and a brief interaction with Allison's work. Then, I will survey the gospel to show that Matthew organized his account of the life of Jesus as an Irenaean recapitulation of Israel's history, in which Jesus replays both major individual roles of that history (Moses, David, Solomon, Elisha, Jeremiah) as well as the role of the nation herself.[11]

---

9. For summaries of the criticisms, see Dale C. Allison, Jr., *The New Moses: A Matthean Typology* (Minneapolis: Fortress, 1993), pp. 293-298; Bauer, *Structure*, pp. 27-35.

10. Jack Dean Kingsbury, *Matthew: Structure, Christology, Kingdom* (Philadelphia: Fortress, 1975), ch. 1. Allison deftly summarizes the case against Kingsburg in "Structure, Biographical Impulse, and the *Imitatio Christi*," p. 136, most devastatingly in the comment that a structural analysis should provide some more illuminating conclusion than that a narrative has a beginning, middle, and end.

11. Though I have not found any scholars who develop this theme as I have done, I make no claim to originality for my fundamental thesis. See Robert Horton Gundry, *The Use of the Old Testament in St Matthew's Gospel: With Special reference to the Messianic Hope* (Leiden: Brill, 1975), p. 210. M. D. Goulder's suggestion (*Midrash and Lection*, p. 233) that Matthew's genealogy sketches the whole of the gospel as a repetition of Israel's history is even closer to my theory.

INTRODUCTION

I.

Bacon suggested that the gospel was structured by an alternating pattern of narrative and discourse, which combine to form five "books." Bacon's point was in part redactional, emphasizing that Matthew modified Mark in order to show that "the chief duty of the twelve" was "to be 'scribes made disciples to the kingdom of heaven,'" sent to teach the world to follow Jesus' commandments. Matthew was "unmistakably . . . of Jewish origin and training, with unbounded reverence for the Law." Torah consists of five books, each of which includes a "body of law introduced by a narrative of considerable length," which narrate Yahweh's "signs and wonders," and Matthew recapitulates this order in his gospel. Matthew was a "'converted rabbi, a Christian legalist,'" whose revision of Mark provided a "Compend of the Commandments of Jesus" under the headings of "Filial Righteousness" (Matthew 5-7), "Duty of Evangelists" (Matthew 10), "Mystery of the Kingdom" (Matthew 13), "Duty of Church Administrators" (Matthew 18), and "Preparedness for the Coming" (Matthew 23-25).[12] Matthew designed his gospel in this fashion as part of an anti-Jewish polemic and a Christian apologetic.[13]

Several of the criticisms of Bacon's analysis are cogent. His decision to label Matthew 1-2 "Prologue" and chapters 26-28 "Epilogue" is not cogent, since both are deeply integrated into Matthew's gospel story: Without a miraculous birth and a resurrection, the story of Jesus has little interest. Further, the lines between "narrative" and "discourse" are not as neat as Bacon assumes, and when Bacon suggests that each book of the Pentateuch alternates between narrative and "legal" material one wonders when he last glanced at Genesis. Nor, despite ingenious efforts to show otherwise, are there any obvious parallels between Jesus' discourses and the specific books of the Pentateuch:

---

12. Bacon, *Studies*, pp. 80-82.

13. Bacon, *Studies*, p. xvi.

Introduction

The Sermon on the Mount is closer to Exodus and Leviticus than to Genesis, the parables of the kingdom have no obvious connection to Leviticus, and the discourse on forgiveness and church discipline in Matthew 18 is not evidently a Christological rewriting of the book of Numbers. Other criticisms land only glancing blows. Kingsbury's suggestion that chapter 23 must be a separate discourse from 24-25 because of the change of location at 24:1, 3 is specious.[14] No one, including Kingsbury, doubts that chapter 13 constitutes a single discourse, since the parable genre and the substantive concern with the "kingdom" runs through the entire chapter, yet Jesus moves from the boat to the house at 13:36.

Bacon's fundamental insight that Matthew, in contrast to the other synoptics, gathers Jesus' teaching into large "blocks" of teaching withstands these criticisms. That this was a deliberate device is evident from the repetition of the concluding (or "transitional") formula (7:28-29; 11:1; 13:53; 19:1; 26:1-2). Repetition as a structuring device is common in the Old Testament,[15] and given Matthew's evident immersion in the Hebrew Scriptures, it is entirely plausible that he would have borrowed this literary device, just as he cites Old Testament texts as prophetic types of Jesus. That Matthew employed this formula five times to mark off five sections of teaching also provides evidence that Matthew intended the structure of his gospel to underscore his theme that Jesus is the fulfillment of Torah (and of all the Scriptures).[16]

---

14. Kingsbury, *Matthew*, pp. 4-5.

15. In the narrative, see the "evening/morning" repetition of Gen 1, and, more broadly, the various formulae invoking "generations" that structure Gen as a whole (2:4; 5:1; 10:1; 11:10; etc.). Lev. 8 employs a "compliance formula" ("as Yahweh commanded Moses") to structure the account of Aaron's ordination. In legal texts, see "and Yahweh spoke to Moses, saying" that structures the tabernacle texts in Exodus 25-31 as a series of seven speeches that recapitulate the words of creation (25:1; 30:11, 17, 22, 34; 31:1, 12). Prophetic texts are structured by "thus says Yahweh" or "oracle of Yahweh."

16. Allison downplays the significance of the numerology by referring to the Jewish and Christian convention of organizing books into five sections (among

Introduction

The value of Bacon's five-discourse structure is most evident when integrated with Matthew's typological hermeneutic, as examined in Dale Allison's richly detailed, deeply researched, and theoretically sophisticated study, *The New Moses*.[17] Allison's thesis is compelling. Typology is clearly central to Matthew's presentation of Jesus. Yet Allison does not, and does not intend to, provide an overall scheme for Matthew. The closest he comes is the suggestion that "the passages in which Moses' tacit presence is the strongest display an order which mirrors the Pentateuch." He makes the point with the following chart:

Matthew	The Pentateuch	
1-2	Exodus 1:1-2:10	infancy narrative
3:13-17	Exodus 14:10-13	crossing of water
4:1-11	Exodus 16:1-17:7	wilderness temptation
5-7	Exodus 19:1-23:33	mountain of lawgiving
11:25-30	Exodus 33:1-23	reciprocal knowledge of God
17:1-9	Exodus 34:29-35	transfiguration
28:16-20	Deuteronomy 31:7-9 Joshua 1:1-9[18]	commissioning of successor

---

others, the Psalter, *Jubilees*, the Megilloth), as well as the conventions of five-act plays and three-volume novels, but he admits that "some of the books I have cited should perhaps be regarded as imitators of the Pentateuch's structure" (*New Moses*, pp. 296-97, including fn. 19).

17. I will take it as given that the writers of the New Testament employed a "typological" hermeneutics in their reading of the New Testament. On this, see G. W. H. Lampe. "The Reasonableness of Typology," in Lampe and K. J. Woollcombe, *Essays on Typology* (Studies in Biblical Theology; London: SCM, 1957), pp. 9-38; Richard M. Davidson, *Typology in Scripture: A study of hermeneutical TUPOS structures* (Andrews University Seminary Doctoral Dissertation Series; Berrien Springs, MI: Andrews University Press, 1981). Less reliable, but still convincing in its main points, is Buchanan, *Typology and the Gospel*, pp. 1-39.

18. *New Moses*, p. 268.

Striking as some correspondences may be, Allison himself is hesitant to make "too much of this common sequence" because many passages are "out of order,"[19] yet he argues that "there is a rough chronological agreement between certain events in the life of Jesus and their typological cousins in the Tanakh, and it is not trivial."[20] One may agree with Allison's comparatively modest claims for his overview, and still find it tantalizingly inadequate as a way of explaining Matthew's ordering of his gospel. Half of the strongly Mosaic passages are exhausted by the end of Matthew 7, strongly Mosaic passages are scattered throughout the book, and large sections do not come into Allison's purview at all. Besides, Bacon's "five discourse" structure fits uneasily in this outline. It would seem that an evangelist who wanted to structure his gospel according to the chronology of the Pentateuch could have done so more straightforwardly. Strong as the Mosaic typology is in Matthew, therefore, it does not seem adequate to account for the gospel's overall architecture.

Allison himself provides data that supports a more compelling solution. He finds allusions to various passages in Deuteronomy in the closing section of the Sermon on the Mount,[21] suggests that the "transitional formula" first used in 7:28-29 echoes Deuteronomy 31:1, 24; 32:45,[22] and notes verbal and conceptual links between Matt 9:35-38 and Numbers 27:15-17 ("sheep without a shepherd") that point to connections between Jesus' commissioning of the twelve and Moses' commissioning of Joshua (Matthew 10:1-3 with

---

19. He cites Matt 14:13-22 and 15:29-39, linked with manna; Matt 21:1-17, which alludes to Moses' return to Egypt on a donkey, Exodus 4:20; and Matt 26:17-25, which combines allusions to Passover and the covenant-making rite of Exodus 24 (*New Moses*, p. 268). These exceptions are not fatal to Allison's point, since the Mosaic resonances of all these passage are, in his judgment, comparatively faint.

20. *New Moses*, p. 268.

21. *New Moses*, pp. 190-191.

22. *New Moses*, pp. 192-194

Numbers 27:18).²³   Matthew 10:1-3, in fact, conflates Numbers 27:18 with Numbers 13:1. From the latter it borrows "sending" (αποστελον in both the LXX and Matthew), while from the former it borrows conferral of authority (LXX: δοξα; Matthew εξουσια). The twelve disciples-made-apostles are "spies" who see that the land can be conquered despite Satan's presence and mastery; they are also "Joshuas" in their authority and faithfulness.

These hints suggest the possibility that the "Pentateuchal" section of Matthew's gospel concludes somewhere near chapter 10, and from that point we move from a Moses/Exodus typology into a Joshua/conquest typology. Given the fact that Joshua is himself typologically similar to Moses,²⁴ it is not surprising that traces of Mosaic typology continue into chapter 10, but these traces become fainter because Matthew has brought another typology to the forefront and allowed the Mosaic typology to recede to the background.²⁵

---

23. *New Moses*, pp. 213-217. Allison considers these allusions fairly feeble: "the presence of a Moses typology in Matthew 10 is not forcibly felt, and it may not be there at all" (p. 217).

24. See *New Moses*, pp. 23-28, and most commentaries on the book of Joshua.

25. Nor is it surprising that Mosaic typology lingers in sections where Jesus is being described as a new David or Jeremiah, since both these, and many others, are already described typologically as "new Moses" figures within the Old Testament. Cf. Goulder, *Midrash and Lection*, p. 228. Allison himself spends a good portion of his book examining the Mosaic typology within the Old Testament, and so it is surprising that he largely leaves this multi-layered Moses behind when he turns to Matthew.

Introduction

As Matthew's story moves on, he makes similar transitions at various points, moving sequentially through the history of Israel with the five discourses, and the surrounding narrative, marking out major periods of Israel's history.[26] This suggestion accounts more fully for the structure of Matthew than any alternative proposals yet made.[27]

---

26. I am not claiming that these sections are neatly sealed off from one another. Jesus is identified as a "son of David" in 1:1, long before Matthew reaches Jesus' recapitulation of the Davidic kingdom. Yet, typological references from different parts of the Old Testament cluster together, and mark out a sequence that runs throughout the gospel.

27. Christopher Smith's ("Literary Evidences") defense of Bacon's thesis and criticism of narrative approaches are welcome, but his argument fails at a number of points. Part of his "literary" evidence for five discourses is the observation that all but one discourse begins as well as ends with a stylized formula. The formula includes a reference to Jesus sitting, the disciples coming to Him, and a reference to the crowds. The exception is the discourse in 10:1, which covers the approach of the disciples by including Jesus' command to the disciples to gather to Him. Chapter 13, likewise, does not begin with this formula; the disciples do not approach Him until 13:10, but that is appropriate since it initiates a "new beginning" of the discourse, now in the house with the disciples only. This becomes problematic when, based on this, Smith claims that the last discourse does not begin until Matt 24, but if the "opening formula" is broken in two in ch. 13, there does not seem to be any reason it could not be delayed to the middle of the final discourse. Further, he argues that narratives introduce the discourses, and that each narrative contains a theme that is picked up in the following discourse. Thus, for instance, the issue of Jesus' authority comes up in chapters 8-9, and this keyword is employed at the beginning of the mission discourse in chapter 10. But this is quite arbitrary: There are numerous verbal and conceptual links between chapters 8-9 and chapter 10, and the issue of authority, as Smith acknowledges, has already come up before chapters 8-9 (cf. 7:29). Why then is "authority" the unifying keyword rather than "demon" or "leper" or "heal" or any number of common terms and themes? Similarly, he characterizes the fourth discourse, chapter 18, as concerned with the "family of the kingdom," but also says that 12:46-50 is the "best introduction to this discourse," even though that passage – introducing the theme of the *fourth* discourse – comes before the *third* discourse. Most fundamentally, Smith's article does not account for Matthew's own agenda because Smith employs the categories of contemporary narrative theory, rather than the categories Matthew himself would have employed – such as typology.

Introduction

II.

The early chapters of Matthew provide *prima facie* evidence of the plausibility of this scheme. First, the sequence of events in Matthew 1-7 closely mimics the sequence of the Pentateuch. Matthew begins his gospel with an overt quotation from the LXX of Genesis: He is writing the βιβλος γενεσεως of Jesus, just as Genesis records the βιβλος γενεσεως of heaven and earth (Genesis 2:4) and of Adam (5:1). Matthew follows with a genealogy, like the numerous genealogies of Genesis (4:16-26; 5:1-32; 10:1-32; 11:10-32; 36:1-43),[28] and recounts a miraculous birth (cf. Isaac, Jacob) to a dreamer named Joseph.[29] Israel has become an Egypt, her king the child-slaying Herod, and Jesus has to escape "by night" (cf. Exodus 12:30) to safety, an event that Matthew sees as a fulfillment of a passage from Hosea that speaks of the exodus (Matthew 2:15; Hos. 11:1). After his water-crossing in baptism (3:13-17), He is tempted in the wilderness for forty days, where He quotes from passages referring to Israel's forty-year sojourn (4:1-11). Ascending a mountain, He instructs His disciples in the righteousness that surpasses that of the scribes and Pharisees (Matthew 5-7), laying before Israel the choice between life and prosperity, death and disaster, a choice

---

28. Only Chronicles devotes so much space to genealogies as Genesis, and it is likely that Matthew is also consciously imitating the Chronicler. For now, simply note that both Matthew and the Chronicler give genealogies that move to the post-exilic period.

29. Cf. Goulder, *Midrash and Lection*, pp. 235-239. The original Joseph ben Jacob is associated with three sets of dreams: He had his own dreams of supremacy over his brothers (Gen 37:5-11), and interpreted dreams for the baker and cup-bearer (40:1-23) and Pharaoh (41:1-36). Matthew's Joseph (also ben Jacob, 1:16) has three dreams (1:20; 2:13, 19). Likewise, the original Joseph brings his family to Egypt, where they find food and safety, as does the later Joseph.

between maintaining their "house" and seeing it dismantled by a rising "river" (cf. Isaiah 8).[30] Schematically, the opening chapters follow the Pentateuch as follows:

Matthew	Old Testament
1:1: Book of Genesis	Genesis 2:4; 5:1
1:1-17: son of Abraham	Genesis 12-26
1:18-25: Joseph the dreamer	Genesis 37
2:1-12: Magi	Nations to Egypt for Joseph; promise to Abraham
2:13-15: Herod kills children	Exodus 1-2: Pharaoh kills children
2:14: Jesus rescued, flees	Exodus 2: Moses rescued, flees
2:19-23: Jesus returns to Israel	Exodus 3-4: Moses returns to Egypt
3:1-12: John announces judgment	Exodus 5-12: Moses/Aaron bring judgment
3:13-17: Jesus passes through waters	Exodus 16: exodus
4:1-11: temptation in wilderness	Exodus 17-19: Israel tempted
4:18-22: Jesus calls disciples	Exodus 18: Moses appoints rulers
chs. 5-7	Sinai and the giving of Torah

Much of this is old hat, and so self-evident that even scholars who resist typological interpretation have a hard time ignoring it. What is often missed, however, is what this implies about the logic of Matthew's typology. Though there are certainly "Mosaic" dimensions to the typology throughout these chapters, the typological thread that provides the continuity is overwhelmingly Jesus-as-*Israel*.[31] Matthew 1:1-17 does not mention Moses, and its

---

30. I agree with N. T. Wright's suggestion that the "house" in view in 7:24-27 is the temple, and this suggests an important chiastic link with Jesus' Olivet Discourse describing the temple's destruction.

31. This point is emphasized by W. F. Albright, *Matthew: A New Translation with Introduction and Commentary* (Anchor Bible #26; New York: Doubleday, 1971), p. 18. Unfortunately, Albright sets this Israel typology in opposition to a "new Moses" typology, which is wholly unnecessary since Moses is the representative Israel.

allusions to Genesis draw on the pre-Mosaic history of the people. Jesus is "son of Abraham" (1:1), who is the father of Israel (Romans 4:1) and not the father of Moses. Though Allison is probably right to discern some hints of Mosaic typology in Matthew's birth narrative, the emphasis on Joseph's role keeps the later chapters of Genesis firmly in mind. Mosaic typology becomes stronger in chapter 2, but even here Jesus is as much Israel as Moses — He does not lead a people out of Egypt-Israel, but is an infant taken, like the surviving firstborn sons of Israel, out of the land.[32] All Israel is baptized in the sea (cf. 1 Corinthians 10:1-4), and all Israel is tempted in the wilderness. When He teaches from the mountain, He is surely a Mosaic figure, but He is also much more, for He does not deliver words from Yahweh but speaks with an apparently underived authority (7:29).

Not only does Matthew repeatedly treat Jesus as the embodiment of the nation, but the sequence of Matthew's narrative follows the order of Old Testament history quite exactly. A few pericopes, to be sure, are more loosely connected to this typological sequence (e.g., John's ministry, 3:1-13), but all the sections that are evidently typological are arranged in the same order they are found in the Old Testament. Matthew 1-7 is the most obviously typological section of his gospel, and if in this section Matthew follows a Jesus-as-Israel typology that is, in its general outlines, chronologically arranged, it is plausible that he would continue that typology straight through.

My second piece of *prima facie* evidence is Matthew 2:15. The precise import of Matthew's use of Hosea is debated and difficult to establish. Whatever the precise nuances, however, one thing

---

32. In some respects, the Mosaic typology in fact works more smoothly for the whole gospel if we understand Matthew 2 not as a reference to the exodus but as a reference to Joseph's move to Egypt or as a typological retelling of Moses' escape to Midian. Judea is the Egypt of Matthew 2, and Jesus withdraws to the "Midian" of Galilee for much of the book, until he returns to "Egypt" in chapter 21, to offer Himself as the Passover Lamb. From this perspective, the "exodus" does not begin until Jesus sends His disciples out of Egypt following His great Passover sacrifice.

is evident: Matthew identifies the "Son" of Hosea 11:1 with Jesus, and Hosea 11:1 is talking about Israel. Were we looking for proof texts, here it is: As R. T. France says, "Matthew's quotation ... depends for its validity on the recognition of Jesus as the true Israel," and notes that Matthew 4 also equates Jesus and Israel through the use of the title "Son."[33] I am far from convinced by Kingsbury's argument that Matthew presents a predominantly "Son of God" Christology, but to the extent that he does, 2:15 indicates that a "Jesus as Israel" Christology is an integral part of any "Sonship" Christology.

In addition to the evidence to be culled from the early chapters of Matthew, the overall arc of Matthew's plot provides a final piece of *prima facie* evidence. Matthew's opening line, we have seen, is quoted directly from the early chapters of Genesis, and Matthew 1 is largely occupied with a numerologically shaped genealogy for Joseph. Matthew clearly begins with echoes of Genesis. At the conclusion of His gospel, Jesus, now endowed with all authority in heaven and earth, commissions His disciples to "Go" to the Gentiles. According to the Massoretic organization, the Hebrew Bible ends with a similar commission, the decree of Cyrus. Cyrus, having received "all the kingdoms of the earth" from Yahweh, God of heaven, commissions Israel to "go up" ($\alpha\nu\alpha\beta\eta\tau\omega$) to Jerusalem to rebuild the temple (2 Chronicles 36:23). In both Matthew 28:18-20 and 2 Chronicles 36:23, we have the following sequence:

    Statement regarding universal authority
        Statement regarding the source of authority
            Commission to "go"

---

33. R. T. France, *Matthew* (Tyndale New Testament Commentaries; Leicester: InterVarsity, 1985), p. 85.

Introduction

Jesus is greater than Cyrus, having received authority in *heaven* as well as earth from His Father, and in the light of that authority he commissions His disciples to "go" (πορευθεντες). Matthew's gospel begins like Genesis and ends like Chronicles, and thus encompasses the entirety of the Hebrew canon.³⁴

III.

Examination of the discourses themselves provides further evidence that Matthew organizes his entire history around the history of Israel. The connections between Jesus' sermon on the mount and the revelation at Sinai are widely recognized, and need not be developed here. As I have suggested above, the second discourse (Matthew 10) begins with a complex of allusions to the twelve spies of Numbers 13 and the commissioning of Joshua as Moses' successor. Jesus' observation that Israel is "distressed and downcast like sheep without a shepherd" (Matthew 9:36), a phrase that occurs near the end of Numbers (27:18), motivates the commissioning, and this suggests a situational analogy between the discourse of Matthew 10 and Moses' sermons to Israel in Deuteronomy: Like Moses, Jesus instructs the heads of a new Israel about their duties when they enter the land.

---

34. This hints at a second analogy between Matthew and Chronicles: Chronicles begins with a genealogy and ends with a commission, and Matthew does the same. On Cyrus as a type of the Messiah, see Isa. 44:28, where Cyrus is pictured as a new Mosaic shepherd who will lead Israel through a dried-up sea; and 45:1, where Cyrus is explicitly described as the "anointed" of Yahweh who "subdues nations before him" and causes kings to shit in their britches. In response to lecture on this topic, James Jordan suggested caution about this canonical argument, pointing out that the order of the Old Testament canon is far from secure and that Ezra and Nehemiah might have been part of an original "Greater Chronicles." Even with this caveat, Matthew still encompasses the history of the world from creation to restoration.

INTRODUCTION

Jesus treats the mission of the Twelve as a quasi-military operation. The apostles are "sheep in the midst of wolves" (10:16), and should expect to face persecution and rejection (10:17, 23). Their ministry will create turmoil among their hearers, turning brother against brother and children against parents (10:21, 35-36). To fulfill their mission, the Twelve need to act with courage, trusting their Father and fearing God rather than man (10:28-29). Jesus announces that he has come to bring a "sword" rather than peace (10:34), and demands a total commitment from His disciples, including a willingness to die for His sake (10:37-39). In exhorting His apostles "Do not fear," Jesus is repeating the words of Moses and Joshua to Israel before the conquest (Numbers 14:9; 21:34; Deuteronomy 1:21; 3:2, 22; 31:8; Josh 8:1; 10:8, 25). The discourse anticipates that some will receive the Twelve, and promises that those who do will, like Rahab, receive a reward (10:40-42). Of course, this conquest is quite different from the original conquest. It is a conquest of liberation and life – the sick healed, dead raised, lepers cleansed, demons conquered (10:8). If this is *herem* warfare, it is directed not against Canaanites, but against Satan and His demons, a *herem* war like that of Elisha. Like Moses, Jesus instructs and sends the Twelve into the land but does not accompany them (Matthew 11:1).

The third discourse has multiple links to the wisdom literature and to Solomon in particular. Jesus begins to speak in "parables," a word first used in 13:3, and used twelve times in the chapter.[35] The LXX employs παραβολη to translate the Hebrew *mashal*, a wisdom term that can be used both of pithy two-line proverbs and extended allegorical narratives.[36] In this chapter above all Jesus employs a wisdom "genre" associated with Solomon.

---

35. The only other uses of the word are in Matthew 15:15; 21:33, 45; 22:1; 24:32. Chapter 13 is, at least in terms of the distribution of the term, *the* chapter of parables.

36. See Hauck, "παραβολη," in *Theological Dictionary of the New Testament* (10 vols.; Gerhard Kittel and Gerhard Friedrich, eds.; Geoffrey W. Bromiley, trans.; Grand Rapids: Eerdmans, 1967), vol. 5, pp. 747-751.

Introduction

Immediately after Jesus finishes his parabolic teaching, he goes to His home country to teach, and the people are astonished at His "wisdom" (13:54). Apart from this reference, "wisdom" is used only in 11:19 and 12:42, the latter a reference to the wisdom of Solomon that so impressed the queen of Sheba. Not only the form but the sapiential content of Jesus' teaching in Matthew 13 is associated with Solomon. Finally, Jesus' parables reveal, for those with ears to hear, the mysteries of the "kingdom of heaven" (13:11), and many of the parables are metaphors of the kingdom (13:24, 31, 33, 44, 45, 47). Though the terminology of the kingdom is widely distributed throughout the gospel, chapter 13 most thoroughly describes the dynamics, future, and demands of the kingdom of heaven.[37]

Skipping Matthew 18 for the moment, we turn to the fifth discourse, which includes both Jesus' polemic against the scribes and Pharisees and His eschatological discourse concerning the temple and Jerusalem (Matthew 23-25). Jesus acts as a prophet in the tradition of Jeremiah and Ezekiel, so that this discourse corresponds to the prophetic works that emerged latter days of the kingdom of Judah. Jesus, like Jeremiah, engages in verbal combat with the priests and leaders of His time, and gives an extended prophecy concerning the destruction of the temple by the Romans.[38] Rhetorically, Jesus' style is very similar to the style of Old Testament prophets. Chapter 23 contains Jesus' most extended and intense condemnation of scribes, Pharisees, and hypocrites, in which He declares eight woes that contrast to the eight Beatitudes of chapter 5. No setting is explicit, but the narrative indicates that this speech takes place in the temple: Jesus arrives in the temple in 21:23, tells parables and engages in debate,

---

37. Goulder (*Midrash and Lection*, p. 364, 388) links Matthew 13 with the harvest feast of tabernacles, which was the setting for the temple dedication in 1 Kings 8.

38. I am convinced that Matthew 24 is about the temple's destruction and not about the end of the space-time universe. For defense, see Wright, *Jesus and the Victory of God* (London: SCM, 1996), pp. 339-368, and Jordan, *The End of the World*.

but never changes location until the beginning of chapter 24. The temple setting establishes a strong link to the temple sermons of Jeremiah 7, 26. Jesus' condemnation of the scribes and Pharisees as "hypocrites," who maintain ceremonial purity while indulging injustice and sin, is reminiscent of Jeremiah's "den of robbers" speech (Jeremiah 7:11), which Jesus quotes upon His arrival in Jerusalem (21:13). Like the "weeping prophet," Jesus laments the rebellion of the city he condemns (23:37-38), and warns Jerusalem she will be left to desolation (23:38; cf. Jer 22:5). Chapter 24:1 records Jesus' final departure from the temple, reminiscent of the departure of the glory of Yahweh from the temple in Ezekiel 8-11.

From this sketch, we discover the following sequence:

MATTHEW	OLD TESTAMENT
Sermon on Mount, 5-7	Sinai Revelation
Mission of Twelve, 10	Deuteronomy: Preparation for conquest
Parables of Kingdom, 13	Wisdom of Solomon
Eschatological doom, 23-25	End of Judah; Babylonian exile

If this scheme works, then the fourth discourse, chapter 18, should have some relation to the divided kingdom period of Israel's history. Though I give a fuller defense of this thesis in the next section, a few hints can be given here. Chapter 18 is often described as the "community rule" for Jesus' disciples, in which He emphasizes that His disciples will be characterized by childlike humility and faith (18:1-3), and warns the community to avoid causing little ones to stumble (18:5-14). Verses 15-20 sketch out the procedures for dealing with sin among the brothers, and Jesus' final parable describes the spirit of forgiveness that must characterize the church (18:21-35).

The discourse assumes that Jesus' disciples will function as a community (εκκλησια) separated from Israel as a whole. In 16:18, the word refers to Jesus' own temple-community that He intends to build on the rock of Peter, and the word has the same connotation in 18:17. Used in the LXX to refer to the "assembly" of Israel (cf. Deuteronomy 4:10), Jesus uses it to refer to the "new

Israel" of His disciples, in contrast to the "Gentiles" outside. Matt. 18:17 goes beyond 16:18, however, in indicating that the new εκκλησια will have its own structures of authority to enforce the community's standards. In short, Jesus is forming an Israel in the midst of Israel, just as Elijah and Elisha had done during the Omride dynasty.[39]

All this may seem a thin reed on which to lean a large theory, but it is a small beginning. Not despising the day of small beginnings, I turn to a more elaborate defense of the thesis, focusing on the narrative of Matthew's gospel to show that his thematic and plot development enflesh the skeleton of the discourses.

IV.

As noted, the Mosaic character of the early chapters of Matthew is evident not only in the mountaintop setting of Matthew 5-7 but in the narrative that precedes the Sermon. If Matthew's typology works out consistently, then we should expect that the narrative between the Sermon and the Mission Discourse would also prepare for a Deuteronomic conquest speech, and the narratives that intervene between the other discourses would also fit into the typological sequence. As will become clear in the discussion below, some of these narrative sequences are more evident than others, and there are more "gaps" in subsequent chapters than in chapters 1-4. Yet, there is sufficient evidence, in my judgment, to conclude that Matthew continues his typological program throughout the book.

In the following pages, I examine the narrative sections between the discourses in turn: Matthew 8-9, 11-12, 14-17, 19-22, and then make a few suggestions about chapters 26-28.

---

39. For more on the typological dimensions of the Elijah-Elisha narratives, see Peter J. Leithart, *1-2 Kings* (Grand Rapids: Brazos Press, 2006).

INTRODUCTION

MATTHEW 8-9

In discussing the sequence of ten miracles in these chapters, Bacon cites the *Pirqe Aboth*, which claims that "Ten miracles were wrought for our fathers in Egypt, and ten by the sea. . . . Ten miracles were wrought in the Sanctuary." On this basis, it has been suggested that Jesus performs ten mighty works in imitation of Moses in Egypt and at the Red Sea. Bacon concludes that Matthew did not intend the parallel, because he judges the ninth and tenth miracles (9:27-34) as an "afterthought" because they come after the "proper climax" of resurrection (9:24-26).[40] Allison likewise argues that a Mosaic typology is doubtful in this section; there are only nine miracle stories, since 9:18-26 combines two healings in one narrative. He admits that the plagues, like the miracles of Jesus, are grouped into three sets of three, but after analyzing the plague narratives he finds the connections with Matthew's gospel fairly weak.[41]

Despite Bacon's and Allison's reservations, I think Matthew intended to present ten miraculous signs in chapters 8-9. Though the stories of the official's daughter and the woman with an issue of blood are intercalated, they are distinct miracles, unlike the healing of the two blind men (9:27-31). Whether the series is to be understood as antitypical to the plagues is another question. There is, after all, another sequence of ten in the Pentateuch, the "ten" rebellions of Israel in the wilderness (Numbers 14:22). That there are ten rebellions as well as ten plagues is significant: It shows that Israel does not remain faithful to the covenant, which is the only way they can avoid suffering the plagues of Egypt (Deuteronomy 28). Many of the ten rebellions take place after Moses receives the

---

40. Bacon, *Studies*, p. 188. Against Bacon, it might be argued that the sequence following the resurrection of the official's daughter actually matches the end of Matthew's gospel quite neatly: After Jesus' resurrection, His disciples come to faith (healed blindness) and go out to preach (healed dumbness).

41. *New Moses*, pp. 207-213.

law on Sinai, just as the ten miracles of Jesus take place after the Sermon on the Mount. The parallel can be made more precise. In the Pentateuchal narrative, Israel remained at Sinai from Exodus 19 through Leviticus, and into the early chapters of Numbers. Numbers 10:11 records: "Now it came about in the second year, in the second month, on the twentieth day of the month, that the cloud was lifted from over the tabernacle of the testimony; and the sons of Israel set out on their journeys from the wilderness of Sinai." This is the first time Israel follows the pillar of cloud from Sinai into the wilderness, and, similarly, in Matthew 8:1 Jesus comes down from the mountain with "great multitudes" following Him. Here he is not only Moses, but Yahweh's pillar that leads Israel during their wilderness sojourn. From this perspective, Matthew 5-7 recapitulates not only the "civil" and "moral" legislation of Exodus 20-24, but the "ceremonial" legislation of Exodus 25-40, Leviticus, and Numbers 1-10. Appropriately, Jesus instructs His disciples not only about how to live but how to worship (6:1-18). Some of the "ten rebellions" occur before Israel ever got to Sinai, but Matthew alters the sequence to record ten miracles after Jesus' Sinai.

Other details of the narrative support these suggestions. Jesus' first miracle after descending the mountain was to heal a leper (8:1-4), and one of the first rebellions after Sinai was led by Miriam, who was made a leper—and healed! (Numbers 12:1-15).[42] The ten rebellions culminate with Israel's refusal to enter to conquer the land, as Matthew's ten miracles lead into Jesus' commission to the Twelve to "spy out" and heal Israel. Jesus' reference to "sheep without a shepherd" echoes, as we have seen, Numbers 27:18, the end of the period of Israel's wandering. Between the judgment and healing of Miriam and the commission of Joshua, Moses faces

---

42. See Bacon, *Studies*, pp. 187-189. Leprosy is strong associated with the Pentateuch. Moses is the first man in the Bible to have a kind of leprosy (Exodus 4:6), but Moses' leprosy is for demonstration purposes only. Miriam is the first to suffer actual leprosy (Num. 12). Leviticus 13-14 give detailed attention to the diagnosis and cleansing of leprosy (cf. Deuteronomy 24:8) and lepers are excluded from the camp of Israel (Num. 5). After the Pentateuch, however, there is not

opposition from Korah, Dathan, and Abiram (Numbers 16-17), and Jesus faces mounting hostility from the Pharisees and scribes (climaxing in 9:34).

Both historically and literarily, the function of Jesus' miracles corresponds to the logic of the "ten rebellions" in the wilderness. Yahweh's judgments on Egypt introduced Pharaoh to the power of Yahweh (cf. Exodus 5:2), and the judgments on Israel were intended to manifest Yahweh's character to His *own* people. Within Israel many lust to return to slavery, so that Israel in the wilderness is all too often a little outpost of Egypt, complete with golden calves. Likewise, Jesus performs ten signs that demonstrate the character of the God of Israel and manifest the nature of His kingdom, but these signs are performed before an uncomprehending Egypt-Israel that fails to recognize Jesus or His Father. Matthew persists in identifying Israel with Egypt (cf. 2:1-15), but in this he is drawing on an Old Testament parallel that manifests this same identity.

By what logic does a series of ten rebellions find a typological antitype in a series of ten miracles, mostly healings? There are three lines of response. First, even in Numbers, the rebellions are often accompanied by miraculous signs, provisions, and even healings. Soon after the exodus, Israel grumbles about the lack of food in the wilderness, and Yahweh gives bread and meat from heaven (Exodus 16:1-21). Israel quarrels with Moses at Rephidim and Yahweh provides water from the rock (Exodus 17:1-7). Miriam is stricken with leprosy when she and Aaron question Moses' leadership, but she is rapidly healed (Numbers 12:1-16). Jesus' miracles thus highlight the mercy Yahweh showed to Israel in the face of repeated rebellion.

---

another leper in the Hebrew Bible until Naaman (2 Kings. 5; cf. the curse in 2 Sam. 3:29). In short, leprosy is a concern in the law, but rarely mentioned elsewhere in the Hebrew Bible. Matthew 8:1-4 is the only account of the healing of an individual leper in the entire gospel (cf. 10:8; 11:5; 26:6). That Jesus begins His ministry of healing with the cleansing of a leper suggests that the typological background is Pentateuchal.

Second, Matthew does not in any case present Jesus as a "straight-line" fulfillment of Old Testament law and prophets. He teaches the counterintuitive message that one should love enemies and accept a second blow on the cheek. In both life and teaching, His fulfillment brings the delight of surprise. Israel, not Egypt, is ruled by the child-killer (Matthew 2), Jesus' baptismal exodus is a departure from *Israel* (Matthew 3), and Jesus, the true Israel, does not fall to the temptations of Satan in the wilderness but resists and triumphs. It is consistent with Matthew's overall program (and Jesus' too), for Jesus to bring healings rather than judgments on the Israel that is wandering like sheep without a shepherd.

Finally, and most decisively, Matthew evidently read the wilderness period through the lens of Isaiah. The one fulfillment formula in these chapters (8:17) quotes from Isaiah 53:17, an indication that Matthew sees Jesus' healing ministry as bringing the final restoration from exile promised in Isaiah. Later (11:4-5), in response to John's inquiry, Jesus Himself cites a related passage from Isaiah (35:5-6) to show that He fulfills the prophet's expectations concerning the healing of blind, lame, lepers, and deaf. Significantly, Isaiah 35 begins with a declaration concerning the desert: "The wilderness and the desert will be glad" (v. 1). The new wilderness experience of Israel will not be one of judgment and destruction but of healing and restoration. As in Israel's first passage from Egypt, but more, "waters will break forth in the wilderness, and streams in the Arabah. And the scorched land will become a pool, and the thirsty ground springs of water" (vv. 6-7; cf. Exodus 17:1-7). Isaiah prophesied that the wilderness of Israel would become fruitful; Matthew writes of the fulfillment of Isaiah's hopes.

In sum, Matthew's typological recapitulation in these chapters can be charted this way:

MATHEW	OLD TESTAMENT
8:1: leave mountain with crowds	Numbers 10:11: Israel leaves Sinai, following cloud

8:2-4: heal a leper	Numbers 12:1-16: Miriam cleansed of leprosy
(healings	Wilderness with overlay of Isaiah 35)
10 miracles	Numbers 14:22: 10 rebellions
9:34: opposition from Pharisees	Numbers 16: opposition from Korah, Dathan, Abiram
9:36: sheep without shepherd	Numbers 27:27: "sheep without shepherd"
10:1f: authority to apostles	Numbers 27:18-24: glory to Joshua
(12 sent into land	Double overlay: 12 spies of Numbers 13-14)
ch. 10: discourse on mission	Deuteronomy: instructions for conquest

---

MATTHEW 11-12

When Matthew 11 opens, we are still in the world of Numbers, Deuteronomy, and Joshua. Expanding on his explanation to John's disciples, Jesus condemns, for the first time in the gospel, "this generation" of Israel (11:16). He is comparing His contemporaries to the Exodus generation, for that generation above all saw the work of God and failed to respond faithfully. Jesus' quotation from Malachi 3:1 in 11:10 confirms this suggestion. Behind Malachi's reference to the "Messenger" ($\alpha\gamma\gamma\epsilon\lambda o\varsigma$) who will "prepare your way" is Yahweh's promise of an Angel to lead Israel to the land (Exodus 33:2).[43] John came as a messenger to lead Israel from exile, but Israel refused to mourn when John played his dirge. Now Jesus comes to offer rest, but they will not dance to His piping.

If the sequence continues, Matthew 11-12 should move forward from the wilderness into the conquest and monarchy period of Israel's history, preparing for the Solomonic "wisdom" discourse in chapter 13. The most striking thing about these chapters is the

---

43. See the superb discussion of Mark's use of Malachi 3:1 in Rikki Watts, *Isaiah's New Exodus in Mark* (Grand Rapids: Baker, 1997), pp. 53-90.

INTRODUCTION

emphasis on rest and Sabbath.[44] Jesus offers to give rest to those who come to Him (11:25-30), and the rest theme continues into the following chapter, where Jesus engages in conflicts with the Pharisees that center on the question of the Sabbath (12:1, 10). Of the ten uses of the word "Sabbath" in Matthew, eight are in chapter 12.[45] While Jesus invokes a Mosaic/exodus theme,[46] in that Moses was (as a new Noah) the rest-giver to oppressed Israel, rest is also prominent in the narrative of the conquest of Canaan and the stories of David. Because of Israel's rebellions, Moses never rested in the land and never gave the people rest in the land; "that generation" never entered rest (cf. Psalm 95). Rest from enemies is promised to Israel (Deuteronomy 12:10) and achieved by Joshua (Joshua 11:23; 14:15). The erection of the sanctuary in the land was to be the sign of rest (Deuteronomy 12), and in Joshua the construction of the sanctuary at Shiloh is the structural center of the second half of the book (Joshua 18:1-7).[47] Now that the "ten rebellions" of Israel have been reversed, Jesus can offer the genuine rest dimly anticipated by His namesake, Joshua. After the missionary discourse (=Deuteronomy conquest discourse) of Matthew 10, Jesus offers the gift of rest.

Israel comes to final rest in the land only after the conquests of David during the reign of Solomon. Joshua's rest was short-lived, soon collapsing into the chaos of the period of the judges, but David was able to achieve "rest on every side from all his

---

44. Boerman ("Chiastic Structure," pp. 316, 320) suggests that the Sabbath dispute in 12:1-8 forms the chiastic center of chapters 11-12, pointing to Jesus' authority over the Sabbath as the main theme of the section.

45. Both numerical indications are significant. The "Ten Words" of Exodus have been repeated as ten Sabbaths in Matthew's account, and the number eight is frequently associated in the Old Testament with moments of new birth. In place of the week-ending Sabbath of the Old Covenant, Jesus brings a new beginning, the first day of a new week.

46. Allison, *New Moses*, pp. 218-233. In support of this, cf. the crucial position of the Sabbath commands in Exodus 31:12-17; 35:1-3.

47. For the structural analysis, see David Dorsey, *The Literary Structure of the Old Testament: Genesis to Malachi* (Grand Rapids: Baker, 1999), p. 94.

INTRODUCTION

enemies" (2 Samuel 7:1, 11), a rest preserved for his son Solomon (1 Kings 5:4). Appropriately, Solomon marks the achievement of rest by building a temple, as Moses had prophesied (Deuteronomy 12). Jesus offers rest, then, not merely as new Moses and new Joshua, but more importantly as David and as the Son of David, the greater Solomon.[48] The Davidic typology becomes explicit in the initial Sabbath debate, in which the Pharisees attack Jesus' disciples for picking grain on the Sabbath, an activity that the Pharisees classify as a form of reaping or harvesting. Jesus responds by appealing to the example of David and his companions, who ate consecrated shewbread from the sanctuary at Nob (12:1-8; cf. 1 Samuel 21). As N. T. Wright has suggested, this response assigns roles to each of the characters in the conflict: The Pharisees are in the position of persecuting Saul or spying Doeg the Edomite; the disciples are the companions of David; Jesus is David Himself.[49] During this encounter, Jesus quotes Hosea

---

48. Jesus offers rest using the image of an easy "yoke" and a light "load." The "yoke" image is sometimes used in the Bible to describe submission to the Torah (cf. Acts 15:10), and thus Jesus might be presenting Himself as a better Moses who delivers His disciples from the Egyptian hardships imposed by the Pharisees and scribes. Yet, the yoke image is also used to describe the rule of Yahweh or of a king (Jeremiah 5:5, where Yahweh is the king; 27:1-22, where Israel is to bear Nebuchadnezzar's yoke). This is the force of the image in 1 Kings 12, where the word is used eight times to describe the "heavy yoke" of Solomon, who had become Pharaoh-like in his oppression of Israel (1 Kings. 12:4, 9-11, 14). Not only does this text share the image of "yoke" with Matthew 11, but both texts oppose "light" and "heavy" burdens and both speak in terms of a son's relation to a father (Jesus-the Father, Rehoboam-father Solomon). Jesus thus describes His own work in direct opposition to the description of Solomon in 1 Kings 12. He presents Himself as a better Solomon, as He has shown Himself to be a better Moses and a better Israel. He is no Rehoboam come to whip Israel with scorpions; nor is He a Solomon who burdens His people with a heavy yoke or loads them down under heavy burdens, as the original Solomon did. He is a true king who offers genuine rest. The association of 11:25-30 with David and Solomon becomes even stronger if we accept Celia Deutsch's suggestion that the pericope is shaped by a "Wisdom Christology" (*Hidden Wisdom and the Easy Yoke: Wisdom, Torah and Discipleship in Matthew 11.25-30* [JSNT Supplement #18; Sheffield: Sheffield Academic, 1987], p. 142).

49. Wright, *Jesus and the Victory of God*, pp. 393-394.

INTRODUCTION

6:6: "I desire compassion, and not sacrifice." Behind Hosea is the prophet Samuel, who cuts through Saul's pious—we might even say, Pharisaical—excuses with "obedience is better than sacrifice" (1 Samuel 15:22-23).[50] After Saul slaughters the priests at Nob, David, knowing Saul will kill him, flees to Philistia until Saul dies (1 Samuel 26-31). Following David, Jesus, knowing the Pharisees are plotting murder, "withdraws" after the encounter with the Pharisees (Matthew 12:14-15).[51] Like David, Jesus is approved by the crowds, but opposed by the leaders of Israel (cf. 1 Samuel 17-18).[52] Jesus' reference to rescuing sheep in the second Sabbath dispute (12:11) may be inspired by the earlier reference to David, drawn from the fold to shepherd Israel.[53]

In the ensuing debates with the Pharisees, Jesus twice mentions the "kingdom" in contexts of violent conflict. His claim that "the kingdom of heaven suffers violence, and violent men take it by force" has been interpreted in a variety of ways, but G. R. Beasley-Murray's argument that it refers to the aggressive progression of the gospel and the violent opposition of the scribes and Pharisees has much to commend it.[54] The conflict of kingdoms comes up again when the Jewish leaders accuse Jesus of exorcising demons by the power of Satan. That Jesus casts out demons by the Spirit

---

50. Hosea's and Jesus' gloss of Samuel is significant, for both translate "obedience" as "compassion."

51. Jesus' kingship is also evident in His "Solomonic" judgment that David's violation of the rules governing showbread was licit. Kingship means making judgments in cases without precedent (cf. 1 Kings. 3:16-28). As Carl Schmitt put it, sovereignty is the authority to rule on exceptions.

52. Lohr ("Oral Techniques," p. 411) notes the intensifying reaction to Jesus throughout these chapters, and claims that the rejection of Jesus is the chief theme of the section.

53. Goulder, *Midrash and Lection*, pp. 328-329.

54. *Jesus and the Kingdom of God* (Grand Rapids: Eerdmans, 1986), pp. 91-96. It is possible that Matthew is showing a progression in the arrival of the kingdom. Early on, John and Jesus warn that the kingdom is "near" (3:2; 4:17, both using ηγγικεν). In 12:28, in what I am suggesting is the "kingdom" section of the gospel, Jesus speaks of the kingdom as already arrived (εφθασεν).

is a sign that the kingdom has come, and Jesus as the greater David is conquering (12:22-28), as the multitudes ask whether His signs show He is "the Son of David" (12:23).[55] There is perhaps a reference to the Spirit-filled David's musical triumph over Saul's "evil spirit" in Jesus' claim to cast out demons by the Spirit (12:28; cf. 1 Samuel 16:13-23). In his climactic condemnation, Jesus explicitly mentions Solomon in His condemnation of the cities who rejected Him and His ministry, and claims superiority to Israel's most accomplished king: "something greater than Solomon is here" (12:42).

Again, these parallels can be charted as follows:

MATTHEW	OLD TESTAMENT
11:1-19: "this generation"	Numbers 13-14: Exodus generation fails to enter rest
11:25-30: Jesus offers rest	Joshua 11:23: Joshua achieves rest
12:1-8: Jesus as David	1 Samuel 21: David and showbread
12:7: compassion, not sacrifice	1 Samuel 15:22-23: obedience not sacrifice
(Jesus persecuted by leaders	David persecuted by Saul)
12:14: Pharisees plot murder	1 Samuel 27:1: Saul plots to kill David
12:15: Jesus withdraws	1 Samuel 27:2: David withdraws to Philistia
12:23: "Son of David"	David as warrior
12:27-28: exorcisms by Spirit	1 Samuel 16: David calms Saul because of Spirit
12:34: mouth speaks from heart	1 Samuel 24:13: wickedness comes from wicked
12:42: Greater than Solomon	1 Kings 3-4: Solomon's wisdom
ch 13: Parables of kingdom	1 Kings 4:32: "Parables" of Solomon

---

55. On Jesus' miracles as signs of Davidic kingship, see especially Lidija Novakovic, *Messiah, the Healer of the Sick: A Study of Jesus as Son of David in the Gospel of Matthew* (Wissenschafliche Untersuchungen zum Neuen Testament, 2.Reihe, #170; Tubingen: Mohr Siebeck, 2003). Novakovic points out that the *Testament of Solomon* describes Solomon as an exorcist (pp. 101ff.).

Introduction

Matthew 14-17

As soon as Jesus finishes His parables of the kingdom, we read the story of John's martyrdom at the hands of Herod. Jesus has already been separating from Israel, but this is the first time we see a direct contrast of Herod's and Jesus' rule. Earlier in the gospel, Herod the Great functioned as a Pharaoh-like figure, but here Herod Antipas is clearly an Ahab. He attacks and kills a prophet, as Ahab permitted the murder of prophets and Naboth (1 Kings 21) and the unsuccessful attempt to kill Elijah (Matthew 14:1-12; 1 Kings 18:4; 19:1-2). Like Ahab, Herod is egged on to attack the prophet by his bloodthirsty wife (Matthew 14:6-8; 1 Kings 18:4; 19:1-2). Like Ahab, Herod is ambivalent, personally reluctant to kill the prophet but too weak to stand up to his wife (Matthew 14:9; cf. 1 Kings 21).

Contrasting to Herod's kingdom is the kingdom that Jesus has described in the parables and which He enacts in the feeding of the five thousand. While Herod serves up prophet's head as the last course of his banquet, Jesus feeds five thousand men, along with women and children, with fives loaves and two fish. That the community gathering around Jesus is the core of a new "Israel" is also evident in the Passover-Exodus sequence: Jesus serves a meal to the multitude (14:13-21), and then crosses the sea at night, walking on the water and joining His disciples in the boat (14:22-33), a sequence repeated a chapter later (15:32-39). This is a "Mosaic" sequence, but in the context of Herod's murder of John, it is an indication that Jesus is the anti-Herod, head of the kingdom of the "true Israel."

Though Jesus is a true Shepherd and king in contrast to Herod, these chapters highlight especially Jesus' role as prophet, specifically as what has come to be called a "leadership prophet," forming a faithful community within a faithless Israel. John has been an Elijah figure from the beginning of the gospel, ministering in the wilderness and adopting Elijah's sartorial sense (3:4). He is again Elijah in the episode with Herod, and Jesus explicitly describes him as Elijah after the transfiguration (17:9-13; cf. 11:14). Elijah appears in his own person at the transfiguration (17:1-8), and of the nine uses of the name Elijah in Matthew, six are in chapters 16-17 (16:14; 17:3-4, 10-12). This cluster of references to Elijah places us in a divided kingdom context, canonically near the center of the book of 1-2 Kings. In one incident, Jesus Himself is an "Elijah-like" figure.[56] When Yahweh sends Elijah from the land, He goes to the region of Sidon, where he assists a widow who has little food and a son to feed, providing food and raising her son from the dead (1 Kings 17:9-24). Similarly, when Jesus goes into the "district of Tyre and Sidon," a Canaanite woman comes seeking help for her possessed daughter. Jesus rebukes her by saying that the bread He brings is for the "children," but she responds by expressing her hope to be among the dogs under the table who receive scraps (15:26-27). Marveling at her persistent faith, Jesus heals her daughter with a word (15:28).

Predominantly John, not Jesus, is Elijah, and if John the forerunner is Elijah, then Jesus, his successor, is another Elisha. Even in the incident with the Canaanite woman, Jesus is Elisha. Elisha too was faced with a woman seeking help for a child, a woman who threw herself at Elisha's feet in the way that the Canaanite woman prostrates herself before Jesus (Matthew 15:25; cf. 2 Kings 4:27). Elisha's ministry revolves around the gift of food, as he heals Jericho's waters (2 Kings 2:19-22), provides food for the sons of the prophets (2 Kings 4:38-41), multiplies loaves to feed a multitude (2 Kings 4:42-44), gives bread to Aramean soldiers (2 Kings 6:20-23), and prophesies an end to the famine during the siege of Samaria (2 Kings 7:1, 18-20). Jesus' ministry is characterized by eating and drinking throughout Matthew (cf. 11:19), but food takes on prominence in chapters 14-16. Jesus feeds five thousand (14:13-21) and shortly after feeds another four thousand (15:32-39).[57] His dispute with the Pharisees centers not

---

56. Buchanan, *Gospel of Matthew*, p. 669.

57. Buchanan, *Gospel of Matthew*, 641, recognizes the Elisha typology.

on Sabbatical practices, as in earlier chapters, but on cleansing rites before meals (15:1-2). When He is not serving a meal, He is using bread as an image, either of the blessings He brings to the children of Israel (15:26), or the teaching of the Pharisees and Sadducees (16:5-12). Of the twenty-one uses of αρτοσ, fifteen are in chapters 14-16 (14:17, 19 [2x]; 15:2, 26, 33-36; 16:5, 7-12). Like Elisha, Jesus performs bizarre miracles—not only multiplying loaves for a multitude but walking on the water and causing Peter to defy gravity (cf. 2 Kings 6:1-7) and sending him to find a coin in the mouth of a fish (17:24-27).

Elisha's ministry involves the formation of a community, known as the "sons of the prophets," an alternative Israel within the idolatrous Israel of Ahab and Jezebel. Elisha ministers life within a culture of death, a ministry of life that divides Israel in two. While Elijah was famously a solo prophet, Elisha is constantly surrounded by "disciples."[58] So also, Jesus organizes a community of disciples and followers around meals, offering them life, within an Israel that is ruled by a murderous son of a murderer.[59]

Elisha has his Gehazi, the bumbling sidekick who gets in the way, cannot manage the miracles of the master, and misconstrues the master's instructions. Gehazi pushes the Shunammite aside

---

58. For more on Elisha, see my *1-2 Kings* (Brazos Press, 2006).

59. Cf. P. F. Ellis's comment that Matthew's gospel divides at 13:35, from which point Jesus turns His attention more exclusively to the Twelve: "Up to 13.35 Jesus speaks to all the Jews. After 13.35, as in Mk. 8:27-46, Jesus bestows the major part of his attention upon the disciples, who, in contrast to the Jews, listen and understand him. Thus, in ch. 13, Jesus turns from the pseudo-Israel which will not accept him (cf. chs. 11-12) to the Church, the true Israel, which believes in him" (*Matthew: His Mind and His Message* [Collegeville, MN: Liturgical, 1974], p. 13, quoted in Bauer, *Structure*, p. 37). Allison ("Structure, Biographical Impulse, and the *Imitatio Christi*, p. 140) makes a similar point: "after so many within corporate Israel have, at least for the time being, forfeited their expected role in salvation-history, an alternative institution is needed. So Jesus establishes his church. That the *ecclesia* is indeed the most important subject of this section appears not only from the ever-increasing focus upon the disciples as opposed to the crowds but also from Peter's being the rock upon which the church is built, because it is precisely in this section that Peter comes to the fore." He cites 14:28-33; 15;15; 16:13-20; 17:24-27 as evidence.

when she comes to Elisha for help (2 Kings 4:27) and is unable to help the Shunammite's son (2 Kings 4:31). He greedily takes Naaman's silver and clothes, and as a bonus also receives the Gentile general's leprosy (2 Kings 5:20-25). He is likely the man of little faith who cannot see the fiery chariots around Elisha and who fears the Aramean soldiers as a result (2 Kings 6:8-17). Yet, he remains enamored of Elisha, and boasts of his master's exploits before the king (2 Kings 8:1-6).

In many respects the disciples resemble Gehazi. When the Canaanite woman seeks help from Jesus, they push her away (15:23). Peter confesses that Jesus is the Christ, the Son of God, but immediately protests, Satanically, when Jesus begins speaking of His death (Matthew 16:13-28). When Jesus comes down from the mount of Transfiguration, he finds disciples at the foot of the mountain ineffectually attempting to cast out a demon (17:14-21), intriguingly the last reference to exorcism in the gospel. Peter, the spokesman of this Keystone Kop band of disciples, becomes prominent only in chapter 14, where his effort to walk on water nearly ends fatally (14:22-33). Prior to that incident, Peter is never singled out for special attention, and this is also the only time in the gospel any individual is described as a man "of little faith" (14:31; cf. 6:30; 8:26). In this "Elisha" sequence, Peter becomes "chief Gehazi."

The two most prominent incidents in this section of Matthew are Peter's confession (16:13-20) and Jesus' transfiguration (17:1-13). The latter is explicitly linked with the Elijah-Elisha narratives by the presence of Elijah, but deeper connections suggest themselves. Peter confesses Jesus as the "anointed One" (Χριστος), and among the prophets Elisha alone is said to be "anointed" (1 Kings 19:16). Elisha, further, appoints Jehu and Hazael to take vengeance against the house of Ahab (2 Kings 8:7-15; 9:1-10), and Jehu is the only king of the Northern kingdom to be anointed (2 Kings 9:6). In the next section, we will see that Jesus the Christ is a new "Jehu," the madman riding into the city with zeal for the honor of God. The transfiguration might be connected with

Introduction

Elijah's ascension in a whirlwind (2 Kings 2), or with the glory of angels that surround Elisha (2 Kings 6:15-17). Like Elisha, Jesus tells His disciples to "fear not" (Matthew 17:12; 2 Kings 6:16).

Though the order of events in Matthew does not match the order in the Elijah-Elisha narratives and though there are Elijah references outside this section, there is a cluster of Elijah/Elisha connections, sufficient to show that Matthew is continuing to show how Jesus recapitulates all Israel's history:

Matthew	**Old Testament**
14:1-12: Herod kills John	1 Kings 19: Jezebel tries to kill Elijah; 1 Kings 21: Naboth
John's death	2 Kings 2: Elijah's departure
(Herod v. Jesus	Divided kingdom; Omrides v. prophets)
14:13-21: Jesus multiplies loaves	2 Kings 4:42-44 Elisha multiplies loaves
14:22-33: Jesus rescues Peter	2 Kings 6:1-7: Elisha makes axehead float
15:14: blind leading the blind	2 Kings 6:8-23: Elisha blinds and gives sight to Aramean soldiers
15:21-28: Syro-Phoenician woman	2 Kings 4:8-37: Elisha raises Shunammite's son
15:23: disciples keep her away	2 Kings 4:27: Gehazi pushes Shunammite away
(Syro-Phoenician woman	overlay with Elijah: raises son in Sidon, 1 Kings 17)
15:29-31: healing on mountain	2 Kings 4:27: Elisha on mountain when Shunammite seeks help; cf 2 Kings 1:9: Elijah sitting on mountain; sick king
15:32-39: 4000 fed	2 Kings 4:38-44: Elisha's food miracles
16:5-12: leftover bread/leaven	2 Kings 4:42-44: leftover bread
16:13-20: Peter's confession	Jesus compared to "Elijah"
(announcement of death	Jesus suffers like prophets, Elijah & John)
16:16: "the Christ"	Elisha is only anointed prophet, 1 Kings 19:16
("anointed for entry to city	Jehu is the anointed Northern king)
16:24: "follow me"	2 Kings 2: Elisha following Elijah

Introduction

16:28: "Son of Man" in glory	2 Kings 2: ascension of Elijah
17:1-13: transfiguration	2 Kings 2: Elijah's departure; John as Elijah
(Elijah and Moses outside the land - now on mountain inside the land)	
17:1-13: transfiguration	2 Kings 6:15-19: Elisha surrounded by angels
17:12: "do not fear"	2 Kings 6:16: "do not fear"
17:14-21: disciples fail to heal	2 Kings 4:29-31: Gehazi fails to heal
17:24-27: fish and tax money	Elisha's odd miracles
ch. 18: community discourse	rules for the "sons of the prophets"

Matthew 19-22

One of the key shifts that takes place at the beginning of Matthew 19 is geographical.[60] From the beginning of Jesus' life, Judea has been dangerous (2:1-18), and at the beginning of His ministry, Jesus withdraws into Galilee when He hears of John's imprisonment (4:12-13). Throughout the intervening chapters, Jesus has been in Galilee (4:23), in Gadara east of the Sea of Galilee (8:28-34), Caesarea Philippi (16:13), occasionally as far as Tyre and Sidon (15:21), but never Judea. Judea is mentioned eight times in the gospel, but never between 4:25 and 19:1. For Jesus, after His Galilean ministry as "Elisha," there is no "Northern kingdom" left, and He turns His attention exclusively toward Jerusalem and Judea. With chapter 19, He turns toward the South, and from there until the final chapter of the gospel He is in Judea and frequently in Jerusalem itself.

---

60. After the fourth discourse, Jesus engages in a debate with the Pharisees concerning divorce. Why is this discussion here? If the typological scheme of Jesus-as-Israel works, then the reference to divorce is apt. While Torah regulates divorce (Deuteronomy24), many of the Old Testament references to divorce concern Yahweh's divorce of adulterous Israel (Isa. 50:1; Jeremiah 3:1, 8; possibly Mal. 2:16). With chapter 18, then, Matthew's gospel moves into an apocalyptic mode in which Jesus announces the Lord's divorce of His bride, who has rejected her husband.

The turn to Judea conflates two moments in the history of Israel and Judah. On the one hand, Jesus' entry to Jerusalem clearly replicates the march of Jehu to Samaria. Like Jehu (2 Kings 9:13), Jesus rides to Jerusalem over a carpet of garments (Matthew 21:8), and both are acclaimed king by their followers (2 Kings 9:13; Matthew 21:5, 9). As soon as He enters Jerusalem on Palm Sunday (21:1-11), He goes to the temple to enact its coming destruction (21:12-16).[61] One of the central events of Jehu's reign was the destruction of the temple of Baal in Samaria (2 Kings 10), and the comparison of Herod's temple to Ahab's is not a compliment to Herod. Following Jehu's massacre of the house of Ahab, Joash narrowly escapes death and comes to reign in Jerusalem, where he famously attends to the disrepair of the temple (2 Kings 12).

Though the triumphal entry clearly has royal overtones ("behold your king is coming," 21:5), the multitudes who announce Jesus' arrival at the capital proclaim Him as "the prophet Jesus" (21:11). For the next several chapters, Jesus is the apocalyptic prophet in the temple. As noted above, this setting connects Jesus with the prophets of the late history of Judah, particularly Jeremiah, who prophesied against the temple in the temple courts (Jeremiah 7, 26).[62] Jesus' cursing of the fig tree is typologically linked to Jeremiah 8:12, and the vineyard parable draws not only on Isaiah 5, but on Jeremiah 12:10-11.[63] Jesus' parable refers to "servants" (=prophets) being "beaten" (Matthew 21:35), and Jeremiah was the only prophet beaten in the Old Testament (Jeremiah 20:2).[64] Those were not far off who believed Jesus to be "Jeremiah, or one of the prophets" (16:14).

---

61. I am persuaded by Wright's interpretation of this event. See *Jesus and the Victory of God*.

62. In the following, I am particularly dependent upon Michael Knowles, *Jeremiah in Matthew's Gospel: The Rejected Profit [sic!] Motif in Matthaean Redaction* (JSNT Supplement Series #68; Sheffield: Sheffield Academic Press, 1993).

63. Knowles, *Rejected Prophet*, pp. 176, 180.

64. Knowles, *Rejected Prophet*, pp. 181-182.

Introduction

The very imagery of Jesus' parables is taken from prophecies concerning Israel's and Judah's destruction. Twice Jesus tells parables about a vineyard owner (20:1-16; 22:33-44) and another about a father who sends his sons to work in the vineyard (21:28), and these chapters contain all ten uses of the word "vineyard" in Matthew's gospel. Matthew 21:33 is clearly quoting from Isaiah 5:1-2, and it's likely that the other references to vineyards, their owners, and their workers allude to this and similar prophetic texts (cf. Psalm 80:8-19; Isaiah 3:14; Jeremiah 12:10; Hosea 2:12). In many cases, the vineyard serves as metaphor for Israel: Planted in the land, cared for diligently by her Lord, but, because it fails to produce fruit, the Lord breaks down every wall of protection and leaves the vineyard to the ravages of the Gentiles. Jesus employs the vineyard imagery in the same way, as an image of an unfruitful Israel whose caretakers will be replaced and destroyed. Jesus warns the Jewish leaders of a judgment that will make the Babylonian exile pale by comparison. The fig tree episode (21:18-22), in context clearly an image for Israel's failures, is similarly drawn from apocalyptic texts of the Old Testament (Isaiah 34:1-15; Jeremiah 8:13-17; Micah 7:1-8).

Matthew uses this combination of geographic/spatial arrangement, imagery, and content to place Jesus as a prophetic figure, a Jeremiah, in a "late monarchy" context, in which he prophesies the coming destruction of the temple and city.

MATTHEW	OLD TESTAMENT
19:1: into Judea	Southern kingdom
20:17: preparing for Jerusalem	2 Kings 11-12: Joash cleansing temple
20:29-34: healing at Jericho	2 Kings 2:19-22: heals waters at Jericho
21:1-11: triumphal entry	2 Kings 9: Jehu rides on robes
21:12-13: temple action	2 Kings 10: Jehu destroys temple of Baal; Joash;
21:13: robbers' den	Jeremiah 7:11: robbers' den
21:18-21: withered fig tree	Jeremiah 8:13: "no figs"; "leaf shall wither"
21:33-46: parable of vineyard	Jeremiah 12:10-11: "ruined my vineyard"

21:35: beaten servant	Jeremiah 20:2: Jeremiah beaten
ch 23: temple discourse	Jeremiah 7, 26
ch 24-25: Olivet discourse	Ezekiel 8-11 (Jeremiah 7:14 with 24:2)

Matthew 26-28

As Michael Knowles has pointed out, the Jeremiah references continue into the final chapters of Matthew:

Matthew	Old Testament
26:28: blood of covenant	Jeremiah 31:27-40 (with Exodus 24:8)[65]
26:28: "remission of sins"	Jeremiah 31:34[66]
26:50-66: Jesus falsely accused	Jeremiah 26: Jeremiah falsely accused[67]
27:3-10: Judas recants	Jeremiah 18, 32 (with Zechariah 11): explicit fulfillment[68]
27:4, 24: "innocent blood"	Jeremiah 26:15: "innocent blood"[69]
27:25: blood on heads	Jeremiah 51:35: blood on Chaldea[70]
27:34: gall	Lam 3:19: "wormwood and bitterness"[71]
27:39: abuse from those who pass	Lam 2:15: "all who pass . . . shake their heads"[72]

---

65. Knowles, *Rejected Prophet*, p. 207.

66. Knowles, *Rejected Prophet*, p. 208.

67. Knowles, *Rejected Prophet*, p. 200.

68. Knowles, *Rejected Prophet*, pp. 53-81.

69. Knowles, *Rejected Prophet*, p. 201.

70. Knowles, *Rejected Prophet*, p. 202.

71. Knowles, *Rejected Prophet*, p. 205.

72. Knowles, *Rejected Prophet*, p. 203.

INTRODUCTION

As the references to Lamentations show, Matthew presents Jesus in the final chapters not merely as the suffering prophet, but as the embodiment of the suffering city, bereft of inhabitants. As a result, the final chapters show that Jesus experiences the exile and restoration of Israel herself in His death and resurrection. The disciples, particularly Peter, play an important role in these chapters; they flee from Jesus, leaving Him wholly isolated before the combined forces of the Jewish Sanhedrin and the Roman Pilate (cf. 26:56; 26:58-75). Jesus is subjected to the Gentile power, as Israel was to the Babylonians, and on the cross He cries out that He has been forsaken even by His God (27:46). As N. T. Wright has argued on other grounds, on the cross Jesus suffers the curse of Israel's, and humanity's, exile, in order to bear that curse away and return humanity to the presence of God.

If the death and burial of Jesus is the exile of Jesus, the resurrection of Jesus is His return from exile. Explicit resurrection texts are comparatively rare in the Old Testament (though Israel always trusted a God who raises the dead), and one of the most prominent is Ezekiel 37, explicitly a prophecy about Israel's restoration from the grave of exile. Finally, the gospel of Matthew ends, as Israel's Scriptures do, with a commission. Matthew has brought us around to the end: Jesus has recapitulated Israel's history in righteousness, and now sends the new Israel to proclaim this news to the Gentiles.

2

New Israel

Israel and Israel's God
Matthew 1:1; 28:18-20

The record of the genealogy of Jesus the Messiah, the son of David, the son of Abraham: – Matthew 1:1

And Jesus came up and spoke to them, saying, "All authority has been given to Me in heaven and on earth. [19] Go therefore and make disciples of all the nations, baptizing them in the name of the Father and the Son and the Holy Spirit, [20] teaching them to observe all that I commanded you; and lo, I am with you always, even to the end of the age. – Matthew 28:18-20

All four gospels reveal Jesus and tell the story of His earthly ministry, but they tell the story differently, with different emphases, audiences, and interests.[1] We can see some of these differences

---

1. For an introduction to the gospels, see my *The Four: A Survey of the Gospels* (Moscow, ID: Canon, 2010).

by looking at the opening chapters of each. Matthew opens with a genealogy. Of the other evangelists, only Luke provides a genealogy, and none of the others begins with a genealogy. Mark has no birth narrative at all. He starts with a quotation from Isaiah and Malachi, and we're off and running. Luke formally addresses Theophilus about his intentions and methods, and then spends two chapters telling about Jesus' birth and childhood. John begins with the famous prologue about the eternal Word made flesh. Each gospel ends differently too. If the shorter ending is original, Mark ends abruptly with fear and dismay and unanswered questions (Mark 16:8). Luke continues his account in Acts, and John emphasizes that he is a witness. Matthew ends with the great commission.

There aren't contradictions among the gospels. They are not telling different stories. But they tell the one story of Jesus differently. How does Matthew tell the story? How does he begin and end? What are his emphases? How does he want us to see Jesus?

Matthew begins his genealogy with a phrase (βιβλος γενεσεως) that alludes to a phrase found ten times in the Greek translation of the book of Genesis. Matthew's phrase, or something like it, is used to structure the book of Genesis, the "book of beginnings." In two passages, the phrase in the Septuagint (LXX) is identical to the phrase that Matthew uses. Genesis 2:4 says, "This is the account of the heavens and earth when they were created," and Genesis 5:1 repeats the phrase, "This is the book of the generations of Adam." Dale Allison argues that Matthew's opening words, βιβλος γενεσεως, should be translated as "Book of the Genesis," a translation ambiguous enough to capture all that Matthew intended—an allusion to the first book of the Bible, a new creation theme, an introduction to the genealogy or birth story. "Genesis" was already established as the title of the first book of the Bible by Matthew's time.[2]

From one angle, the closing verses of the gospel conclude this "new Genesis" theme. The risen Jesus brings His disciples together and commissions them to take the gospel to the Gentiles. And the basis for this commission is that Jesus has received "all authority in heaven and on earth," a phrase from the first verse of the Bible.[3] Jesus, whose story begins as a "book of Genesis," ends as a new Adam.

There is another allusion in the Great Commission. The Great Commission is very similar in its structure and its message to the Decree of Cyrus the Persian King who gave Israel permission to return to Jerusalem to rebuild the temple:

> Now in the first year of Cyrus king of Persia—in order to fulfill the word of the Lord by the mouth of Jeremiah—the Lord stirred up the spirit of Cyrus king of Persia, so that he sent a proclamation throughout his kingdom, and also put it in writing, saying, Thus says Cyrus king of Persia, 'The Lord, the God of heaven, has given me all the kingdoms of the earth, and He has appointed me to build Him a house in Jerusalem, which is in Judah. Whoever there is among you of all His people, may the Lord his God be with him, and let him go up!
> -2 Chronicles 36:22-23

Cyrus makes his decree on the basis of his authority, an authority that comes from the "God of heaven." His authority extends to "all the kingdoms of the earth." Jesus claims a wider authority; He claims authority in heaven too. But Cyrus's authority is as extensive as any human's can get. Also, Cyrus instructs the people to "go up" and build the temple and city of Jerusalem, the house of Yahweh. Jesus also tells His disciples to go, and go under the authority of the Lord of heaven and earth. Jesus, of

---

2. Allison, *Matthew: A Shorter Commentary* (Continuum, 2004), pp. 1-2.

3. See Jonathan T. Pennington, *Heaven and Earth in the Gospel of Matthew* (Supplements to *Novum Testamentum*; Leiden: Brill, 2007), p. 345.

course, tells His disciples to go from Judea *to* the Gentiles, instead of returning *from* the Gentiles to Jerusalem. His instructions send His disciples out to places they've never gone before, not back home. The trajectory of the journey is radically different, but the instruction is the same.

Matthew begins his gospel with a genealogy, and even uses the word "Genesis"; he ends with a commission to go to the Gentiles. He begins with an allusion to Genesis and ends with a commission that is reminiscent of the decree of Cyrus. Jesus is first presented as the New Adam. At the end, He is the greater Cyrus.

The full import of this comes out when we realize that the Decree of Cyrus is at the very end of the Hebrew Bible, at least as the canon is presently organized. Matthew writes a gospel that begins with an allusion to the second chapter of Genesis and ends with a commission that alludes to the final chapters of 2 Chronicles. Matthew's account of the story of Jesus moves from the Alpha to the Omega of the Old Testament, from A to Z, from creation to restoration. The story of Jesus is a repetition, a recapitulation, of the story of Israel as recorded in the Old Testament.

This is filled out by the way that Matthew writes his gospel as a whole. It's not just at the beginning and end, but in the middle. As discussed in more detail in the introduction, many commentators have noticed that Matthew's gospel is organized by five large discourses: The Sermon on the Mount (Matthew 5-7), instructions for mission (Matthew 10), parables of the kingdom (Matthew 13), instructions about forgiveness and discipline (Matthew 18), and the Olivet Discourse (Matthew 23-25). If Matthew shows Jesus reliving the history of Israel, it would make sense if these discourses matched different periods of that history. The narrative of Matthew 1-4 leads up to a Sinai scene, as Jesus relives the early history of Israel. In Matthew 5-7, Jesus preaches on a Mountain, talks about the righteousness required of His disciples, and teaches concerning the Law. He is the new Moses, and also Yahweh Himself revealing His commandments to His people. The next discourse is in chapter 10, where Jesus gives instructions to the Twelve as they embark on ministry. That is reminiscent of Moses, who gives instructions to the twelve tribes concerning their conquest of the land. Like the original Joshua, Jesus, who bears the name of the conqueror, comes to proclaim that Yahweh is king of His land. In chapter 13, Jesus tells parables, a form of wisdom literature, about the kingdom. He is the sage king, the new Solomon.

By the time we get to the next discourse (ch. 18), Israel and especially her leaders have rejected Jesus and His disciples. Jesus withdraws, and He devotes His time to training His disciples to live together as a community. In this divided kingdom period, Jesus is like a new Elisha, following John, the new Elijah, and forming communities of the prophets. Finally, chapters 23-25 are a large prophecy against the temple and city of Jerusalem. Jesus condemns the Pharisees with a series of eight woes then launches into a prophecy of the destruction that will come on Judah and Jerusalem within "this generation." He is a new Jeremiah, preaching against the temple and city of Jerusalem.

Between the "Genesis" genealogy at the beginning and the "Decree of Cyrus" at the end, Matthew has told the story of Jesus as a recapitulation of the story of Israel. Jesus does it right; He keeps the covenant; he is the obedient Adam reversing the sin of the first Adam, the obedient Israel undoing the failure of the first Israel. He goes to the wilderness and resists temptation. He conquers the land with words of healing and power. He is faithful in the face of the attacks of the people and of Herod. In his death and resurrection, Jesus relives Israel's exile and return. Jesus is Israel, living through the history of Israel in order to undo that sinful tragedy.

Jesus is Israel, but Jesus is more than Israel. He is also Israel's God. The genealogy in chapter 1 makes this point too. As noted above, two passages in Genesis use precisely the same phrase as Matthew does. In both of the Genesis passages, the phrase does not, as in Matthew 1:1, introduce a genealogy but a list of descendants. Genesis 5:1 introduces the descendants of Adam, and Genesis 2:4 also introduces a series of "generations."

In Genesis 2:4, the "heavens and earth" are the "parents" who generate (through God's work) plants, mist, a garden, a man. Adam's mother is the earth, as his father is the God of heaven; he is taken from the mother-dust, and his Father breathes life into Him from heaven.[4] In both places where Genesis uses the same phrase as Matthew, the text describes those things that come *from* the one named. If Matthew uses the phrase in the same way, then Jesus is being presented not only as the descendant of those named (though he is that, 1:16) but also as the progenitor of those listed. Israel's history is *initiated* by Jesus, even as it also *climaxes* in Jesus. This is neatly captured by the chiastic structure of Matthew's genealogy—moving from Jesus-David-Abraham (v. 1) and then through Abraham (v. 2) and David (v. 6) to Jesus (v. 16). Jesus is the first Man and the Last Man, the first Israelite and the final Israelite. He is not only Omega. He is Alpha. He is not only Israel, but Israel's God.

The genealogy implies that the history of Israel that Jesus relives is also a history of God. Jesus not only recapitulates the great human heroes of Israel's history, but relives Yahweh's dealings with Israel. From this angle, we can see that Jesus' parable of the vineyard sums up the entire gospel (Matthew 21). The owner of the vineyard cared for the vineyard. He provided a wall, built a tower, and put in a wine press. Then he rented the vineyard to servants and went on a long journey, leaving the tenants in charge of the vineyard. But the tenants didn't honor the owner of the vineyard. When he sent servants to collect the rent, the tenants beat them and chased them away. Finally, the owner sent his son, and instead of honoring the son, the tenants killed him, in hopes that they could seize the vineyard for themselves.

---

4. Throughout Genesis, similar phrases introduce genealogies. Genesis 10:1, for instance, introduces the "generations of Shem, Ham, and Japheth," and then goes on to list those who are born from them, and the events generated by those generations.

The Father is the owner of the vineyard, who keeps sending His servants to find fruit. In Matthew, Jesus is all those servants and prophets that Yahweh sent to Israel to call her to follow the covenant. Jesus is Moses, Joshua, Solomon, Elisha, Jeremiah. These servants who came in God's name enacted God's own coming. The advent of a new ruler was God's own Advent, and the coming of a prophet was Yahweh's own coming. As Jesus tells it in the parable, Israel's history manifested a constant pattern of rejection. God came to Israel in Moses, and He was rejected. God came to Israel through kings and prophets, yet Israel refused to listen to her Lord. God came to Israel through Solomon, and Elisha, and Jeremiah, and yet Israel rejected the servants of Yahweh.

In Jesus, Yahweh comes in flesh; Yahweh comes in person, as the Son, greater than Moses, Joshua, Solomon and all the rest put together. Israel *still* rejects him.

But the God of Israel doesn't stop coming. After His servants have been rejected countless times, after He has been rejected time without number, He keeps coming and will not give up coming. Israel's history is a story of a spurned husband, of a scornful wife. But it's a story of a spurned husband who refuses to give up on His bride. His bride spurns Him and finds other husbands, but He woos her back. He is the relentless, the pursuing Hound of Heaven.

And this is the message of the final act of this drama, the resurrection of Jesus. Yahweh comes in flesh; Israel's Father comes as Israel's Son, and He is rejected yet again. But the resurrection shows that He will not allow rejection to have the final word. He will not let Israel's rejection stand. He keeps coming back even after Israel thinks they have killed Him. His love will not let Israel rest; in His love, He will not allow Israel to reject Him forever. This is great good news, the gospel of God, the gospel that reveals God as He is, the gospel that reveals God. Matthew's gospel reveals that God is Love. Matthew's gospel reveals that God is *relentless*, death-defying Love.

Son of David, Son of Abraham
Matthew 1:1-17

The record of the genealogy of Jesus the Messiah, the son of David, the son of Abraham: ² Abraham was the father of Isaac, Isaac the father of Jacob, and Jacob the father of Judah and his brothers. ³ Judah was the father of Perez and Zerah by Tamar, Perez was the father of Hezron, and Hezron the father of Ram. ⁴ Ram was the father of Amminadab, Amminadab the father of Nahshon, and Nahshon the father of Salmon. ⁵ Salmon was the father of Boaz by Rahab, Boaz was the father of Obed by Ruth, and Obed the father of Jesse. ⁶ Jesse was the father of David the king. David was the father of Solomon by Bathsheba who had been the wife of Uriah. ⁷ Solomon was the father of Rehoboam, Rehoboam the father of Abijah, and Abijah the father of Asa. ⁸ Asa was the father of Jehoshaphat, Jehoshaphat the father of Joram, and Joram the father of Uzziah. ⁹ Uzziah was the father of Jotham, Jotham the father of Ahaz, and Ahaz the father of Hezekiah. ¹⁰ Hezekiah was the father of Manasseh, Manasseh the father of Amon, and Amon the (F)father of Josiah. ¹¹ Josiah became the father of Jeconiah and his brothers, at the time of the deportation to Babylon. ¹² After the deportation to Babylon: Jeconiah became the father of Shealtiel, and Shealtiel the father of Zerubbabel. ¹³ Zerubbabel was the father of Abihud, Abihud the father of Eliakim, and Eliakim the father of Azor. ¹⁴ Azor was the father of Zadok, Zadok the father of Achim, and Achim the father of Eliud. ¹⁵ Eliud was the father of Eleazar, Eleazar the father of Matthan, and Matthan the father of Jacob. ¹⁶ Jacob was the father of Joseph the husband of Mary, by whom Jesus was born, who is called the Messiah. ¹⁷ So all the generations from Abraham to David are fourteen generations; from David to the deportation to Babylon, fourteen generations; and from the deportation to Babylon to the Messiah, fourteen generations. – Matthew 1:1-17

We are surrounded by lists; we construct lists all the time. Pop music has its continuous Top 50 lists, and the *New York Times* has a regular best-sellers list. Many of us are fascinated by the lists of nominees for the academy awards, glance at the Sports pages to see who is leading the NL West in batting average or homeruns, and peruse the gossip columns full of lists of who attended what party with whom, who is dating whom. We check out the leading scorers and rebounders in the NBA. The Guinness Book of World Records is in its umpteenth printing.

We may be fascinated by lists, and we look at them a lot. But we don't think of a list as a high form of literature. No form of writing is lower on our scale of literary value than a list. We use lists to head to the grocery store, to check off to-do items, to determine who gets a wedding invitation or what we're going to get someone for Christmas. We might sit still to watch the credits after a movie, but we usually don't think of the list of names as an important part of the movie. Credits appear in literature only when they are safely tucked behind or before the text on an acknowledgements page. If we are postmodernists, we might put a list in the middle of a story just because it doesn't belong there. Umberto Eco loves to include long lists in his novels, because he loves to play with conventions.

Pre-modern people, though, loved lists, and pre-modern literature—classic literature—is full of lists. Think of the list of names in the *Iliad* Book 2. Homer asks the Muse to guide him as he begins the list; only with the Muse's help can he "tell the lords of the ships, the ships in all their numbers."[5] The author of Beowulf provides a genealogy every time he introduces a character, like a Southern matron who cannot say a name without giving a family tree and explaining who married whom. Pre-moderns would have agreed with Umberto Eco, "Lists are the most necessary literary accessories of all."

Biblical writers loved lists too, and they used them a lot. Genealogical lists are among the most popular kinds of lists in Scripture. The book of Genesis is full of genealogical lists, particularly in chapter 10 where the writer lists the seventy or so nations that descended from the sons of Noah. Numbers, as the title suggests, includes long lists of names and a census of Israel, and

---

5. *Iliad* 2.582-3 (Fagles translation).

Chronicles begins with a lengthy genealogy. The New Testament begins with the genealogy we're looking at today, and there is another genealogy in Luke that appears to trace the lineage of Mary rather than Joseph. And there's a chapter in Revelation that is little more than a list of tribes. Genealogical lists in particular are used for a number of purposes. They show relations of Jews and nations. They are a short and easy way to show the continuity of Israel over time, to show how God's purposes are being worked out in the history of His people. Perhaps most importantly, genealogical lists establish credentials for office. Lists show that priests are descended from Aaron, and thus are qualified to serve as priests; lists show descent from David.

The Biblical writers also pack a lot of important information and theology into the lists. The list of descendants of Noah in Genesis 10 is a framework for understanding the Gentile world throughout the Bible. There are 70 or so descendants, and after this chapter the number 70 is used throughout the Bible as a symbol of the Gentile nations. We learn about the relationships among the various nations—that Sidon is the firstborn son of Canaan, for instance, which helps us anticipate what kind of character the Sidonian princess Jezebel will be. We learn that the Philistines are related to the Egyptians, and this helps us grasp the significance of the Philistines in Israel's history. The two lists of tribal numbers in the book of Numbers show that God has given Abraham an abundant seed, as He promised. There is a census at the beginning of the book, and another toward the end, and the numbers of Israelites nearly identical—which shows that, in spite of all the judgments that fell on Israel during their wilderness wanderings, the Lord has preserved a nation. More subtly, many of the numbers in the book of Numbers have some astronomical significance. They are multiples of the cycles of astronomical bodies, proving that the Lord has given Abraham a seed like the stars of heaven. The genealogy in the first nine chapters of Chronicles is organized in a great chiasm, which centers in chapter 6 on the Levites, and also highlights the two royal tribes of Judah and Benjamin at either end of the genealogy. And the whole thing is set within a genealogy that begins with Adam and ends with the list of returnees from Babylonian exile—in other words, Israel's history is set within the history of the nations.

Matthew shows the same interest in packing lists not only with factual information but with theology and instruction. The list of Jesus' ancestors contains a summary of redemptive history, a preview of Gentile inclusion, and a foreshadowing of the coming of the kingdom. Matthew organizes the genealogy numerically, in three groups of fourteen generations. There are fourteen names between Abraham and David, if you include both of them. In the next phase, you need to exclude the first name, David, from the list in order to get fourteen. In the last section of the list, both Jeconiah and Jesus have to be included to get fourteen names. When we compare this scheme to the genealogy in Chronicles, it is clear that Matthew has adjusted the list to make it fit this scheme. There is a gap in the list, particularly in verses 8-9, as several generations of the descendants of David are not included. This is not only because Matthew wants to fit the list into a numerical pattern, but because those who are excluded (including Joash) were Davidic descendants associated with the house of Ahab. Matthew follows a precedent set by the writer of Kings. When the writer of Kings deals with Athaliah, he treats her as if she never reigned in Judah at all (2 Kings 11). He gives her reign no opening, no closing, no summary. She stands outside the normal pattern of history. Matthew does something similar with all of the Davidic kings who descended from the union of Athaliah and Joram. Matthew shows a judgment on the Davidic kingdom that runs to three or four generations.

What is Matthew after with the numerology? One possibility is that he is hinting at a sevenfold structure: 3×14 is 42, equivalent to 6×7. This might be related to the symbolism of a week, which Daniel also uses in his prophecy of seven weeks of years. There are two weeks of generations between Abraham and David, two weeks of generations between David and the deportation, two more weeks between Jeconiah and Jesus. Six weeks of generations are between Abraham and Jesus, and that means that Jesus is the first name in the seventh seven, the beginning of a new week, the week of the new creation. Jesus comes in the "seventh" position, the sabbatical position, in this creation-genealogy. After the ups and downs of Israel's history, Sabbath—a super-Sabbath, a 7 x 7 Sabbath, a Jubilee Sabbath—has arrived in Jesus. Jesus brings Sabbath as the New Moses, delivering us from the bondage of Egypt. He brings Sabbath as the new Joshua, subduing the land to peace and delivering an inheritance. He is David, putting down our enemies on every side. Jesus comes to deliver Israel from the burdens imposed by hypocritical Pharisees. And He comes to release our burdens, the burdens of our sins, the burdens of the law, the burdens of anxiety and fear. He comes to announce the year of Jubilee, which took place in the year after the seventh sabbatical year, the year when slaves are released, when all Israelites returned to their ancestral lands, the year that saw Israel reordered and put right. Jubilee means the end of exile, and Jesus comes as Lord of Jubilee.

In addition, Matthew has organized the genealogy around the name "David." Some Old Testament genealogies are organized numerologically to highlight a particular name. Genesis 46 is organized around the number seven, the numerical value of the name "Gad," whose name is seventh on the list and who has seven sons. According to W. D. Davies and D. C. Allison, "We read that all the persons of the house of Jacob were seventy, that seven of Judah's descendants went to Egypt, that the sons of Jacob by Rachel were fourteen, and that Bilhah bore to Jacob seven persons in all. Moreover, Gad, whose name has the numerical value of seven . . . is placed in the seventh position and given seven sons."[6] Matthew does something similar with the name "David." In Hebrew, David's name has three consonants: the numerical value of "David" is fourteen. Besides, David's name is the fourteenth in Matthew's list, and the name is repeated three times outside the genealogy proper (vv. 1, 17). The shape of the

---

6. Davies and Allison, *Matthew 1-7* (International Critical Commentary; London: Continuum, 2004), p. 164.

genealogy confirms that David is the high point of the whole genealogy: from Abraham to David, Israel waxes to its height; from David to the deportation, the Davidic kingdom wanes; but after another fourteen generations appears a second David, Jesus, who restores the kingdom of David. As we go through Matthew, we'll see that Jesus comes preaching about the kingdom of God or the kingdom of heaven. He announces that the Davidic kingdom is being restored, and that He, as the last Davidic king, extends the kingdom of David even more widely than David did.

Genealogies are particularly important for the qualification of priests, since priests had to descend from Aaron and later from Zadok, the high priest at the time of David. Many of the names in the last third of Matthew's list are strongly associated with the priesthood. Abiud is a version of Abijah, one of the sons of Aaron. There is a Zadok, the name of David's priest, and Eleazar, another son of Aaron. After the exile, the Davidic kingdom was never restored, and the high priests began to take on civil as well as liturgical functions. During the period after the Maccabean Revolt, the high priest held the highest civil office, and sometimes he even held the title of king. Jesus is the Davidic king, but Matthew also shows that He transcends the Davidic kingship by being a king-priest. He transcends the Aaronic priesthood by being a priest-king. He combines the offices, and He shows Himself to be the priest after the order of Melchizedek.

Matthew also highlights some other themes by including a number of women in the genealogy. This is not unprecedented in biblical genealogies, but it is rare. Four women are included: Tamar (v. 3; Genesis 38), the daughter-in-law of Judah who dressed as a prostitute, seduced Judah, and gave birth to his twin sons, Perez and Zerah; Rahab (v. 5; Joshua 2), the prostitute of Jericho who hid the Israelite spies and whose house was saved as a result; Ruth (v. 5), whom we know from the book of Ruth; and "the wife of Uriah," Bathsheba (v. 6; 2 Samuel 11-12). Why would Matthew include women at all, and why particularly these women? Why not Sarah and Rachel and Abigail?

All but Ruth are connected with some scandal, and it is often said that Matthew includes these women to show that God's purposes triumph over human sin. That is certainly true, and leads into the intriguing climax of a fifth woman: Mary! Each of the women gave birth in circumstances that might have seemed immoral or scandalous. So did Mary. But the Jews over time had come to recognize each of the women named in the genealogy as a paragon of virtue, and Matthew hints that Mary is in the same position. Though the circumstances of her pregnancy were questionable, Jews should not be surprised or reject Jesus or Mary on that account. Joseph represents the typical Jewish reaction to Mary's pregnancy, but then is changed. Matthew wants the Jewish readers of his gospel to do the same, as they've done with Tamar, Rahab, Ruth, and Bathsheba.[7]

While true, Matthew could have done it without mentioning any women. He makes this point clearly enough by including Manasseh in the genealogy (v. 10; 2 Kings 21). Besides, most of these women are commended for their righteousness. Judah says that Tamar is "more righteous than I," and James commends Rahab the prostitute for her living, working faith (Genesis 38:26; James 2:25). Ruth was fairly aggressive in pursuing Boaz, but she was doing it under her mother-in-law's instructions, and she is never condemned for anything. Bathsheba committed adultery, but David was the predator in that situation.

Matthew includes these women because all are Gentiles, or (in Bathsheba's case) members of a Gentile household. Tamar was a Canaanite, Rahab also a Canaanite (a resident of Jericho), Ruth a Moabitess. Bathsheba, though an Israelite, was married to a Gentile solder of David's and is named in this genealogy in relation to her husband. From the moment Jesus appears, He incorporates Gentile flesh and blood—four of them, from the four corners of the earth—into His body, His physical body. Gentile "brides" incorporated into the Bride of God, Israel. Including Gentiles is

---

7. Edwin Freed, "The Women in Matthew's Genealogy," *JSNT* 29 (1987), pp. 3-19.

not some second-thought on God's part. He included Gentiles in the body of His Son from the beginning. The women show that Jesus comes as the fulfillment of the promise to Abraham, to bless the Gentiles through the seed of Abraham. Jesus is the son of Abraham, the true seed, in whom Gentiles are *already* blessed.

Twice in his genealogy, Matthew refers to "brothers." Jacob was the father of "Judah and his brothers," and at the time of the deportation to Babylon "Jeconiah and his brothers" were born to Josiah. This initiates a theme in Matthew's gospel, the theme of the church as a brotherhood. Alongside Judah and his brothers, and Jeconiah and his brothers, Matthew talks about Jesus and His brothers. At the heart of this is a redefinition of what counts as family. Family is not blood-based. It's faith-based, and obedience-based. When Jesus is told that his mother and brothers wait to see Him, He says that His mother and brothers are those who do the will of the heavenly Father (12:50). Later, Jesus says that no one should be called Rabbi because "you are all brothers" (23:8). Throughout the gospel, Jesus teaches us how we are to behave toward brothers. In the Sermon on the Mount, He prohibits anger against a brother (5:22-24) and tells us to remove the logs from our own eyes before we try to pick out the speck in our brother's eye (7:3-5). Jesus gives us a procedure for dealing with our brother's sins (18:15). He warns that the Father will not forgive us if we don't forgive our brothers from the heart (18:35). This is not a peripheral issue for Matthew. We are all brothers toward one another because we are all brothers to Jesus and sons and daughters of the same heavenly Father. A key test of discipleship is how we treat our brothers.

The genealogy of Jesus thus contains a Christology: Jesus is the son of Abraham, bringing blessing to the Gentiles, the true Davidic king, and an heir also to the priesthood. He is the priestly Messiah, the priest-king after the order of Melchizedek. The genealogy of Jesus also shows what God is up to with the history of Israel. It shows that Israel does not exist for herself. Matthew doesn't want to give us a pure-blood genealogy. He wants to show that in Jesus, in His own body, flows the blood of Canaanites and

Moabites and the wife of a Hittite. And when He begins to gather His corporate body, He incorporates us as members, so that in Jesus people from every blood, from every race, from every tribe and tongue are combined in one person, in the one New Man, Jesus. In this way, the genealogy at the beginning anticipates the conclusion, when Jesus the Jew-Gentile son of Abraham and David sends the Eleven to proclaim His kingdom to the nations.

Conceived of Mary by the Spirit
Matthew 1:18-25[8]

Now the birth of Jesus Christ was as follows: when His mother Mary had been betrothed to Joseph, before they came together she was found to be with child by the Holy Spirit. [19] And Joseph her husband, being a righteous man and not wanting to disgrace her, planned to send her away secretly. [20] But when he had considered this, behold, an angel of the Lord appeared to him in a dream, saying, "Joseph, son of David, do not be afraid to take Mary as your wife; for the Child who has been conceived in her is of the Holy Spirit. [21] "She will bear a Son; and you shall call His name Jesus, for He will save His people from their sins." [22] Now all this took place to fulfill what was spoken by the Lord through the prophet: [23] "Behold, the virgin shall be

---

8. Matthew 1:18-2:23 sorts out into a neat chiasm:

A. Joseph, angel, dream, Jesus born
    B. Wise men search for Jesus: to Herod
        C. Wise men visit Jesus: dream
            D. Joseph, dream flee to Egypt
        C'. Herod tricked by wise men
    B'. Herod kills children
A'. Joseph, angel, dream, Jesus settles in Nazareth

Sections A, D, and A' are particularly intimately related. Each is about a dream of Joseph in which an angel appears. In all three, Mary and the child are mentioned. Each includes a fulfillment formula. In the D and A' sections, the commands of the angel begin with a command to rise, a "resurrection" command: "Arise and take the Child and His mother" (vv. 13, 20).

with child and shall bear a son, and they shall call his name Immanuel," which translated means, "God with us." [24] And Joseph awoke from his sleep and did as the angel of the Lord commanded him, and took Mary as his wife, [25] but kept her a virgin until she gave birth to a Son; and he called His name Jesus.
— Matthew 1:18-25

According to the Nicene Creed, the one Lord Jesus Christ was "incarnate by the Holy Ghost of the Virgin Mary." This has been the confession of the church since the earliest centuries. In the past few centuries many have challenged or rejected it. Some reject the Virgin conception and birth of Jesus because they don't believe such things can happen. Others reject this doctrine because they think it's mythological. They point to legends of miraculous births and divine-human births in mythologies throughout the world, and conclude that this is just another example of that kind of mythology. This often reduces to the first objection: Once upon a time, human beings had no idea where babies came from, but now we know that virgin births can't happen. Some, however, question the virgin birth because they say the New Testament doesn't teach it very clearly or consistently. Mark and John don't mention Jesus' miraculous birth and neither does Paul. So, they argue, it couldn't be all that important. Many things appear in only one or two books of the Bible, and yet we believe them. Why should every book cover everything?

There is no doubt after all, that both Matthew and Luke teach that Jesus was conceived in the womb of Mary when she was a virgin. Matthew says that Mary was found to be with child "before they came together" (v. 18). That might be "before they were married," but the phrase could also have a sexual connotation—namely, that Mary became pregnant before she had sexual relations with Joseph. Mary is explicit in Luke, "I know not a man."

Verses 22-23 provide the prophetic basis for this event. It is the first of over a dozen fulfillment formulae in Matthew's gospel. Jesus comes to fulfill the law and the prophets, and

Matthew shows us this by frequently citing Scripture that Jesus is specifically fulfilling. The life of Jesus is shaped the way it is because it is shaped in fulfillment of prophecy.

There is some debate about Matthew's translation here. Isaiah uses a Hebrew word (*alma*) that can be translated simply as "young woman" and doesn't necessarily connote "virgin." Hebrew has another word for "virgin," and Isaiah does not use that term in Isaiah 7. Matthew quotes in the Greek, which in the LXX had already translated "alma" more explicitly as "virgin" (παρθενος). That Greek word is a reasonable translation of the Hebrew. Though the Hebrew word doesn't necessarily mean "virgin," it means a young girl of marriageable age, and the assumption would be that she is a virgin. Isaiah 7 is the only passage where the word *alma* is used in connection with childbirth, so a child born to an *alma* is an odd happening. Isaiah says it is a sign. To be a sign, it must be out of the ordinary run of things.

Unfortunately, some who rightly defend the doctrine of the virgin conception and birth of Jesus don't go much further to think about what it means. What does it tell us about Jesus? About God? Why would God the Son become incarnate in this fashion? Many have thought that Jesus' conception of a Virgin was designed to bypass original sin. Elaborate theories have been developed to show that the stain of original sin is passed from the male rather than the female. So long as Jesus didn't have a human father, he was free from original sin, even if he had a human mother. Jesus was free from sin of all sorts (Hebrews 4:15), but this doesn't seem to be the rationale for the virgin conception of Jesus. Why wouldn't Jesus have picked up original sin from Mary, after all? To protect against this conclusion, the Roman Catholic Church has resorted to the doctrine of the Immaculate Conception, which refers to Mary's own freedom from original sin. To make sure that Jesus was free from *all* stain of original sin, Mary also has to be free from original sin. But then you have a regression that goes back along Mary's whole genealogy.

Matthew's point is different. He says nothing about Jesus' sinlessness here. The emphasis is on Jesus as the Deliverer from sin, not on Jesus' own freedom from sin. This episode is framed as part of a creation story. Like 1:1, verse 18 uses the word "genesis" (γενεσις, translated "birth"). In this creation context, the references to the Holy Spirit (vv. 18, 20) allude back to Genesis 1:2. Mary is the "earth" over which the heavenly Spirit hovers to form a new creation. Joseph rising from sleep to take his wife reminds us of Adam in the garden (Genesis 2:18-25), taking Mary as his wife just as Adam took the newly created Eve as his wife.

This virgin birth is thus a sign of God's new initiative, of God's new creation, which begins with the creation of the new Man, Jesus. Our salvation does not come—it *cannot* come—from inside humanity. We are not capable of saving ourselves. God has to come in from the outside if we are going to be saved. We cannot repair the damage of sin or construct a new creation by our own initiative, by our own reproduction, by our own expertise or power. The virgin birth passes a judgment on *all* human efforts at self-salvation, all our prideful pretense that we can put the world right through political or technological or educational means. If the world is going to be put right, God must enter the world from the outside, because everything that comes from within humanity is corrupted and weak.

We can also note Isaiah's and Matthew's use of the name Immanuel, "God with us." The virgin birth means that Jesus is God with us, God in human flesh, God who has taken on human nature to be with His people and to save us. The virgin birth thus tells us something about the nature of Christ. It is not as if Joseph and Mary had a son who later became the Son of God. It is not as if there was a pre-existing human being who was later infused with Godness. Rather, the virgin conception and birth shows that Jesus only exists *as* the humanity of the Son of God. There is not even a single moment when the humanity of Jesus exists by itself. It is always, from the moment of conception, the humanity of the Son of God. It is God's humanity. And this means that Jesus really is God-with-us, God near us, God entered into human nature, into human history, in the fullest possible sense. There is no distance between God and Jesus, not even for a single second. Donald Macleod has written, "God was involved in a peculiarly direct and intimate way in the creation of his humanity. To deny the virgin birth and introduce instead human sexual activity is to distance God unacceptably from the production of the Holy One."[9] To touch the humanity of Jesus is to touch the humanity of God. To see and hear Jesus is to see and hear God in human flesh. Because of the Virgin Conception and Birth, Jesus truly is, in the most direct way possible, both *God* and *with us*.

We can explore this further by looking at the prophecy quoted in verses 22-23. Matthew quotes only one verse, but the whole story is in view. Isaiah prophesies in the context of a political crisis in the Southern Kingdom of Judah. Assyria is on the rise to the East, and in order to resist Assyria, the Northern Kingdom of Israel, led by Pekah, and Aram, led by Remaliah, ally to force Judah to join the alliance. Ahaz of Judah refuses to join the alliance, and so these two kings propose to attack Jerusalem, topple Ahaz, and put a more sympathetic king on the throne. Isaiah assures Ahaz that he need not fear Pekah and Remaliah (v. 4), because the Lord has said "it shall not stand nor shall it come to pass" (v. 7). Yahweh is still the head of Jerusalem, and he will crush the heads of Samaria and Damascus. To further reassure Ahaz, Yahweh offers, through Isaiah, to give the king a sign. Though a wicked king, Ahaz pretends to be pious and says he won't test the Lord by asking for a sign (v. 12). Isaiah sees this as itself a test of the Lord's patience and announces that the Lord will give a sign anyway, the sign of the pregnant virgin, the sign of the miracle son, whose name will be called Immanuel. In its initial significance, the sign is a sign of victory over Israel and Aram: "before the boy will know enough to refuse evil and choose good, the land whose two kings you dread will be forsaken" (v. 16). Pekah and Remaliah will be defeated before the boy is full grown.

---

9. McLeod, *The Person of Christ* (Contours of Christian Theology; Downers Grove: IVP, 1998), p. 39.

In other words, the prophecy is about the birth of a child who will be called "With us God," and that's in the context of a military threat to Judah. The promise that God will be with Judah is a promise that He will be a deliverer for His people. This annunciation reminds us of Old Testament annunciations of Ishmael (Genesis 16) and Samson (Judges 13). Just as the Lord sent Moses, and Samuel, and Samson through miraculous births to be the saviors of Israel, so the Lord is going to do the whole thing over again by sending one as a savior. The prophecy of Isaiah 7:14 is directly related to verse 21: "You shall call His name Jesus, for it is He who will save His people from their sins." This new Immanuel won't save His people from Egypt, Philistia, Babylon, or Rome, but from their worst enemy, Sin (v. 21). Jesus the Virgin Born comes as the One who will achieve the victory of God. The sign of the virgin birth is a sign of victory over enemies. To say that the Son of God has been born of a virgin, and is therefore God with us, is to say that God is with us as our protector, defender, victor, savior.

But the prophecy of Isaiah goes on, and we need to recognize the double-sidedness of the prophecy. Ahaz attempted to sound pious and godly: "Oh, no, I won't test God by asking for a sign even when He's offered a sign. I might test God by worshiping idols. I might test God by constructing an altar on the model of an altar I saw once in Damascus. But test God by accepting His offer of a sign—Oh, no, I'm too pious for that." Because of his false piety, which Isaiah knows is a form of unbelief, the sign of God With Us is not only a sign of victory, but a sign of impending judgment. After the prophet promises that Yahweh will remove the kings, he says that a much more powerful enemy is going to come: Assyria. Yahweh will whistle for the Assyrians like a beekeeper whistles for his bees; Assyria will come like a razor and remove all the glory-hair of Judah. The birth of the child means that God is with Judah, but the presence of God can be comforting or condemning depending on our faith. If God comes near to a disobedient, faithless people, it can only mean destruction.

This too is part of the story of Matthew's gospel. As soon as he's quoted from Isaiah 7, he gives us an example of a king very like Ahaz, a wicked king who acts piously by pretending to want to worship the king alongside the wise men, a king who refuses to acknowledge the sign that is given, the sign of Immanuel. Herod cannot rejoice at the news of a new king, whom he sees as a rival to his own power. Many Jews receive Jesus, but Jerusalem, the center of Jewish leadership, is hostile to Jesus from the beginning. Rather than receive Jesus, Israel's leaders prefer to play the role of court scribes to the bloodthirsty power-monger, Herod. Jerusalem confirms its reputation as the city that kills prophets; she will be left desolate as a result (cf. Matthew 23:37-38).

By his very name, Joseph the adoptive father of Jesus brings to mind the Joseph of Genesis, and, as we have seen, there are many similarities between them. Both receive dreams and act on them. Both go to Egypt in order to protect their families. Both are righteous men, threatened by their own countrymen, by brothers. Within Genesis, Joseph ben Jacob fulfills the promises to Abraham. Yahweh told Abraham that through his seed, all the families of the earth will be blessed. Though this promise is fulfilled completely in Jesus, it is also fulfilled within the book of Genesis itself. Joseph is the seed of Abraham who blesses the nations by providing food for a famine-stricken world. Joseph the father of Jesus too fulfills the promises to Abraham, and in much the same manner. He goes to Egypt in order to ensure that the promises to Abraham will be fulfilled. He follows the Lord's instructions to ensure that there is food for a hungry world. Jesus is the true bread that has come down from heaven, and Joseph acts repeatedly to ensure that this bread is preserved for the nations to eat. Joseph son of Jacob became a great ruler, the second ruler of Egypt. Joseph the father of Jesus does not rule Egypt, and he does not even rule in Israel, but he is still a king. He is called "son of David" (Matthew 1:20); he administers the law with mercy; he receives revelation by dreams, as Solomon, Nebuchadnezzar, and others kings did. As a king, Joseph ensures that the people have bread. Joseph the father of Jesus is obedient to the vision so that the bread of life born at Bethlehem, which is the house of bread, can be preserved as bread for the Gentiles.

In keeping with the allusions to the Joseph story, the coming of the wise men in the following section is also a story of Gentile "invasion." Isaiah prophesied that Assyrians would come and attack the land of Judah, and that Immanuel was a sign of that coming attack. God will be with Judah through Assyria as well. In Matthew's gospel, when Herod-Ahaz refuses to acknowledge the sign, the Lord brings in Gentiles to worship what the Jewish king refuses to worship. Jesus' birth is a sign: Jews refuse the sign, Gentiles accept it. In this story is foreshadowed the great reversal that takes place in the gospel.

The contrast in Matthew is not simply between Jew and Gentile. Jesus, after all, gains a wide following among the Jewish people. Multitudes follow Him and become disciples. The difference is a difference within Israel as well as between Israel and the Gentiles. The difference is between those who are leaders in Israel, part of the establishment, residents of the capital city, and those who are in the villages and countryside. The difference is between the powerful, whose power is threatened by Jesus' popularity, and the poor and weak who follow Him. Jesus is not only a challenge to Judaism; he is specifically a challenge to wealthy and powerful Jews.

Of course, this reversal is also prophesied. Stars represent rulers, and the appearance of a new star tells the magi that a king has been born (cf. Numbers 24:15-19). The magi come to pay homage to King Jesus, like the Queen of Sheba who came to see Solomon's court (1 Kings 10) and in fulfillment of prophecies about the Gentiles streaming to Jerusalem to offer their riches to the God of Israel (Isaiah 60:4-9). The last is a prophecy about the future of Jerusalem, the fact that the Gentiles will assist in building up the house of the Lord and will make the house glorious and full of the treasure of the Gentiles. That was true of Solomon's temple, which was full of the plunder of the Gentile nations that David conquered. But these Gentiles will willingly bring their treasures, like Cyrus sending material back with the exiles.

This is what the sign of Immanuel means. God is with us, and those who trust and believe and obey can be confident in the face of all enemies, in the face of Sin and Satan and Death, in the face of Rome and Assyria and Pekah and Remaliah. But God with us threatens the rich and powerful who resist God, who put a pious face on their unbelief. Immanuel is a sign of the rising and falling of many in Israel. He still is. Jesus is God-come-near, God-with-us, God-become-man. That is a sign of life unto life, and a sign of death unto death. The only right response in the face of this sign is humility, repentance, and faith. Immanuel has come: Repent and believe the good news.

Magi from the East
Matthew 2:1-12

Now after Jesus was born in Bethlehem of Judea in the days of Herod the king, magi from the east arrived in Jerusalem, saying, [2] "Where is He who has been born King of the Jews? For we saw His star in the east and have come to worship Him." [3] When Herod the king heard this, he was troubled, and all Jerusalem with him. [4] Gathering together all the chief priests and scribes of the people, he inquired of them where the Messiah was to be born. [5] They said to him, "In Bethlehem of Judea; for this is what has been written by the prophet: [6] 'And you, Bethlehem, land of Judah; are by no means least among the leaders of Judah; for out of you shall come forth a ruler who will shepherd My people Israel.'" [7] Then Herod secretly called the magi and determined from them the exact time the star appeared. [8] And he sent them to Bethlehem and said, "Go and search carefully for the Child; and when you have found Him, report to me, so that I too may come and worship Him." [9] After hearing the king, they went their way; and the star, which they had seen in the east, went on before them until it came and stood over the place where the Child was. [10] When they saw the star, they rejoiced exceedingly

> with great joy. [11] After coming into the house they saw the Child with Mary His mother; and they fell to the ground and worshiped Him. Then, opening their treasures, they presented to Him gifts of gold, frankincense, and myrrh. [12] And having been warned by God in a dream not to return to Herod, the magi left for their own country by another way.
> – Matthew 2:1-12

For many in the modern period, Christianity has been seen as an apolitical religion. This has been a convenient myth for modern people. The modern world was born in an age of religious war. After the Reformation, Europe entered a period of protracted and often vicious conflict that left large portions of Western Europe devastated. In the aftermath, politicians and theologians and philosophers decided they had to do something to make sure that nothing like this ever happened again. For many, the most obvious thing to do was to exclude religion from the political sphere. Religion was dangerous and divisive in politics, and it had to be driven away to bring peace and quiet. To do that, they had to change the meaning of "religion."[10] For about a millennium, Christianity permeated the political life of Western Europe. Western Europe was Christendom, Christ's realm. Kings took oaths to the Triune God at coronations and thought about the implications of the Ten Commandments for developing laws. If religion were going to be excluded from political life, it had to be turned into something that was not inherently political. It had to be spiritualized.

Surprisingly, the Christians who have been most eager to follow this program are not liberals and virtual unbelievers, but conservative Bible-believing Christians. While many liberals have substituted politics for faith, many Bible-believing Christians have often dispensed with the political dimensions of their faith

---

10. Very little of this standard account of the rise of modern secular politics is true. For a devastating critique, see William T. Cavanaugh, *The Myth of Religious Violence: Secular Ideology and the Roots of Modern Conflict* (Oxford: Oxford University Press, 2009).

altogether. So, when Jesus' preaching is summarized in the political phrase the "kingdom of God," we mentally translate it to a "spiritual" kingdom. When Jesus is declared the king of the Jews, we immediately say, "Well, his kingdom is not of this world." When Paul tells Christians to submit to the ruling authorities, we say, "See, Christianity is not political at all. We just go along with the authorities."

There is superficial plausibility in these responses. Jesus Himself does say, "My kingdom is not of this world," and Paul does indeed say that we should submit to ruling authorities. But submitting to authorities is not an "apolitical" position; it's a particular kind of politics. Jesus doesn't deny that He is a King or that He has a kingdom. He denies that His kingdom is like the kingdom of Herod, Pilate, or Caesar; but He admits He is a King with a kingdom. Jesus said that the children of this world are in their generation wiser than the children of light. Herod the Great—paranoid, power-hungry, unscrupulous—recognizes something about Jesus that many faithful believers do not recognize: He knows that when Jesus is called the "son of David" and "king of the Jews," it is a political claim and a political threat. Herod can see the inexorable political logic: Jesus claims to be King of the Jews, Herod claims to be King of the Jews. They cannot both be right. If both claim to be kings, and they do, then conflict is inevitable. Inevitably, Jesus' advent provokes fear and rage from other pretenders to the throne. Jesus' mere presence on earth, even as a little baby, is already a political act, God's challenge to the political status quo, God throwing down the gauntlet to Herod and all earthly rulers like him. Jesus' birth comes with the exhortation of Psalm 2: "Now therefore, O kings, show discernment; take warning, Judges of the earth. Serve the Lord with reverence, and rejoice with trembling. Kiss the Son, lest He be angry and you perish in the way."

Remember that the whole book of Matthew follows the storyline of the whole Old Testament. Jesus is Israel living through the entirety of Israel's history in order to redeem it. Jesus is also Israel's God living through again His pursuit of Israel, His covenant-history with His bride. Joseph of Nazareth is parallel to the Joseph of the book of Genesis: Both are righteous men who dream (1:20), both go to Egypt with their family (2:14), and both return (2:21). By the time we get to the beginning of chapter 2, though, the typology has moved to the Exodus. The story of the wise men and Herod is set in this Exodus context. Pharaoh had his court magicians; Herod is surrounded by the chief priests and scribes (2:4). Pharaoh killed innocent Hebrew children; so does Herod (2:16-18). When Moses was a young man, he killed an Egyptian, and had to leave Egypt. He went to Midian, where he stayed until the Lord sent him back to deliver His people. Jesus too goes out of the land and is later going to return.

The locations have become ironically reversed. Israel has become an Egypt, and Jesus, the new Moses, has to flee to *Egypt* for safety. This has happened before. In Jeremiah's prophecy, Jeremiah describes Judah in terms that recall the condition of Egypt, and he instructs the faithful within Jerusalem to "go out" of Jerusalem as they once went out of Egypt. Jeremiah announces an exodus, but not an exodus from a Gentile land. He announces an exodus from the land of Israel. Yahweh turns His weapons on Judah (21:8-10; 29:17ff). Jeremiah warns the people to "go out," an "exodus" exhortation, but the place they are to exit is not Egypt or Babylon but Israel.

This inverted exodus replays the early life of Jesus. At Jesus' birth, Israel has reached a similar nadir. Israel has become an Egypt. The Lord turns His weapons against Israel and calls His faithful people to "go out" in a new Exodus. If Herod is a new Pharaoh, Jesus is a new Moses, who gathers a people to lead them out from under the oppressive hand of Herod. This is one of the political effects of Jesus' coming: Those who become disciples of Jesus serve another king. They are liberated from the tyrannical political systems of this world. We may still submit to earthly rulers, but we do that for the sake of our heavenly ruler, Jesus. We submit to earthly kings not because they are our ultimate authority but because we are obeying the instructions of Jesus, our true King. This is destabilizing, and rulers like Herod cannot help but suspect that we are disloyal. Gentile magi come to worship Jesus. Matthew's genealogy includes four Gentile women, anticipating the inclusion of Gentiles in the new Israel. The story of the wise men reiterates this theme. The magi come to pay homage to King Jesus, like the Queen of Sheba who came to see Solomon's court (1 Kings 10) and in fulfillment of prophecies about the Gentiles streaming to Jerusalem to offer their riches to the God of Israel (Isaiah 60:4-9). Though Israel has become an Egypt, the Lord is beginning to form a new Israel out of non-Israelites.

But something more radical is going on here. The magi are not just on a par with the queen of Sheba and other Gentiles who visited Solomon but who then remained Gentiles. The magi are much more like Israel herself. The magi follow the star to Jerusalem, a star that is capable of marking out a single house where Jesus is born (v. 9). As unbelievers like to suggest, this is not really possible for a star. Stars cannot stand above houses. What they see in the sky and what leads them, is the glory-cloud.[11] It is star-like, but not a literal star. The magi follow the star just as Israel had followed the pillar of cloud and fire from Egypt. They travel from the east and enter the land from the east, just as Israel did. They come into the land to worship the true king of the land, Jesus. In other words, the magi are not merely Gentile God-fearers, but the beginning of a new Israel, which is going to consist of Jews and Gentiles. They are the true Israel, the firstfruits of the Gentiles.

Jews already reject Jesus, and Gentiles already worship Him. But that is not the precise contrast in Matthew's gospel. Joseph and Mary, after all, are Jews, and they honor the new King. It's true that Herod and the Jewish leaders are troubled (v. 3). Herod cannot rejoice at the news of a new king, whom he sees as a rival to his own power. Rather than receive Jesus, Israel's leaders prefer to play the role of court scribes to the bloodthirsty power-monger, Herod. Jerusalem confirms its reputation as the city that kills

---

11. See James B. Jordan, "Star over Bethlehem: A Snapshot of Dominion," *Geneva Review* 25 (1985), pp. 1-2.

New Israel

prophets (cf. Matthew 23:37-38). Jerusalem is the place where the opposition to Jesus begins. Jerusalem is where Jesus will be killed. Jerusalem is where the chief priests and scribes and Pharisees are concentrated. When Jesus is in Galilee, huge crowds gather to follow Him, to listen to Him, to become His disciples. Jesus wins the devotion of many Jews throughout Judea as well. The ones who stand in stubborn opposition are not the Jews per se, but the Jewish leaders.

This is part of the message of the prophecy quoted from Micah 5 about the birthplace of the Messiah. Fulfilling prophecy, Jesus is born in Bethlehem, the "house of bread" and the city of David. Early in his prophecy, Micah condemns the rulers of Judah "who hate good and love evil, who tear flesh from their bones, and who eat the flesh of my people, strip off their skin from them, break their bones, and chop them as for the pot and as meat in a kettle" (Micah 3:1-3). Judah is ruled by a cannibal king, but Micah also promises deliverance through a faithful king. Micah 5, quoted in Matthew 2:6, tells the story of a siege and the birth of a child who will deliver Israel and bring peace (Micah 5:1-5). This ruler is said to "go forth" from Bethlehem, to depart from Bethlehem as a conqueror. In contrast to the devouring shepherd, Herod (cf. Ezekiel 34), Jesus comes to "shepherd My people Israel" (Matthew 2:6). In Micah 5, however, the wording is different. Matthew quotes it in a way that suggests that Bethlehem has some standing in the cities of Judah. In Micah, however, the statement is opposite: "as for you, Bethlehem Ephrathah, too little to be among the clans of Judah, from you One will go forth for Me to be ruler in Israel." Micah emphasizes the smallness and insignificance of Bethlehem; Matthew emphasizes its prominence.

Both of course are true. Bethlehem was a little and sometimes despised town. It was implicated in some of the evils recorded in the book of Judges and had a reputation as a moral cesspool. But this little and sometimes despised town first became the city of David and then the birthplace of David's greater son. It is marginal but becomes a new center. It is despised, but it takes on a high reputation. It is "too little to be among the clans of

Judah," and yet it is also "by no means least among the leaders of Judah." And this points to the character of Jesus' kingdom and the political effects of Jesus' advent. Jesus challenges corrupted, violent, established rulers. He is not a threat to established authority simply because it is established. But He is a serious threat to established rulers who use their power for evil, who kill innocents, who rule with brutality. And He challenges these established rulers by coming from the margins and gathering an army from the margins, by gathering His followers from among the victims of those rulers. He challenges these rulers by calling worshipers from the east, and from Galilee, to be a new Israel.

This is the way that God continues to challenge corrupt powers since the time of Jesus. The gospel is a royal announcement, a declaration that the King of the Jews has been exalted to become King of everything. The gospel calls kings and rulers in particular to submit to the High King. At the same time, through the gospel, God is gathering together the weak and the lame, the blind and the deaf, the despised and the rejected, to become the nucleus of His own kingdom. Matthew's birth story thus exemplifies the politics of God, which is also expressed by Paul in 1 Corinthians: "God has chosen the foolish things of the world to put to shame the wise, and God has chosen the weak things of the world to put to shame the things which are mighty; and the base things of the world and the things which are despised God has chosen, and the things which are not, to bring to nothing the things that are, that no flesh should glory in His presence. But of Him you are in Christ Jesus, who became for us wisdom from God—and righteousness and sanctification and redemption—that, as it is written, "He who glories, let him glory in the Lord." The circumstances of Jesus' birth foreshadow the ways of His kingdom. The kingdom of God subverts the kingdoms of this world, and the kingdom of God grows to encompass the entire earth.

God's Plan Unfolding
Matthew 2:13-23

Now when they had gone, behold, an angel of the Lord appeared to Joseph in a dream and said, "Get up! Take the Child and His mother and flee to Egypt, and remain there until I tell you; for Herod is going to search for the Child to destroy Him." [14] So Joseph got up and took the Child and His mother while it was still night, and left for Egypt. [15] He remained there until the death of Herod. This was to fulfill what had been spoken by the Lord through the prophet: "Out of Egypt I called My son." [16] Then when Herod saw that he had been tricked by the magi, he became very enraged, and sent and slew all the male children who were in Bethlehem and all its vicinity, from two years old and under, according to the time which he had determined from the magi. [17] Then what had been spoken through Jeremiah the prophet was fulfilled: [18] "A voice was heard in Ramah, weeping and great mourning, Rachel weeping for her children; and she refused to be comforted, because they were no more." [19] But when Herod died, behold, an angel of the Lord appeared in a dream to Joseph in Egypt, and said, [20] "Get up, take the Child and His mother, and go into the land of Israel; for those who sought the Child's life are dead." [21] So Joseph got up, took the Child and His mother, and came into the land of Israel. [22] But when he heard that Archelaus was reigning over Judea in place of his father Herod, he was afraid to go there. Then after being warned by God in a dream, he left for the regions of Galilee, [23] and came and lived in a city called Nazareth. This was to fulfill what was spoken through the prophets: "He shall be called a Nazarene."
– Matthew 2:13-23

One of Matthew's themes is that Jesus fulfills the Scripture, that the gospel, as Paul puts it at the beginning of Romans, announces that what was promised by the prophets in the holy Scriptures is now fulfilled in Jesus (Romans 1:1-4). That is the theme running through this passage. Matthew 2:13-23 is divided into three episodes, each of which concludes with a statement about events "fulfilling" prophecy (2:15, 18, 23). His move from Israel to Egypt fulfills the words of Hosea 11:1: "Out of Egypt I called my son." Herod's slaughter of infants in the region around Bethlehem fulfills the prophecy of Jeremiah 31 about Rachel weeping for her children that were not. Jesus' final settlement in Nazareth fulfills a teaching of the prophets in general, that the Messiah would be known as a Nazarene. Jesus' movements, His places of residence, His escape from an early death, all of this was mapped and planned centuries before. There is nothing accidental. The whole history of Jesus, from His descent from David and Abraham through the moves of His early childhood to His eventual death and resurrection, all was planned beforehand and revealed in pieces by the prophets of Israel. As the incarnate Word (John 1:1, 14), He lives out the script of the written Word.

What are the specific prophecies that Jesus fulfills here? What does this tell us about the work of Jesus? What does it mean for us who are disciples of Jesus? The first quotation is from Hosea 11:1. Threatened by the magi's news about the birth of a king, Herod plans to kill Him. But the Lord intervenes with yet another dream (1:20; cf. 2:19, 22) and sends Joseph to Egypt. This fulfills, Matthew says, the prophecy of Hosea. Hosea 11 is one of a number of summaries of Israel's history found in the prophets. These are all stories about the Lord's kindness, faithfulness, and generosity to His people, and also about His people's consistent rejection of her Lord and consistent refusal to walk in His covenant. Hosea 11 begins with a reference to the exodus from Egypt, but goes on to talk about Israel's idolatry and the Lord's subsequent judgment. At the same time, Hosea expresses the Lord's anguished appeals to His son to return to Him, and also expresses His enduring love for a people that will not have His love. He cannot give up Ephraim in spite of Ephraim's sins and idolatries. And Hosea says that even though the Lord will punish Ephraim for their sins, He will not leave them in the grave of exile forever. He will roar and call them back trembling from Egypt and Assyria

All this is in the background of Matthew. Jesus is the "son" who comes out of Egypt. He is the true Israel who lives Israel's history. But this Israel is not going to be like the Israel of old. This Israel will fulfill the Scriptures entirely, not only in the providential mapping of His life, but also in His complete obedience and submission to the Father. Jesus as the true Israel also expresses the Father's longing for Ephraim, His sympathy, the churning of His heart. The Son's arrival is the result of this divine anguish, this inner churning of the Father. Matthew is showing us that the God of Israel cannot give up on His people. Though some in Israel will be destroyed, in the end all Israel will be saved.

But the fulfillment is not straightforward. It is ironic. We expect Hosea 11 to be quoted instead somewhere around verse 20, when Joseph leaves Egypt and returns to Israel. The quotation is not out of place. As Israel leaves Egypt at night, so Joseph leaves *Israel* by night (v. 14), and this confirms that Matthew sees Israel as the new Egypt. When he quotes Hosea 11:1 (v. 15), he is making the same point: Israel was Yahweh's firstborn (Exodus 4:22-23), called out of Egypt; Jesus, the true, faithful Israel, the Son of Yahweh, is called from the threatening world of Herod's kingdom. In order for Yahweh to fulfill His yearnings in bringing Israel from Egypt, He must bring Israel out of Israel. He must call Israel, Jesus, His Son, from the Egypt of Herod's kingdom. This is the way that the ultimate fulfillment of Hosea's prophecy will be accomplished. Salvation comes when the Father calls His Son from Egypt. The new exodus occurs when Jesus leads His people out.

After Joseph has fled to safety, Pharaoh Herod sets about slaughtering all the newborn male children around Bethlehem (v. 16). This is literally over-kill. Herod looks for one child, but he kills dozens. This too is part of God's predestined purpose for the Messiah. Even this tragic event fulfills a prophecy made centuries before Jesus was born, by Jeremiah 31:15. Even the tragedy of the slaughter of infants is enclosed within God's plan for His Son. Jeremiah 31 is mainly a joyous passage about Israel's return from exile, and it includes a number of parallels with the story of Jesus: The returning exiles are described as a "virgin" (Jeremiah

31:4) and as Yahweh's firstborn son (31:9, 20), and the exile is the "salvation" of Israel (31:7). Matthew quotes the gloomiest verse in the entire chapter. It alludes to the story of Rachel's death near Bethlehem, and it applies this to the exile. He imagines Rachel watching her children streaming away from the land into exile, lamenting and mourning for the children who are going to the Babylonian grave, who "are no more." Though he quotes this gloomiest verse, he intends his readers to bring the entire chapter to mind. He wants to show that the end of exile only occurs through exile, the pleasant salvation that he prophesies about is only going to come through the shedding of blood. This becomes more apparent when we examine another quotation from Jeremiah in Matthew's gospel. Matthew is the only New Testament writer to name Jeremiah. He quotes him both here and in 27:9 (where Judas returns the thirty pieces of silver, which purchases a "field of blood"). The sequence from slaughter to salvation is part of God's purpose. Redemption comes through sorrow, and the Lord calls children who "are not" (Matthew 2:18) back to life. Again, the early life of Jesus foreshadows the end. The slaughter of the children constitutes the birth pangs of the birth of a new Israel, just as Jesus' betrayal and slaughter on the cross is the birth of a new creation.

Verses 19-21 are closely parallel to Exodus 4:19-20, which describes Moses' return from exile in Midian. In both cases, the Lord tells someone who is exiled from his homeland to return home. In both cases, a man travels with his wife and son to return to the land. There is no donkey in Matthew, but most of the paintings of the flight into and return from Egypt throughout the history of Christian art have depicted Joseph with Mary on a donkey, an indication that artists have interpreted the story in Matthew through the story in Exodus. The one key change is that Joseph returns to "the land of Israel" (Matthew 2:21), while Moses "returned to Egypt" (Exodus 4:20). Here again, Matthew is showing us that Israel has become Egypt.

Joseph's settlement in Nazareth also fulfills prophecy. Nowhere in the Old Testament is it said that the Messiah will be a Nazarene. Matthew knows this. He is not claiming to quote a particular passage. In verses 15 and 17, Matthew says that events fulfill "what is spoken through the prophet, saying," but in verse 23, he uses the plural, "prophets." He's not quoting a particular verse but summarizing a teaching found in several passages. He also doesn't use the phrase word "saying," and this change suggests that he's not quoting a statement but a theme.

What prophets teach that the Messiah be a Nazarene? And what does that mean? Matthew's point turns on a multiple Hebrew pun. Nazirites (Numbers 16) were "holy" warriors, so Jesus' hometown reveals Him as God's holy one (cf. Mark 1:24). The Messiah, Matthew is saying, is prophesied as being a holy one, and particularly a holy warrior. The Hebrew word for "branch" is *netzer*, and this is a name for the Davidic Messiah (Isaiah 4:2; Jeremiah 23:5; Zechariah 3:6; 6:12). Further, Jesus' hometown reveals Him as the Davidic "branch," growing from the dead stump of Jesse: "There shall come forth a Rod from the stem of Jesse, and a Branch shall grow out of his roots. The Spirit of the Lord shall rest upon Him, the Spirit of wisdom and understanding, the Spirit of counsel and might, the Spirit of knowledge and of the fear of the Lord" (Isaiah 11:1). "Branch" and "holy one" come together in Isaiah 4:3, in a context that describes Israel's restoration after exile. The Branch from David is going to be the Holy Warrior of Yahweh, who is going to bring Israel from exile and into the redemption. Nazareth was an unimportant town in a despised region, so Jesus' hometown reveals His humility.

Matthew's use of Scripture has some interesting implications for how we read the Bible and the Old Testament in particular. Matthew doesn't offer a proof text but a teaching that emerges from a number of texts. Yet, he describes this teaching as the teaching of the prophets. There are truths revealed not only in single texts of Scripture but also in common threads among various passages of Scripture. These teachings have the same authority as the direct quotations. Matthew also indicates that we need to read poetically, even punningly, if we are going to understand how Jesus fulfills the prophets. He does not always fulfill prophecy in a straightforward, literal manner. Sometimes that is true – as when the soldiers gamble for Jesus' robe at the foot of the cross or He dies on the cross with no bone broken. Other times, the fulfillment is more subtle. Who would think, reading the Old Testament passages about the branch or the Nazir, that the Old Testament was teaching something about the Messiah's hometown? We have to be alert not only to the poetry and puns of Scripture, but also to the providential orchestration of history, if we're going to understand the Scriptures rightly.

What does all this mean for us? We are the body of Christ, and His life-history becomes our life history. Jesus recapitulates the history of Israel, and He does it right. And in so doing, He also anticipates the history of the church. The history of the church is marked by periods of oppression. At times, Herod has been on the throne of the new Israel. But when that happens, the Lord always rescues His sons, and He prepares a new, fruitful land for them. The history of the church is marked by persecutions. But the Lord never leaves the blood of the infants unavenged. Rachel's lamentation gives way to rejoicing, and blood leads to redemption. Disciples of the Nazarene, we are all Nazarenes. We are all holy warriors, consecrated for battle. We are all branches in the Branch, who is growing into the dominant tree of the forest. We all share our Savior's humility, so that we can share His glory.

John the Baptist
Matthew 3:1-17

Now in those days John the Baptist came, preaching in the wilderness of Judea, saying, ² "Repent, for the kingdom of heaven is at hand." ³ For this is the one referred to by Isaiah the prophet when he said, "The voice of one crying in the wilderness, make ready the way of the Lord. Make His paths straight!" ⁴ Now John himself had a garment of camel's hair and a leather belt around his waist; and his food was locusts

and wild honey. ⁵ Then Jerusalem was going out to him, and all Judea and all the district around the Jordan; ⁶ and they were being baptized by him in the Jordan River, as they confessed their sins. ⁷ But when he saw many of the Pharisees and Sadducees coming for baptism, he said to them, "You brood of vipers, who warned you to flee from the wrath to come? ⁸ Therefore bear fruit in keeping with repentance; ⁹ and do not suppose that you can say to yourselves, ' We have Abraham for our father'; for I say to you that from these stones God is able to raise up children to Abraham. ¹⁰ "The axe is already laid at the root of the trees; therefore every tree that does not bear good fruit is cut down and thrown into the fire. ¹¹ As for me, I baptize you [a]with water for repentance, but He who is coming after me is mightier than I, and I am not fit to remove His sandals; He will baptize you with the Holy Spirit and fire. ¹² His winnowing fork is in His hand, and He will thoroughly clear His threshing floor; and He will gather His wheat into the barn, but He will burn up the chaff with unquenchable fire." ¹³ Then Jesus arrived from Galilee at the Jordan coming to John, to be baptized by him. ¹⁴ But John tried to prevent Him, saying, "I have need to be baptized by You, and do You come to me?" ¹⁵ But Jesus answering said to him, "Permit it at this time; for in this way it is fitting for us to fulfill all righteousness." Then he permitted Him. ¹⁶ After being baptized, Jesus came up immediately from the water; and behold, the heavens were opened, and he saw the Spirit of God descending as a dove and lighting on Him, ¹⁷ and behold, a voice out of the heavens said, "This is My beloved Son, in whom I am well-pleased."
– Matthew 3:1-17

For many modern Christians, conservative or liberal, the New Testament often seems quite different from the Old. The Old Testament was a corporate religion, centered on membership in a nation, the nation of Israel. The New Testament is an individual religion, which has to do with my own individual standing before God. The Old Testament is a physical religion, all bound up with food laws and sacrifices and blood and water. The New Testament is a spiritual religion; Christianity in contrast to Judaism is all about God's relation to the soul and the soul's relation to God.

But the beginning of Jesus' ministry shows that this is not the case. In every one of the gospels, the beginning of Jesus' ministry is John's ministry. John is the forerunner, the first witness in God's final prosecution of His lawsuit against Israel. John and Jesus both preach repentance and coming judgment; both offer a way of life for Israel; both oppose the Pharisees and Sadducees; both are prophets. Wrath is coming on Israel (Matthew 3:7), and the Lord sends a double witness to warn Israel. John's ministry shows that the contrasts between Old and New Covenant do not work. John is clearly concerned with the nation of Israel. He is a prophet calling the people of God to repentance, signified by baptism. There is wrath coming (v 7), and the Jews should not think they'll escape wrath simply by being children of Abraham, since God is able to raise up children of Abraham from stones (v. 9). There is no shift in John's preaching from corporate concerns to individual concerns. He preaches against and about Israel. When He comes preaching repentance and coming judgment, Jesus preaches exactly the same message. John and Jesus are both preaching in regard to the corporate situation of the people of God. Both address the dangerous condition that the nation of Israel faces.

At the center of John's preaching is baptism. Mark is even more direct than Matthew (1:4): John comes "preaching a baptism." The content of his preaching is baptism, the sign of repentance and inclusion in the Israelite remnant that will survive the judgment. In other words, there's a physical, material sign associated with membership in the company of John's disciples. There is no contrast between a materially-based religion in the Old Covenant and a purely spiritual religion in the new. From the beginning, and to this day, Christianity, the new covenant, is bound up with things, with material realities. In fact, John's ministry is not a break in the history of Israel at all. It is a continuation of that history, the completion of that history. John's ministry fulfills a prophecy of Isaiah. John is the voice crying in the wilderness (v. 3; Isaiah 40:3), which is what Isaiah promised. This comes in a section of Isaiah where the prophet promises an end to the exile in Babylon. The previous chapter ended with a warning that Israel would go into Babylonian exile, but he immediately moves into a promise. The exile will end with the Lord's forgiveness of His people, with the glory of the Lord being revealed, with the coming of the Lord. Yahweh will come, and in preparation for His coming all the mountains will be cast down and the high places raised up. A way will be prepared for Yahweh's arrival, which is the end of the exile—Yahweh's return to His land, to His people, to His city and temple.

Israel has been back in the land for several centuries, but at the same time they have not seen the complete fulfillment of the promises of return. Now they are going to see that. They are still in exile not because they are under the dominion of Rome but because they are under a much worse oppression. When the Pharisees and Sadducees come to John, he addresses them as a brood of vipers, children of the devil not children of Abraham. Israel, especially her leaders, is under the dominion of the devil (John 8). Israel must prepare for the coming of Yahweh and for the end of exile. He baptizes in the wilderness (v. 1) and at the Jordan (v. 5) because his baptism ritually enacts that return; those baptized by John cross the Jordan from exile back into the land (cf. Ezekiel 36).[12]

It's not only the explicit quotation that marks John as a continuation of the history of Israel. It's his demeanor, clothing, and diet. He is playing a role, consciously. And the role that he's playing communicates to Israel what is about to happen. Verse 4 tells us about John's clothing and diet. He wears a garment of camel hair with a leather belt around his waist. The leather belt and rough hairy garment identifies him as Elijah, who is described in 2 Kings 1 as a "Baal of hair" who has a "leather belt" at his waist (v. 8). John is Elijah, the Elijah prophesied by Malachi, who comes before the great and terrible day of the Lord to restore the fathers to children and children to fathers, who will be the forerunner of the blazing fire that will burn in Israel and consume all the chaff

---

12. N.T. Wright, *Jesus and the Victory of God* (Christian Origins and the Question of God; Minneapolis: Fortress, 1992), p. 160.

(Malachi 4:1, 4-6). Elijah came to Israel during the darkest period of her history, during the time of Ahab. Herod is a new Ahab, and as Elijah, John is warning that Herod's kingdom will be destroyed. Those who want to survive and flourish must attach themselves to the new Elijah and to the coming new Elisha.

John's diet links him with the wilderness. Locusts are food of the wilderness. So long as Israel dwells in the land, she cannot be renewed. They have to be taken from the land, turned into Gentiles, and then reincorporated into the land by returning to the land through the Jordan. That is the process of renewal. Locusts are instruments of judgment in the Old Testament. While locusts are clean, it is more common in the Old Testament to read of locusts eating than of them being eaten. And in some passages (Joel 1-2), locusts are symbolic of invading, consuming Gentile nations who threaten Israel. Israel has been eaten up by the locusts of various Gentiles for centuries, but John consumes locusts. He eats the eater, and those who repent and receive His baptism will also consume the consumers. The locusts will be eaten up into the body of the prophet. In a sense, John eats Gentiles. The honey is *wild* honey, and locusts often represent invading Gentile armies. Eating is an act of incorporation, and by eating this "Gentilic" food, John anticipates the inclusion of Gentiles. The message is: "Forsake the old Jewry. Become incorporate with John as gentiles, and become a New Israel at the Jordan."[13]

Honey is associated with the land throughout the Old Testament. To eat honey means to eat the good of the land, to be restored to the land. John baptizes at the Jordan, enacts a ritual river-crossing for those who are going to return to the land of Israel and eat from its goods. But this is wild honey, the honey of the wilderness, reminiscent of the honeyed taste of manna (Exodus 16:31). It's a taste of the honey of the land of milk and honey, but only a taste. The full enjoyment will come later. John is telling Israel that they can be renewed only by reverting to the

---

13. Much of the discussion of John's diet depends on comments made by James Jordan on a private email discussion group.

wilderness, only by ceasing to be Israel and then being restored to being Israel. And this message comes against the background of a warning of great judgment coming upon Israel. When the King comes, He will burn in wrath against Israel's sins and chop down all the haughty trees (v. 10). When the King arrives, He will review His people to dole out rewards and punishments as appropriate. The coming of the king means the coming of Judgment, the coming of fire. John uses the word "fire" three times (vv. 10, 11, 12) to describe the purging, judging advent of the King.

John alludes to Psalm 74, which describes the destruction of the temple as the devastation of a forest, and he alludes to Isaiah 10:15-19, which describes Assyria as Yahweh's axe. Another Gentile power threatens Israel, and John calls Israel to repentance before it is too late. In fact, it is too late. Judgment is coming. Israel is going to suffer devastation, which means de-templarization. The axe is already at the foot of the tree. The only thing to do is to repent and trust in Yahweh for salvation, hoping that He will bring new life to His people on the far side of the catastrophe. But John knows that he is only the beginning. Another is coming who will baptize with the Spirit and fire, who will remove whatever chaff remains after threshing (vv. 11-12). The final catastrophe of Israel is on the horizon. Those who repent will be vindicated on the other side of exile. It is well to remember that the temple was built on the threshing floor of Araunah the Jebusite. John's prediction about the clearing of the threshing floor anticipates the cleansing of the temple.

John's placement in the wilderness, his baptism in the Jordan, his diet and clothing, indicate that Israel will pass through a radical renewal before they can be brought out of the exile they are currently in. They have to be wrenched from the land, dwell in the wilderness all over again, and return to the land. Israel has become Egypt, and for Israel to become new, she must go through a massive exodus, which is what John is enacting. Some of the Jews don't want this. They think they are fine already, just by being descended from Abraham. John warns them that this is not the case, and that only fruitful trees will survive the judgment that's coming. Being a descendant of Abraham is not enough, if they don't have the faith of Abraham or bring forth the fruit of Abraham.

Jesus comes to John for baptism (v. 13), and John objects that Jesus should be the one baptizing. Jesus insists that righteousness must be fulfilled (v. 15). What does he mean by this? Of course, Jesus doesn't need to confess His sins, and He doesn't need to be baptized in order to be cleansed from anything. It is true, as many have said, that in receiving baptism from John, Jesus is identifying with the people He's come to save. He is Jesus, and His name means that He will save His people from their sins. But He saves His people by identifying fully with their sins. As the incarnate Son, He does not keep His distance from a sinful people. He doesn't tell them to shape up, and leave them to do it themselves. He submits to baptism and acknowledges that He is among a sinful people, that He is one with them.

The reason that Jesus gives for being baptized, however, is that He must fulfill all righteousness. What does this mean? If we take "righteousness" as obedience to the commandments of God, then we're left with a puzzle: Where did God command this? Perhaps because John is a prophet, his instructions are to be taken as divine commandments. But there appears to be something else going on here. The vast majority of Matthew's uses of the verb "fulfill" have to do with the fulfillment of prophecy (cf. 2:15, 18, 23), and that is likely what Jesus is referring to here. He consciously, and obediently, conforms to the will of His Father by fulfilling prophecy. Early in his life, he fulfilled prophecy without any human consciousness of doing so. But now He comes as the one who fulfills the plan of the prophets consciously and deliberately. "Righteousness" in the prophets, however, not only refers to personal morality, but to God's establishment of right order and justice (cf. Isaiah 51:4-8). In submitting to baptism, Jesus becomes the Spirit-filled instrument for establishing God's righteousness (cf. Isaiah 11:1-10).

We are baptized into Christ, and in a sense we share in His baptism. His is, in a sense, the "one baptism for the remission of sins," and all other baptisms are applications of this one baptism. But if Jesus' baptism makes Him an instrument of righteousness, so does ours. That's what Paul says in Romans 6: We die with Christ in baptism, and having died to sin we live to righteousness. Our bodies become instruments of doing righteousness rather than instruments of sin. The account of Jesus' baptism also indicates something not only about Jesus but also about the baptisms of believers.

As Jesus is coming from the water, the heavens open (v. 16). In Jesus, heaven and earth, estranged since Adam's fall, are rejoined (cf. Matthew 28:18).[14] The agent for joining heaven and earth is the Spirit, who descends on Jesus in the form of a dove (v. 16). When we are baptized, we don't see heaven opened, of course, but we do know that the heavenly Spirit has been poured out and that the baptized is incorporated by the Spirit into the body of Christ, the temple of the Spirit. Through baptism, we are joined to the earthly people that share in a heavenly life. We are joined to the Spirit-filled people of God. The dove recalls Noah's dove, which flew over the waters of the flood and brought news of new life on earth. Ultimately, the dove hovering over Jesus alludes back to Genesis 1:2: In Jesus the new creation is taking form through the brooding of the Spirit. We too are made new creatures through baptism. We are given a new name, incorporated into a new community, given a new past and a new future, a new mission toward the world outside. The Father speaks from heaven to identify Jesus as Son and Servant (v. 17). The Father's announcement conflates Psalm 2 and Isaiah 42: Jesus is the Royal Son, the Davidic King and new Adam, who will be installed on Zion, and He is the Servant of Yahweh, whose suffering will bring redemption to His people. Again, we are baptized into this one baptism. And in Christ, we become kings in the King, and servants of Yahweh in the Servant of Yahweh.

---

14. See Pennington, *Heaven and Earth in the Gospel of Matthew*.

John's baptism is a preparation for judgment. Those who go through the waters of baptism, repenting and confessing sin and bringing forth the fruit of repentance, will be saved. And so for us: We go through the waters of Christian baptism, confessing our sins and bringing forth fruit of repentance, and we will stand in the judgment. As we are baptized, and as we display the faith of Abraham, we are children of Abraham, heirs of the land, heirs of the world. And we will eat the honey of the land.

In the Wilderness
Matthew 4:1-11

Then Jesus was led up by the Spirit into the wilderness to be tempted by the devil. ²And after He had fasted forty days and forty nights, He then became hungry. ³And the tempter came and said to Him, "If You are the Son of God, command that these stones become bread." ⁴But He answered and said, "It is written, 'Man shall not live on bread alone, but on every word that proceeds out of the mouth of God.'" ⁵Then the devil took Him into the holy city and had Him stand on the pinnacle of the temple, ⁶and said to Him, "If You are the Son of God, throw Yourself down; for it is written, 'He will command His angels concerning you'; and 'On their hands they will bear you up, so that you will not strike your foot against a stone.'" ⁷Jesus said to him, "On the other hand, it is written, 'You shall not put the Lord your God to the test.'" ⁸Again, the devil took Him to a very high mountain and showed Him all the kingdoms of the world and their glory; ⁹and he said to Him, "All these things I will give You, if You fall down and worship me." ¹⁰Then Jesus said to him, "Go, Satan! For it is written, 'You shall worship the Lord your God, and serve Him only.'" ¹¹Then the devil left Him; and behold, angels came and began to minister to Him.

– Matthew 4:1-11

We pray that our Father will not lead us into temptation, and that He will deliver us from evil. This is part of the prayer that Jesus taught us to pray, and our petition is reinforced by the promise of James: "Let no one say when he is tempted, 'I am being tempted by God'; for God cannot be tempted by evil, and He Himself does not tempt anyone" (2:13). This promise is implicit in the nature of God: God is wholly good, and therefore cannot be tempted. He cannot wish or intend evil. It is an insult to God's goodness to believe that He is capable of tempting us. We pray that God would not lead us into temptation with the full assurance that it would be contrary to His eternal character to do so.

And yet, Matthew records that Jesus received the Spirit at His baptism, and that this Spirit led Him into the desert, where the devil was waiting to tempt Him. In fact, the point can be made more strongly: The syntax suggests that the purpose for which the Spirit led Jesus into the wilderness was so that He might be tempted by the devil. The Spirit led Him "to be tempted" (the Greek is an infinite expressing purpose). It's not just that the Spirit led Jesus to the wilderness for some other purpose, and the devil happened to be there. The Spirit led Jesus into the wilderness for the express purpose of being tempted.

Jesus goes to the wilderness in order to fulfill righteousness, in order to continue re-living Israel's history, and to do it right this time. We've been looking at this theme from the beginning: Jesus is the true Israel, recapitulating and summing up all of Israel's history but reversing Israel's failures. Jesus was born in an Israel ruled by Herod, a king who kills babies. Jesus was called out of this Egypt, crossed through the waters of the Jordan, and fittingly He immediately goes into the wilderness. Once Jesus has passed through the waters, the Spirit He received at baptism leads Him to the wilderness, as Israel was led through the Red Sea by the Spirit-pillar. For forty days and nights, He is tempted as Israel was for forty years, and He resists.

He is the true Israel, and He is also the true Adam, who refuses to eat forbidden fruit and refuses to seize authority that has not been given to Him. Jesus is the first of a new kind of Israel, and the first of a new sort of human, one that does not bow before Satan but rebukes him. Unlike the first Adam and the first Israel, Jesus keeps the fast. But that just raises the question more intensely: It seems that the Lord has been leading His people into temptation for a long time. So, we are left with some serious questions. Does God tempt, or doesn't He? Does He lead us into temptation, or not? Does He put His children in harm's way? Is there a dark side to God? Is He looking for reasons to send us to hell, constructing reasons when none presents itself naturally?

Part of the answer is to recognize that the word "tempt" can have more than one meaning. On the one hand, God does not tempt anyone because He does not desire that we do evil. He does not tempt as the devil tempts. The devil tempts us with the specific hope that we will rebel against God. He tempts us because He wants us to sin. He is trying to seduce us to do wrong, because He is a liar and a murderer from the beginning. God doesn't do that. That's what James is saying. God may put the devil in our path; He may send us to the wilderness where the devil is waiting to pounce. But He does not put the devil in our path in order to get us to fall. Yet, on the other hand—in a passage very relevant to this text—Moses exhorts Israel to remember that the Lord led them through the wilderness "that He might humble you, testing you, to know what was in your heart, whether you would keep His commandments or not" (Deuteronomy 8:2). God *does* tempt by testing us, when He puts the pressure on us, when He knocks out the props that we rely on, in the sense that He leads us into deserts to hunger so that the things hidden in our hearts will be revealed. God tests us by threatening us with the loss of a job, or by actually taking a job from us. He tests us with our children. He tests us in our marriage. He tests us by making us wait for things we want far longer than we want to wait. That's what He is doing with Jesus, because that is what He was doing with Israel. And it's perfectly typical for God to bring such times of testing in the immediate aftermath of some great Spiritual gift. God created Adam, gave him life and the garden and a bride, and then immediately He brought the serpent to the garden gate to test His newborn son. God brought Israel out of Egypt, and immediately they were plagued by Amalekites snipping at their heels, and they were faced with hunger and thirst and the other dangers of the wilderness. God brings the true Israel, Jesus, through the waters of the Jordan, fills Him with the Spirit, and then sends Him off to be tested.[15]

This is the way the Father worked with His Son Israel, and His Son Jesus. It's the way He works with all His sons. He gives us the Spirit, exhorts us to follow the Spirit, and then the Spirit leads us into the valley of death or into the howling waste. But these tests are for our good. This is how our Father brings us to maturity, by placing devils and satans and accusers and dangers in our way. He is not seducing us to evil. He intends it to strengthen our hands for war, so that we grow in faith and hope in God. He tests us so that we will be prepared for greater tests, more intense battles, later on.

Satan's three temptations form a progression. He moves from a temptation about physical hunger to a temptation to test God instead of humbly obeying Him to a temptation to receive the kingdoms of the earth. The temptations also progress spatially. Jesus moves from the desert to the pinnacle of the temple to a mountain from which he can view the kingdoms of the earth. The climactic scene on the mountain in chapter 4 anticipates the mountain in chapter 28, where Jesus declares Himself to have received all authority, not by bowing to Satan but by obeying His Father to the death. Jesus is the true Israel, and He is faced with the same series of temptations that Israel faced when they

---

15. Between Matthew 4 and 19, there is no mention of Judea or the region "beyond the Jordan." Once He hears of John's arrest, Jesus withdraws to Galilee (4:12), and doesn't come back until 19:1. As soon as He steps back into Judea, the Pharisees come to "test" Him. Apart from 16:1, this word hasn't been used since chapter 4 either—and then it was used of Satan ($\pi\epsilon\iota\rho\alpha\zeta\omega$ means "test" or "tempt"). The testing in 16:1 takes place in Galilee, but the instigators are "Pharisees and Sadducees" who "come up," presumably from Jerusalem. For Matthew, Judea is the place of testing, the place where Satan assaults Jesus. Jesus returning to Judea is like Moses returning to Egypt after his sojourn in Midian. As soon as Moses tries to cross the boundary to Egypt, the angel of the Lord confronts him; as soon as Jesus arrives in Judea again, the Satanically-inspired Pharisees are there to tempt Him.

were in the wilderness.[16] When Israel had passed through the Red Sea at the Exodus, they immediately went into the wilderness and realized they had no water or bread. They began to grumble against Moses and the Lord that the only water was bitter, and the Lord brought sweetened water. They grumbled about their lack of bread and wished they were in Egypt, and the Lord rained bread from heaven.

Each of the passages Jesus quotes are from accounts of the wilderness wanderings of Israel. Moses commented on this in Deuteronomy, saying that the Lord caused Israel to hunger in the wilderness for forty years to test them and to see what was on their heart. This is the very passage that Jesus quotes in response to the first temptation of Satan: Israel was supposed to learn that man does not live by bread alone but by every word that proceeds from the mouth of God (Deuteronomy 8:1-4). They were to learn to rely on the Lord for their bread, not grumbling against Him but trusting that whether He gave them life or death, He would do them good. No sooner had Israel received bread and meat from heaven than they again found that they lacked food. They grumbled again against Moses and the Lord, and this time, they added to their sin of grumbling the sin of testing the Lord. Exodus 17:7 says, "And [Moses] named the place Massah and Meribah because of the quarrel of the sons of Israel, and because they tested Yahweh, saying, 'Is Yahweh among us, or not?'" They put God to the test here in the sense that they reserved their trust in Him until He had demonstrated His power. Devastating Egypt, opening the Red Sea, sweetening the water, and raining bread from heaven were not enough to win their trust. Like the village atheist who dares God to strike him with lightning, they said, "You're going to have to do that again before we believe that You are with us. Prove yourself." Jesus alludes to this very incident

---

16. See Austin Farrer, *The Triple Victory: Christ's Temptation According to St. Matthew* (Cowley Publications, 1990).

when he responds to the devil's second temptation: "You shall not put Yahweh your God to the test, as you tested Him at Massah" (Deuteronomy 6:16).

Finally, while Israel waited at the foot of Sinai for Moses to reappear from the cloud, they constructed a golden calf at the foot of the mountain and bowed down to worship it. Lusting for bread and testing the Lord, they added the sin of idolatry, throwing themselves before the golden calf, worshiping Satan. Jesus could be alluding to this very incident when He responds to the third temptation: "You shall fear Yahweh your God, and you shall worship Him, and swear by His name. You shall not follow other gods, any of the gods of the peoples who surround you, for Yahweh your God in the midst of you is a jealous God; otherwise the anger of Yahweh your God will be kindled against you, and He will wipe you off the face of the earth" (Deuteronomy 6:13-16), which is precisely what the Lord threatened to do after the golden calf incident. Israel lusted after bread and grumbled against the Lord. Israel tested Yahweh at Massah and Meribah. Israel turned to worship Satan. Jesus is faced with precisely these three situations in this order. And Jesus succeeds in overcoming these temptations. He trusts God for His bread, He refuses to test God, and He does not succumb to idolatry. He is the true Israel, reversing the sins of the first Israel.

There's another crucial dimension to this as well. Jesus is Israel. But Jesus is also Moses. That's evident in the fact that He fasts for forty days. In Deuteronomy 9, Moses refers to two different forty-day fasts. The first came before he received the tablets of the law: "I remained on the mountain forty days and nights; I neither ate bread nor drank water. . . . And it came about at the end of forty days and forty nights that Yahweh gave me the two tablets of stone, the tablets of the covenant" (Deuteronomy 9:9, 11). After the people had worshiped the golden calf, their climactic moment of rebellion against the Lord, Moses again threw himself before the Lord to plead with Yahweh to turn from His wrath against Israel: "I fell down before Yahweh, as at the first, forty days and nights; I neither ate bread nor drank water, because of all your sin which you had committed in doing what was evil in the sight of Yahweh to provoke Him to anger" (Deuteronomy 9:18). Jesus is an intercessor in His resistance to temptation, the new Moses whose obedience to His Father intercedes for his people.

The forty-day fast also reminds us of Elijah. Elijah fasted for forty days and nights in a similar situation. Israel had been following Baal, but Elijah had destroyed the altar and prophets of Baal in the great confrontation at Mount Carmel. Then Jezebel again seized the initiative, and Israel again began to follow idols. Fed by an angel, Elijah took off toward Horeb to bring charges against Israel, to intercede *against* them as Moses had interceded *for* them. Along the way, Elijah fasted for forty days and nights. Like Moses, he came before the Lord at Horeb having fasted for forty days and nights. Through Moses' intercession, Israel was saved from destruction. And in spite of their lust for bread, in spite of their grumbling, in spite of their testing God, in spite of their idolatry, the Lord led them to a good land, and they received their inheritance, a land flowing with milk and honey, the land of many nations stronger and more numerous than Israel. Moses' intercession was appropriate to the situation. By fasting, he did the opposite of what Israel had been doing. Israel had complained they had no bread; Moses refused bread. Israel murmured and put God to the test at the waters of Massah; Moses drank nothing for forty days. Israel set up an idol to lead them into the land, and bowed to it; Moses destroyed the idol and threw himself before the Lord.

Jesus doesn't merely obey where Israel disobeyed. He is faithful where Israel was unfaithful. He keeps the fast—refusing to eat bread and to turn stones into bread, refusing to test the Lord, refusing to bow before Satan. Because He is the new Moses as well as the new Israel, because He intercedes by His fasting and His faithfulness, His people will be saved. Jesus is our champion, defeating Satan without our help. He is also our example, showing us how to defeat Satan. The tests that Jesus endured are perennial temptations. When God turns up the heat and the pressure, when the Spirit leads us into the desert where there is no water or bread, we are tempted in precisely the ways Israel and Jesus were.

We are tempted to seek our life and help from someone other than God. We try to serve God and obey Him. We follow Jesus faithfully, and then realize that He's led us into the wilderness instead of a garden. We feel that He's led us into a trap, and we are tempted to look elsewhere for our help. We are tempted to seek to live by bread alone and not by the word of God. When we are in the wilderness, we are tempted to test God. If God is God, we say, He should be here. He should intervene. We are tempted to question whether God is among us or not. Prove yourself, we demand of God. And we are tempted to abandon Jesus for some other Master. When God leads us into the wilderness, it seems that we have no good reason to serve Him. We're not getting much out of it. Following Jesus just brings us difficulty and pain. Perhaps another Master will do us better. Perhaps another Master will bring us to green pastures and still waters. Perhaps we can find a Master who will give us all things, but who won't burden us with a cross.

How do we resist these temptations? It is often remarked, accurately, that Jesus responds to Satan with the Word of God, a spiritual weapon powerful for tearing down the fortresses of the world. But we should also notice what the quotations from Scripture say. We defeat Satan by living on the Word that proceeds from the mouth of God, feeding on it with hunger that surpasses our hunger for bread. We defeat Satan by trusting God, not by testing Him. We defeat Satan by worshiping and serving God alone. When we do those things, Satan slinks away and angels gather to minister to us. So, we resist Satan in the hope that we will gain the victory over him.

In this sense, the temptation is a preview of the entire gospel. Jesus, the Son of God, becomes flesh, and He enters the wilderness of this world, the wilderness that Israel has become. He assumes all human frailties and undergoes all the tests that Israel and all humanity have endured. He is "tested" or tempted here by the devil, directly, as he will be tested by the Jewish leaders throughout the remainder of His ministry among His people. Three times Matthew records the Jews testing Jesus (16:1; 19:3; 22:34-34), and when He hangs dying on the cross, the Jewish leaders echo Satan's challenge to Jesus' Messianic sonship: "If You are the Son of God, come down from the cross" (27:40); "let Him now come down from the cross, and we shall believe in Him" (27:42); "He trusts in God; Let Him deliver Him now, if He takes pleasure in Him; for He said, 'I am the Son of God'" (27:43).

Like the gospel as a whole, the story of Jesus' temptation is not a story of defeat but a story of triumph. Matthew ends the account of the temptation by recording that angels came and served Jesus (4:11). Adam was created among the hosts of angelic sons of God, but he lost that status by submitting to a beast. Throughout the Old Testament, Adamic humanity was under guardians and managers, sons treated like slaves. Adam was made a little while lower than angels, but now Jesus the Last Adam is exalted above the angels, and angels minister to Him. Satan leaves the desert, and he awaits a more opportune time to test Jesus again. But Jesus has already passed this test, and He will pass all the others as well. Winning the first battle, He already wins the war. And we all share in that victory as we follow Jesus who was led by the Spirit. The Spirit leads us into deserts to hunger and thirst. The Spirit places on us the painful burden of the cross. The Spirit leads us to places of testing, where Satan tempts us to fall down and worship him. As we follow Jesus, live by the Word that proceeds from His mouth, trust Him, and worship Him alone, we too trample Satan under our feet.

THE KINGDOM OF HEAVEN COMES NEAR
Matthew 4:12-25

Now when Jesus heard that John had been taken into custody, He withdrew into Galilee; ¹³ and leaving Nazareth, He came and settled in Capernaum, which is by the sea, in the

region of Zebulun and Naphtali. ¹⁴ This was to fulfill what was spoken through Isaiah the prophet: ¹⁵ "The land of Zebulun and the land of Naphtali, by the way of the sea, beyond the Jordan, Galilee of the Gentiles — ¹⁶ the people who were sitting in darkness saw a great light, and those who were sitting in the land and shadow of death, upon them a light dawned." ¹⁷ From that time Jesus began to preach and say, "Repent, for the kingdom of heaven is at hand." ¹⁸ Now as Jesus was walking by the Sea of Galilee, He saw two brothers, Simon who was called Peter, and Andrew his brother, casting a net into the sea; for they were fishermen. ¹⁹ And He said to them, "Follow Me, and I will make you fishers of men." ²⁰ Immediately they left their nets and followed Him. ²¹ Going on from there He saw two other brothers, James the son of Zebedee, and John his brother, in the boat with Zebedee their father, mending their nets; and He called them. ²² Immediately they left the boat and their father, and followed Him. ²³ Jesus was going throughout all Galilee, teaching in their synagogues and proclaiming the gospel of the kingdom, and healing every kind of disease and every kind of sickness among the people. ²⁴ The news about Him spread throughout all Syria; and they brought to Him all who were ill, those suffering with various diseases and pains, demoniacs, epileptics, paralytics; and He healed them. ²⁵ Large crowds followed Him from Galilee and the Decapolis and Jerusalem and Judea and from beyond the Jordan.
– Matthew 4:12-25

Jesus' ministry is linked to John's ministry. John baptized Jesus. When John is arrested, Jesus withdraws to Capernaum, and later on, when Herod beheads John, Jesus withdraws again to a lonely place by Himself. His ministry imitates John's. John's ministry and life foreshadow Jesus'. John says, "Repent, for the kingdom of heaven is at hand." Jesus says, "Repent for the kingdom of heaven is at hand." John fights with the Jewish leaders, and Jesus will too. John falls afoul of Herod, and Herod kills him, foreshadowing the death of Jesus after trials before Herod and Pilate.

Jesus is not simply another John, however. As John predicted, there is a progression. John said, "I baptize with water, but He who is coming after me is mightier than I, and I am not fit to remove His sandals; He will baptize you with the Holy Spirit and fire." John foreshadows Jesus, but Jesus is far greater. The relationship between John and Jesus is like that between Elijah and Elisha. John is an Elijah figure—dressed in camel hair, alone in the wilderness, denouncing the leaders of his time, persecuted by a vacillating king and a far more determined queen. John is the paradigm of the lone prophet, calling the nation to repentance and predicting judgment. Jesus is not alone, and Jesus is not in the wilderness. He calls disciples, visits synagogues, travels from town to town, goes to Jerusalem. He is Elisha, gathering a group of disciples who will carry on His mission and ministry. Jesus' ministry is also like Elisha's in the fact that it is largely a ministry of mercy.[17]

Listening to John, we think that there's a great judgment coming, and that it will be carried out by the "One who comes after me." John says that this one comes with a winnowing fork to clear the threshing floor, gather the wheat, and burn the chaff with unquenchable fire. He comes to baptize with the Spirit and fire. What does Jesus do when He comes? Not what we expect.

The first thing that Matthew tells us about Jesus' public ministry is its location. As soon as Jesus hears that John is taken into custody, He moves from Nazareth, in Galilee, further north, to the northern reaches of the Sea of Galilee, to Capernaum-By-the-Sea. Galilee is mentioned only five times in the Old Testament. It's mentioned in passing in Joshua 20:7 and 21:32, because the city of Kadesh in Galilee is set aside as a city of refuge in the land of Naphtali. The first time that Galilee figures into a story is in the reign of Solomon. Solomon has had good relations with Hiram the king of Tyre for some time, but those relations sour a bit late in Solomon's reign. Hiram was the Gentile who helped build the temple of Yahweh in Jerusalem, and to honor Hiram, Solomon sold him twenty cities in the northern part of Israel, in the land of Galilee (1 Kings 9:10-13). Not only were these cities given over to the hands of a Gentile king, the king of Tyre, but the area is

---

17. For more on the relation of Elijah and Elisha, see my *1-2 Kings*.

described as *kabul*, which is usually etymologized (following Josephus) as "worthlessness," though sometimes seen as referring to the "mortgaging" of the towns of Galilee, the sale of the towns to Hiram. The Talmud says that the word means "sterile" or "bound," as with chains of gold and silver. The LXX translates the words as "boundary," or "march-land," connected with the Hebrew *gebul*, border. There still is a village by the name Kabul in this area. Galilee is mentioned again in 2 Kings. First, Pul king of Assyria invades, and Menahem extracts money from the men of Israel to pay him to go away. In the following generation, during the reign of Pekah, Assyria returns: "In the days of Pekah king of Israel, Tiglath-pileser king of Assyria came and captured Ijon and Abel-beth-maacah and Janoah and Kedesh and Hazor and Gilead and Galilee, all the land of Naphtali; and he carried them captive to Assyria" (2 Kings 15:29). It's no wonder that the land of Zebulun and Naphtali, the region of Galilee, was considered a place of darkness.[18] Towns had been sold to the Gentile Hiram and pronounced worthless. This region was the first to go into exile, and the Assyrians resettled Gentiles in the land (2 Kings 17). Galilee was not a thoroughly Gentile region, but it was considered a borderland, not quite fully Gentile but not quite fully Jewish either.

The despised and darkened land of Galilee, Galilee of the Gentiles, will not remain in darkness forever. The day will dawn in a land of night. Isaiah 9 comes at the end of a prophecy concerning the Aramean crisis in Judah. Rezin of Aram and Pekah of Israel are ganging up on Ahaz of Judah to force Judah into an anti-Assyrian alliance. Isaiah warns that the Lord is going to bring the bees of Assyria (Isaiah 7:18-19) to invade Judah; the

---

18. The name "Zebulun" contains a promise of restoration. Like all the names of Jacob's sons, "Zebulun" is a pun. When Leah bore a sixth son to Jacob, she said, "God has endowed me with a good gift; now my husband will dwell (zabal) with me, because I have born him six sons." Matthew records the fulfillment of this hope, for Jesus withdraws from Judea to Galilee to "dwell" in Capernaum (Matthew 4:13). Zebulun becomes truly Zebulun, the place of dwelling for the divine husband of Israel.

Euphrates that will submerge Israel (in the generation after Ahaz) is going to overflow into the land of Judah until it nearly drowns the land (8:5-8). In this situation, many in Judah - those who are following mediums and spiritists rather than the law of Yahweh —are awaiting a dawn that will not happen (8:20). Those who do not go to the Torah and testimony of Yahweh will never see the day dawn. Darkness will cover them, "distress and darkness, the gloom of anguish; and they will be driven into darkness" (8:22). Yet, there will be a dawn, and Matthew tells us that dawn happens with Jesus. But how is this a judgment? How does this fulfill the expectation of John that the One who comes after is going to bring a winnowing fork in order to separate wheat and chaff?

It's a judgment because the dawn doesn't happen in Judah. Instead, day dawns far away, in the land of Zebulun and Naphtali. In Isaiah's day, the Northern kingdom was already collapsing, but Isaiah says that dawn will come in the land that Tiglath-pileser had already begun to conquer (2 Kings 15:29; 16:1). In context, the prophecy of hope simultaneously condemns Judah, or a large portion of Judah at least. The dawn will not come from Ahaz. Though the throne of David is going to be re-established (9:7), yet the glory of that throne will first be apparent in "Galilee of the Gentiles" (9:1). Eventually, the light will extend to all Israel, but the day dawns from the north (where God's throne is, Psalm 48:2). This of course fits neatly into Matthew's story. Matthew 4:12 says that Jesus withdrew from Nazareth to Capernaum when John was taken captive. The wickedness of Judah forces the light to withdraw to the northern extremities of the land, where the kingdom of the new David first begins to take shape among the semi-Jews of Galilee. The fact that light dawns in Zebulun and Naphtali sends a message of condemnation to Judea and her king, Herod the king of darkness and, behind him, the devil. Isaiah pointed Jewish hopes toward Galilee, but that is a condemnation of Judah, David's own tribe.

Jesus, like Elisha before him, was a minister to Gentiles. He goes to Galilee of the Gentiles, and people come to Him from the Decapolis, a confederation of ten Hellenistic cities to the east of the

Sea of Galilee. This too is a judgment against Judah. The God of Israel turns from Israel to the nations to provoke Israel to jealousy (Deuteronomy 32:16-21). From His base in Capernaum, Jesus begins proclaiming the kingdom (4:17). He immediately begins to gather assistants, calling the four cornerstones of a new Israel, the four pillars of a new temple, the first disciples who will spread to the four corners of the earth. Like Elijah calling Elisha from his plowing (1 Kings 19:19-21), Jesus calls Simon and Andrew, and then James and John, from their fishing. Like Elisha, these four leave their work and their families to follow Jesus. Andrew and Peter are casting nets into the sea, but when Jesus commands them to follow Him, they leave their nets behind and follow Him (v. 20). The call of James and John is even more radical. They are in the boat with their father Zebedee, and when Jesus calls them, they leave not only the boat but also their father in order to follow Jesus (v. 22).

This is consistent with the radical demand that Jesus makes throughout the gospel. He calls people from an established way of life. He calls people from their families. He says that they have to be willing to leave everything behind if they are going to be His disciples. His disciples must be willing to hate father and mother for his sake. When someone wants to go back and bury his dead father, Jesus says, with scandalous indifference to filial duty, "Let the dead bury their dead." The command and claim of Jesus overwhelms even the highest of natural affections and demands. Of course, Jesus also promises that we receive more back than we renounce; everyone who leaves father and mother to follow Jesus receives back fathers and mothers a hundredfold (Mark 10). There is a promise of increase, but the demand is radical and requires faith in Jesus, because the promise of increase is not immediately apparent.

For Peter and Andrew, James and John, this is a call to ministry alongside Jesus that is unique. For these and the rest of the twelve, ministry with Jesus becomes a lifetime vocation. Not every believer is called to this kind of service, but every believer *is* called by Jesus to reorient everything in life around Him, around Jesus.

Even if you don't leave your home, you have to live in your home as a disciple of Jesus. Even if you don't leave your nets and boats and business behind, you are called to follow Him. This is not a call to some elite shock troops of the kingdom. Every subject of Jesus' kingdom, of the kingdom of heaven, is called to restructure their time, their spending of money, their desires and hopes, their actions, their plans, their child-raising, their marriages, their work, their leisure in radical ways. From the roots up, everything is to be redirected toward Jesus.

While Elisha ministered among the landed Israelites, the disciples will fish in the Gentile sea. Matthew is already beginning to show the scope of Jesus' work. That scope will become fully explicit at the end of the gospel, when Jesus announces His authority over heaven and earth and sends the disciples to the Gentiles to make them disciples. But there is another implicit reversal. The image of "fishers of men" is not new with Jesus. The prophets of the Old Testament already spoke of people who were "fishers of men." But in the Old Testament, "fishers of men" is connected with judgment. Prophets speak of Gentile nations invading the land to capture Israel and remove them from the land (Jeremiah 16:16; Amos 4:2). In these passages, "fishing for men" is a picture of invasion and exile. Yahweh threatens that Gentiles are going to come into the land and remove the Israelites. They are going to pursue them until they find them. There will be no place to hide. Those who are captured will be pulled from the sea and taken into exile in Babylon, among the Gentiles.

Jesus uses the image in the same way. He expects the disciples to seek out and capture people, eventually Gentiles, from the sea of nations. He's talking about a kind of invasion. Jesus and His disciples are going to go through the land and the world, pursuing men and capturing them, pulling them out. But in a central way, Jesus uses the image differently. The disciples are going to capture Jews and Gentiles from the sea of nations to gather them into the kingdom (cf. Matthew 13:47-50). They are not being hunted and fished for to take them into exile. They are going to be hunted down and fished to bring them back *from* exile and brought into a good land, the land of God's kingdom.

Does this fulfill the expectations of John? Is this a judgment? Yes, it is, because Jesus' disciples will fish and then separate the fish. They will gather Jews from their exile among the nations, and Gentiles from the sea, and bring them into the kingdom. But they are not going to bring every fish into the boat of the church.

Jesus' main message throughout His ministry is that the kingdom of heaven has come near (vv. 17, 23). He is the herald that announces the coming of a new ruler. What does this mean? It means, first of all, that God is going to take charge of a world that has rebelled against Him. It is often said that the word "kingdom" in the New Testament means first of all "reign," and not "realm." I think it implies realm, but one of the central messages of Jesus is that God is going to start reigning. Of course, God has been reigning forever and will reign forever. He does what He pleases, and no one will stop Him or say to Him, what have you done? But the world has not acknowledged that rule. During the Old Testament period, God didn't bring His rule to bear in a complete way. He "winked" at sin. No longer. He's going to take charge, and He's going to put things back the way they should be. Injustice has filled the earth, but God is going to right injustice. War has filled God's earth, but God is going to bring peace. Violence has filled the earth, but God is going to form a humble and meek new humanity. All this depends on God taking His throne, and this is what Jesus is saying: God is about to take His throne, and He's about to deal with all the injustice, evil, sin, and wickedness. To prepare for God's arrival and the new order He is going to establish, the people must repent or else face God's terrible judgment.

In a king's absence, discipline at court becomes lax. Servants slouch when they serve at the table, and they are stealing food from the pantry. The steward has been fudging some of the books. Military discipline is not what it should be. Now, here comes a herald who says, "The king is coming. He's going to take his throne again and start reigning for good." What would you do if you were a servant in the palace? You should straighten up. That's John's message, and that's Jesus' message: The king is at the door. God is beginning to reign, beginning to reign already in Jesus Himself. So repent.

Jesus uses the phrase "kingdom of heaven" to describe this reality. Some have thought that Jesus, following Jewish scruples, is avoiding the use of the word "God." But Jesus also speaks of the "kingdom of God." He's not superstitious about the word "God." He uses the phrase "kingdom of heaven" to highlight one aspect of what He's announcing. He's talking about the reestablishment of the original harmony of creation. Because of Adam's sin, heaven and earth have been disrupted and alienated. Earth has rebelled against the God of heaven, and the life of earth has not been reflecting the life of heaven. But that's about to end. Heaven is going to come back into harmony with earth, so that the will of God will be done on earth as in heaven.

God is going to take the throne and assert Himself actively in the world, turning back the evil and rebellion of humanity. But what will that look like? What effects does it have on earth? As John said, this is a separation and a judgment. Jesus doesn't heal everyone. Not everyone is willing to come to Jesus for healing. When Jesus heals some and leaves other unhealed, when He delivers some demoniacs and not others, then those who refuse to receive Him are condemned already. But the accent is on the grace of God, operative in Jesus. What it shows us is that the kingdom comes as a kingdom of healing, righteousness, restoration, renewal, resurrection. Verses 23-24 give us a portrait of the effects of God's rule on earth. When God begins to reign, His truth will be taught in the synagogues, He will triumph over every kind of disease, He will put Satan to flight, and He will gather a new humanity from the four corners of the earth.

3

ON THE MOUNTAIN

SITTING TO TEACH
Matthew 5:1-2[1]

When Jesus saw the crowds, He went up on the mountain; and after He sat down, His disciples came to Him.[2] He opened His mouth and began to teach them.   – Matthew 5:1-2

---

1. Jesus' sermon can be outlined and overviewed in various ways. The sermon is framed by references to multitudes (5:1; 7:28-29), and by Jesus' ascent (5:1) and descent from the mountain (8:1). Further, the concluding warning and promise (7:24-27) echoes some themes of the Beatitudes (5:1-12). Within this frame, the structure of the sermon is roughly chiastic:

    A. Beatitudes, 5:1-12.
   B. Salt and Light, 5:13-16.
    C. Jesus fulfills law and prophets, 5:17-20.
      D. "You have heard that it was said" (so-called "antitheses"), 5:21-48.
       E. Righteousness before God/hypocrisy, 6:1-18.
        F. Seek the kingdom/no worry, 6:19-34.
       E'. Judgment and hypocrisy, 7:1-5.
      D'. Prayer, 7:6-11.
    C'. Doing the law and prophets, 7:12-14.
   B'. False prophets/bad fruit, 7:15-23.
    A'. Hear Jesus' words and do them, 7:24-27.

Sitting is Jesus' characteristic posture for teaching. He sits in a boat on the Sea of Galilee as He tells parables of the kingdom (13:1-2). He sits on a mountain near the Sea of Galilee, and the people bring their lame and deaf and blind to be healed (15:29). He sits to deliver the prophecy of judgment against Jerusalem and its corrupted temple. He promises He will come again and sit on His throne to pass judgment (19:28; 25:31), but already in His earthly ministry, He teaches as one enthroned, teaching as one having authority and not as the scribes.

To teach, He sits on a *mountain*. Jesus' whole history in Matthew can be told as a series of mountain experiences, moving through seven mountains.[2] Satan's climactic temptation and Jesus' climactic victory over temptation takes place on a mountain: Jesus begins His conquest on a mountain. Jesus teaches from a mountain, and He prays on a mountain (14:23). He ascends a mountain to heal, and His glory is shown on the Mount of transfiguration, a sign of the approaching glory of His coming (17:1ff). He delivers the Olivet discourse from a mountain, and the great commission from still another mountain. On a mountain, Satan offered the kingdoms of the earth; on a mountain, Jesus announces that He has received all the kingdoms of the earth, not by bowing to Satan but by obedience to His Father. He will tell His disciples they are the light of the world and a city set on a hill. Before they become the city of light, Jesus is on the mountain as the light that lights the city. On the mountain, He is the light that cannot be put under a basket, and His words are a lamp to the feet of His disciples and a light to their path.

Mountains are where heaven and earth meet. Going up a mountain is an ascent from earth toward heaven.[3] In Isaiah 14:13, the king of Babylon claims to sit on the mountain, which represents an ascent to heaven and an enthronement. On the mountain, Jesus is enthroned in a high place, a place near heaven, to bring the

---

2. I am taking this from an unpublished paper by Warren Gage, "The Theme of Matthew: Jesus, the True Moses" (1998).

3. See James Jordan, *Through New Eyes* (Eugene, OR: Wipf & Stock, 2000).

words of the kingdom of heaven to the people on earth. He is on the mountain to reconcile heaven and earth, so that God's will will be done on earth as it is in heaven.[4] Jesus Himself *is* the mountain that connects heaven and earth. Jesus is the ladder that descends from heaven so that humanity can return to God. Eden was on a mountain, and Jesus is the new man establishing a new Eden. The temple was on a mountain, and Jesus is the new temple, from which the law of the Lord flows like living water. The mountain is the symbol of the kingdom in Nebuchadnezzar's vision (Daniel 2), and Jesus on the mountain is the King in His kingdom. The first creation centered on a mountain, the mountain of Eden, and all subsequent new creations have had central mountains—Ararat of Noah, Moriah of Abraham, Sinai of Moses, Zion with David, the restored Zion of Isaiah's prophecies, and the mountain of the kingdom in Daniel's prophecy.

After Jesus sits, the disciples come to Him and He begins to teach. Around Sinai, and around the tabernacle, there was a circle of priests and Levites, and then a larger circle of the multitudes of Israel. Israel was organized in concentric circles around the Torah kept in the Most Holy Place. Israel was organized in concentric circles around the tabernacle, God's dwelling place. So the disciples, perhaps the four called in the previous chapter, perhaps more, come to Jesus to hear the Word from the living temple.

The disciples are not the only ones who hear. By the end of the sermon, we learn that the multitudes have heard what Jesus says: "the multitudes were amazed at His teaching" (7:28). These multitudes are the ones that Jesus has already healed: "all who were ill, taken with various diseases and pains, demoniacs, epileptics, paralytics." (4:24).[5] Multitudes follow Jesus, gather round Him on the mountain, marvel to hear Him speak as the

---

4. See Jonathan Pennington, *Heaven and Earth in the Gospel of Matthew* (Supplement to *NovumTestamentum*; Leiden Brill, 2007).

5. Dale Allison, "The Structure of the Sermon on the Mount," *JBL* 106:3 (1987), pp. 423-445.

enthroned teacher of Israel. These are the multitudes who will become the city on a hill, with Jesus (the Lamb) as the light that illumines the city.

The multitudes are redeemed multitudes, already brought out of Egypt, already delivered from bondage to Satan, the curse, death, and illness. The multitudes are saved multitudes, and Jesus gives His instruction to those who have already received His grace. These are the crowds that always come to hear Jesus. Jesus doesn't teach people so that they might begin to follow Him, so that they might be healed, so that they can save themselves. He delivers, and *then* He speaks, like Yahweh leading Israel from Egypt to speak to them at Sinai.

Jesus says that His disciples must exhibit a righteousness that surpasses the righteousness of the scribes and Pharisees. That can be taken as the central theme of the sermon. But what does it mean? How does the righteousness Jesus requires go beyond the righteousness of scribes and Pharisees?

Many different interpretations have been offered in the history of the church. Some have interpreted the sermon as a frontal assault on Torah. Torah was God's will and God's law for the Old Testament, but now Jesus brings a new law that is not only different from but in many ways directly contrary to the law of Moses. Perhaps the righteousness of the scribes and Pharisees is inadequate because they are still paying too close attention to the law. This is *not* what Jesus says. On the contrary, He says that He has not come to abolish but to fulfill the law and prophets. He is not an opponent of Moses. Whatever He means by "fulfill," it can't mean "abolish." Further, Jesus goes on to say that the smallest letter or stroke of the law will not pass from the law until all is accomplished. He is clearly endorsing the law in its "jots and tittles" — a "jot" being a "*yod*," the smallest letter of the Hebrew alphabet, and a "tittle" being a tiny part of a letter that distinguishes one letter from another. Not the least part of the law is going to be annulled. And in the next verse Jesus says that status in the kingdom of heaven is determined by one's attitude toward "the least of these commandments." Keeping and teaching the least of the commandments of the law is the way of greatness in the kingdom. In chapter 5, Jesus even follows the order of the Torah, the sequence of the Ten Words of the old covenant (Exodus 20). He contrasts the interpretations of the law that were given "of old" with the views of the demands of the law itself. And as he runs through these things, we can see that they follow the order of the second half of the Ten Words. Jesus deals with murder (sixth commandment), then adultery (seventh commandment), then divorce (which is linked to the eighth commandment in Deuteronomy 23), then to false oaths (ninth commandment concerned with false witness), and then finally a statement about vengeance, which is related to covetousness in the tenth commandment. The Sermon also follows the order of the case laws in Exodus 21-23 to some degree.

Virtually nothing in Jesus' teaching is unprecedented in Judaism. There is nothing that a Jew could not have concluded from a diligent study and meditation on the law. When Jesus says that we are not to hate, He is echoing Leviticus (Leviticus 19:17-18). When Jesus says, "Love your enemy," He generalizes from the law (Exodus 23:4-5) and repeats Solomon (Proverbs 25:21-22). When He teaches us that lust is a form of adultery, He's saying no more than what the Tenth Commandment required (Exodus 20:17). Jesus is not correcting the law but the practical and pedagogical distortions of the law that were widespread in Judaism.

Some have thought Jesus' teaching differs from that of the Jewish leaders because He does not give commandments. Jesus speaks words of grace and mercy, not words of demand. The Old Testament was law; the new is grace, and grace makes no specific demands. This interpretation fails to account for the sermon too. There are *many* imperatives in the sermon, and Jesus' demands are not less strict than the Torah's. If anything, He makes more demanding demands.

Some have thought that Jesus emphasizes the *internal* demands of the law. Instead of focusing on externals, like the scribes and Pharisees, Jesus focuses on the internal attitudes and desires. The scribes and Pharisees are concerned with the act of murder, adultery, or the details of oaths. Jesus focuses on anger, lust, and truth in the inner parts. The scribes and Pharisees are concerned with external action; Jesus is concerned with internal attitude. But this doesn't work either. Jesus does address attitudes, but so did the Mosaic law. And Jesus commands *doing*, not just attitudes. When He warns against practicing righteousness before men, He doesn't go on to say that what matters is our hearts. He commands a different set of *practices* concerning alms, prayer and fasting. He doesn't say, "Do these things with a different attitude." He says, "*Do* them *differently.*" If you think turning the other cheek is only an attitude, you haven't done much of it.

Some have suggested that the sermon gives us an impossible ideal that we can never fulfill. Perhaps the whole design of the sermon is to drive us to a kind of holy despair about our own sinfulness, so that we throw ourselves on the imputed righteousness of Christ. But this is not what Jesus is talking about. He describes right living, righteousness in actual life, and He gives instruction about what that righteousness involves throughout this sermon.

One of the keys to understanding the teaching of the sermon is to get a handle on the meaning of the word "righteousness." "Righteousness" doesn't always mean conformity to a standard of behavior. When Paul talks about the righteousness of God exhibited in the gospel, He is talking about the righteous, powerful action of God in Christ that restores sinners to God and mends the world (Romans 1:17). God's righteousness is not conformity to rules but redemptive action that displays God's faithfulness to His Name and covenant. This is why Isaiah can speak of "righteousness" and "salvation" as parallel realities (cf. Isaiah 45:8; 46:13; 51:5-6, 8; 56:1). That's the kind of righteousness exhibited in Jesus' own life, and it is the kind of righteousness He demands of His disciples. He comes as the embodied righteousness of God to bring in the restoration of all things, the kingdom of heaven. His instructions tell us how *we* can participate in that restoration. He commands a new set of practices, but they are practices that go beyond the righteousness of the scribes and Pharisees because these practices, these habits, these actions break through the perverse customs and habits of sinful humanity and bring restoration.

Many believe that after Matthew 5:20, Jesus teaches with a series of dyadic contrasts.[6] The elders teach only an external and visible conformity to the law, and Jesus teaches something deeper. The ancients say, "Don't murder," but they imply that we need not worry overmuch about hatred. Don't commit adultery, but don't worry overmuch about lust. Jesus deepens the commandment, so that it applies to desires, attitudes of the heart. But Jesus is not simply contrasting external and internal. He analyzes the cycles of sin and gives instruction for breaking through those cycles.

On murder: Jesus doesn't merely say, "You have heard, 'do not murder,' but I say don't hate." Rather: "You have heard, 'do not murder,' and those who murder are liable to court; but I say that anger and insults leave you in danger of the court; *therefore*, leave your offering and go be reconciled to your brother." The commandment is *not*: "Don't be angry." Jesus' commandment is: "Go be reconciled." *That* is the greater righteousness, not simply avoiding the anger but acting in a way that breaks through the cycle of anger and insult that leads to murder. That's the redemptive righteousness that Jesus demands. Jesus' teaching on lust is similar. He doesn't simply contrast "don't commit adultery" with "don't lust." Jesus does deepen the commandment against adultery by insisting that lust is *already* adultery, not merely a prelude to it. But then He goes on to give a commandment: Cut it off. Remove the offending organ. *That* is the greater righteousness, not simply avoiding lust.

The righteousness Jesus looks for is not merely avoidance of heart sin. The righteousness that He demands involves surprising, creative, redemptive action that gets at the root of the sin and cuts it. It's not enough to avoid anger; in fact Jesus doesn't even say, "Don't be angry." Rather, His *command* is that you take the

---

6. In the following and throughout my exposition of the Sermon, I depend heavily on Glen Stassen, "The Fourteen Triads of the Sermon on the Mount: Matt

initiative to be reconciled to a brother. It's not enough to avoid lust; in fact, Jesus doesn't say "Don't lust." Rather, he tells you how to respond to lust, how to break through the chains of lust, in order to have chaste relations with women. You need to cut off the organ that offends. It's not enough to avoid hating enemies; you need to do good to them, to break through the habits of hatred, counter-hatred, escalating hatred, that destroy life.

This, Jesus says, is the kind of righteousness the Torah *always* intended. At the center of the Law are righteousness, mercy, and truth (Matthew 23:23). The rest is detail. Jesus teaches how to keep Torah as an adult. He lays out the way of true righteousness.

This is the righteousness of faith. In 6:34, near the structural center of the Sermon, Jesus assures His hearers that if they pursue the righteousness they've described before, they can be sure that they will have all they need for life. This is answering a real question, a question that arises from the instructions He's given. In fact, in this section, Jesus is directly addressing the question of whether He's put an impossible standard before us. Jesus says, Don't resist by evil means; give to Him who asks. Give your coat to the one who asks for a shirt, and go a second mile, and turn the other cheek. It might seem that following Jesus' instructions will result in constant deprivation: If we give away our cloaks, we'll be naked; if we go the second mile, we'll get tired; if we take the second slap, our faces will be constantly bruised.

Our reaction is to say, "Get real, Jesus! This may all be great for a perfect world. But we don't live in a perfect world. We live in a hard world, and you've got to cut some corners, break some eggs, defend yourself, take a little bit of vengeance, if you're going to survive." Jesus says, No. The whole issue comes down to trust. Do you trust your Father to give you what you need if you do what Jesus says? Do you trust that you'll still have clothes if you keep giving them away, that you'll still have bread if you are generous, that you'll still have a face if you keep giving up your cheeks for a punching bag? Trust your Father, Jesus says, and obey my

---

5:21-7:12," *JBL* 122:2 (2003), pp. 267-308.

commandments. Trust your Father, and live a righteousness that surpasses the righteousness of the scribes and Pharisees. Trust your Father, and live out the righteousness of that faith.

Blessings of the Kingdom
Matthew 5:1-16

When Jesus saw the crowds, He went up on the mountain; and after He sat down, His disciples came to Him.² He opened His mouth and began to teach them, saying, ³ "Blessed are the poor in spirit, for theirs is the kingdom of heaven. ⁴ Blessed are those who mourn, for they shall be comforted. ⁵ Blessed are the gentle, for they shall inherit the earth. ⁶ Blessed are those who hunger and thirst for righteousness, for they shall be satisfied. ⁷ Blessed are the merciful, for they shall receive mercy. ⁸ Blessed are the pure in heart, for they shall see God. ⁹ Blessed are the peacemakers, for they shall be called sons of God. ¹⁰ Blessed are those who have been persecuted for the sake of righteousness, for theirs is the kingdom of heaven. ¹¹ Blessed are you when people insult you and persecute you, and falsely say all kinds of evil against you because of Me. ¹² Rejoice and be glad, for your reward in heaven is great; for in the same way they persecuted the prophets who were before you. ¹³ You are the salt of the earth; but if the salt has become tasteless, how can it be made salty again? It is no longer good for anything, except to be thrown out and trampled under foot by men. ¹⁴ You are the light of the world. A city set on a hill cannot be hidden; ¹⁵ nor does anyone light a lamp and put it under a basket, but on the lampstand, and it gives light to all who are in the house. ¹⁶ Let your light shine before men in such a way that they may see your good works, and glorify your Father who is in heaven. – Matthew 5:1-16

Jesus begins the Sermon on the Mount with a poem, a song. Nine times he repeats the word "blessed" (Greek μακαριος), and in the first eight of these blessings Jesus adopts the same structure: Blessed are X, for they shall receive Y. The first and last of the eight end with the same blessing: The poor in spirit and the persecuted are both promised the "kingdom of heaven." The first four blessings alliterate on the Greek letter "p." "Poor" is πτοχοι, "mourn" is πενθουντες, "meek" is πραεις and "hunger" is πεινοντες. Some of the promised outcomes pick up the same alliteration: "Spirit" is πνευμα, and "comfort" is παρακαλεω. In all, the first four beatitudes contain thirty-six words—3 × 12—and the last four have the same number of words, for a total of seventy-two.[7] The number of Israel is the basis for the pattern, and the number of the nations of the earth—70—is also hinted at (cf. Genesis 10). These are the blessings on the new Israel, the true Israel, which encompasses the seventy nations.

Jesus begins His sermon with a poem, and Jesus' poem alludes to an earlier poem, a poem from the prophet Isaiah. In Isaiah 61, the prophet speaks of one anointed by the Spirit who is going to arrive to announce a restoration of Israel. The prophet promises that the afflicted or poor will receive good news. He says that those who sorrow will be bound up. He says explicitly that those who mourn will be comforted and that their mourning will turn to celebration and rejoicing. And he promises that righteousness will flourish in the land.

In Isaiah, the promise is one of national restoration, as becomes clear if we look at the larger context—from Isaiah 40 to the end of Isaiah 61. William Dumbrell says that these chapters of Isaiah "operate as a review of the community expectations whereby the redeemed community awaits to enter into the blessings of the promised restoration." Isaiah 40:1-9 shows the redeemed gathered to Zion, expecting God's arrival in their midst, and the chapter moves toward a reiteration of the promises to Abraham concerning the restoration of the land. By the time Isaiah gets to chapter 61, these blessings of restoration are about to break out, but they haven't yet. It is almost dawn, but dawn hasn't come yet.

---

7. The most complete discussion of the poetic features of the Beatitudes is found in H. Benedict Green, *Matthew, Poet of the Beatitudes* (London: Continuum, 2001).

The Spirit-endowed messenger tells the people to hope in God to restore Zion, and chapter 61 goes on to detail the physical restoration of Zion. The Spirit-anointed messenger "comes to a depressed community and brings them the resplendent note of actualized redemption."[8]

The Beatitudes have often been interpreted as descriptions of internal experiences of believers. Comfort, satisfaction, mercy, seeing God are all seen as blessings that have to do with my emotional state. God's "blessing" is to make us feel better. Certainly there is a personal and emotional component to blessing, but in the light of Isaiah 61, that's not all that Jesus is talking about. He's talking about the *situation* of His people. They will be placed in a *condition* of blessing and happiness. This is what Jesus is announcing to the multitudes and the disciples who gather around Him from the corners of the land. The promises of Isaiah are on the verge of fulfillment. Israel is about to be restored, and all Israel's sorrow is about to be turned into laughter; all Israel's cursing is about to be turned into blessing.

Jesus declares the coming of blessing. What does it mean to be "blessed"? Humanity began in a state of blessing (Genesis 1:28). Adam was blessed in that the Lord gave him the ability to be fruitful, multiply, fill the earth, subdue it, and rule it. The Lord blessed Adam by giving him the ability to flourish and so to fulfill his purpose in creation. Jesus uses a form of blessing that is found in many Psalms and other parts of the Bible. A blessed man is like a fruitful green and growing tree (Psalm 1:3; 92:12-15), a blessed woman like a vine (Psalm 128:3). Because of sin, we don't flourish; our hopes and plans are frustrated. Jesus comes to announce blessing, which is to say, life, abundant life.

To achieve a blessed state, things must be turned around radically. Israel knew, and Jesus agrees, that the world was not as it should be. Yahweh had promised to raise up Zion as the chief mountain and fulfill His promises to Abraham. He had promised

---

8. W. J. Dumbrell, "The Logic of the Role of the Law in Matthew V 1-20," *Novum Testamentum* 1 (1981), pp. 8-9.

that His people would ride the high places of the earth. It hadn't happened yet. But Yahweh had come through before. When poor persecuted Hannah mourned and hungered for righteousness, He raised up her son Samuel to put Israel back on track (1 Samuel 1-2). They hoped Yahweh would do the same again, on a grander scale.

This hope is so real that Jesus' disciples are blessed already in the present. Most of the promised blessings are stated as future blessings. Those who mourn shall be comforted. Those who are meek will inherit the earth. Those who are merciful will receive mercy. But the first and the last are in the present tense: "Theirs *is* the kingdom of heaven." This is a sign that the blessings of the kingdom are ours now, and not merely in the future. This is a hint that the promised restoration is already happening in Jesus' lifetime, and that it happens throughout the history of the church. In the midst of poverty and want, in the midst of mourning and hunger, in the midst of persecution, we are in a happy situation, in a blessed situation. In the midst of this incomplete restoration of things, we already know that we are in a blessed situation.

Jesus announces blessing to Israel, restoration, abundant life for the people of God. But the blessings Jesus pronounces are counter-intuitive. He comes to fulfill these hopes, but He seems to fulfill them in a paradoxical way. Poverty, sadness, hunger and thirst, and persecution are the very opposite of blessing. Is Jesus changing the standards so radically that he says now poverty and hunger and sadness are blessings? Or is he saying that these social conditions are merely metaphors for spiritual conditions? That may be plausible in Matthew. Jesus doesn't bless "the poor" but the "poor in spirit." He doesn't promise satisfaction to the hungry, but to those who hunger and thirst for righteousness. He's spiritualized all these social conditions, and we might plausibly conclude that Jesus is not at all concerned about real poverty, real hunger, real sadness, real oppression. He's interested in the virtues and spiritual dispositions that correspond to these social and economic circumstances.

This is plausible if we look only at Matthew, but when we look at the way Jesus pronounces blessings in Luke 6, the social dimension is unavoidable. Jesus doesn't pronounce blessings to the "poor in spirit," but simply to the "poor." He doesn't bless those who are hungry for righteousness, but the hungry. And He also includes woes against the rich, the full, the happy, because they are going to face judgment later. We need to read both gospels together. The gospels are movements of a symphony, not self-standing books. And when we read them together, we realize that Jesus is talking about *both* social condition *and* the response to that condition, a quality of the heart and soul. In themselves, poverty, sadness, hunger are not blessed conditions. "Poor" here doesn't mean having one TV instead of two; it is begging poverty, utter destitution. That's not blessing, that's not flourishing abundant life. The blessing is that those who are poor will be put in a *different* situation, as heirs of the kingdom.

But Jesus is not saying that people inherit the kingdom *simply* by being deprived of food and drink and the necessities of life. We shouldn't eliminate the social dimensions. But we also can't reduce Jesus' message to a "social gospel." Jesus announces blessings to those who are not blessed, offers abundant human life to those who are not living abundantly. But it's not their social condition as such that qualifies them for the blessing. It is repentance, and repentance that manifests itself in humility, hunger for righteousness, mercy, purity of heart, peaceableness. He refers to people who are in desperate social and economic conditions, but whose attitude in the midst of those conditions is one of dependent trust in God to change their conditions. Those are the ones who will inherit the kingdom.

Jesus thus picks up an Old Testament theme, one that had already begun to identify "the poor" with "the righteous." Hannah celebrates because God "raises the poor from the ash heap" (1 Samuel 2:8). Psalm 113:7 says the same: "He raises the poor from the dust, and lifts the needy from the ash heap." David describes himself in the Psalms as "this poor man," the one oppressed by his enemies and crying out to the Lord for deliverance (Psalm

34). Israel looks to the Lord who gives justice to the poor. "Poor" means one who is oppressed, deprived, attacked. The poor is the righteous man who is assaulted and under oppression for his righteousness. It is a social condition; but it's a social condition that's directly tied to a spiritual condition.

Verses 11-12 provide a key perspective on all the beatitudes. Structurally, these verses stand out. Verse 10 forms a frame with verse 3, both pronouncing the blessing of the kingdom of heaven. Verses 11-12 don't give a new blessing but expand the blessing of verse 10 by describing the kinds of persecution, and the basis for joy in persecution, in more detail. Those who are persecuted for the sake of righteousness are blessed because they have a great reward in the kingdom, and because they are sharing in the persecution of the prophets. These verses also stand out because this blessing is far longer than the others. It's as long as the two sets of four—thirty-five words by itself. It is also in the prominent place of being the last of the blessings.

These literary details suggest that this final ninth blessing, the blessing that surpasses and spills over the structure of eight, is the key to the whole series. The first four beatitudes describe the condition of those who are persecuted for righteousness' sake. They are poor because they might be cast out from their families and friends and networks of contacts. They mourn because they seem to be in a wretched condition. They might be so destitute that they are without food and drink. Their condition is one of social and economic hardship, hardships that they suffer because of persecution for Jesus' sake. Jesus preaches good news to the poor, and He pronounces blessings on the poor. He is especially assuring those who follow Him that, whatever deprivations they suffer as a result, they are and will be blessed by receiving the kingdom. Jesus comes to announce good news to those who are marginal, outcasts, oppressed, mocked, scorned, treated with contempt by the powerful elites of the day. And the good news is that Jesus is going to turn things around, so that the poor will receive justice.

Justice for the poor is not a secondary theme in Jesus' ministry. It is a direct implication of the coming of the kingdom. Jesus the king has come. God is taking His throne. God is setting things right. And that means that all the greedy grasping rich who grind the faces of the poor and trample them underfoot are going to get theirs. As Psalm 72 promised, the King will "vindicate the afflicted of the people, save the children of the needy, and crush the oppressor." Jesus is that King, and He's calling oppressors to repent or face an exceedingly ill-tempered Judge.

We don't want to hear this. This makes us uncomfortable. We rich Americans don't want a Jesus who is a defender of the poor, because we know how rich we are. We spiritualize—it's the poor in spirit Jesus is talking about, so we don't have to worry about the poor in cash. We justify our complacency—"the poor are always with you" is from Jesus Himself. But Jesus doesn't let us off the hook. The coming of the kingdom is the coming of justice, God's assault against oppression, God's vindication of the poor. And when the kingdom comes, Jesus expects us to have the same attitude that He has. He expects us to take a stand with the weak and helpless, and not with the strong oppressors. We are all wealthy, unbelievably so, and Jesus expects us to use our wealth not to shield us from the needy, but to provide for the needy and to defend and assist the vulnerable and weak. This is what it means to be the light of the world.

For Jesus, social justice does not come through political means. It comes through repentance, and it comes through the practice of the life of righteousness that Jesus describes in the rest of the sermon. But the fact that Jesus doesn't look for political salvation *does not* mean he's uninterested in social justice. This is what the kingdom brings—it is good news to the poor, gladness to those who mourn, satisfaction for the hungry, justice for the unjustly oppressed.

The demand of the prophet Micah is the demand of Jesus: What does God require of you but to pursue justice, to love mercy, and to walk humbly with your God?

Salt, Light, and the Law
Matthew 5:13-20

> You are the salt of the earth; but if the salt has become tasteless, how can it be made salty again? It is no longer good for anything, except to be thrown out and trampled under foot by men. [14] You are the light of the world. A city set on a hill cannot be hidden; [15] nor does anyone light a lamp and put it under a basket, but on the lampstand, and it gives light to all who are in the house. [16] Let your light shine before men in such a way that they may see your good works, and glorify your Father who is in heaven. [17] Do not think that I came to abolish the Law or the Prophets; I did not come to abolish but to fulfill. [18] For truly I say to you, until heaven and earth pass away, not the smallest letter or stroke shall pass from the Law until all is accomplished. [19] Whoever then annuls one of the least of these commandments, and teaches others to do the same, shall be called least in the kingdom of heaven; but whoever keeps and teaches them, he shall be called great in the kingdom of heaven. [20] For I say to you that unless your righteousness surpasses that of the scribes and Pharisees, you will not enter the kingdom of heaven.
> – Matthew 5:13-20

Most of the Beatitudes in Matthew are in the third person. "Blessed are the poor in spirit, for *theirs* is the kingdom of heaven." "They shall be comforted," "they shall inherit the earth," "they shall be called the sons of God." In verses 11-12, Jesus addresses the persecuted directly: "Blessed are *you*." That second-person address continues into verses 13-16. "You are the salt of the earth" follows immediately from an exhortation to rejoice and be glad in the midst of slander, persecution, and insult. And this continues into verse 14: "You are the light of the world" and, implicitly, "you are a city on a hill." This is the same you that he addressed in talking about the persecuted.

Jesus is still addressing the persecuted when he says "You are the salt of the earth." But we should also notice that these are all second-person plurals: "you all." Jesus addresses more than one person. He addresses a community of people; the persecuted community that is the church is the salt and light. The church acts as salt by living together as a people. The church is light insofar as it is an organized polity, a polis, a city on the hill that cannot be hidden.

But what do these images mean? What does it mean for the church, the persecuted disciples of Jesus, to be the salt and light of the world and the city on a hill? We can consider these images individually first, and then consider them together, because they form a pair of symbols.

So, first, what does salt mean? Under the Old Testament system, Israel added salt to every offering at the tabernacle and temple. Yahweh tells Israel to include salt in every grain offering, but then He goes on to say, "With all your offerings you shall offer salt" (Leviticus 2:13). This is not restricted to grain offerings; the flesh offerings should also include salt. In various places in Leviticus, the sacrifices are described as the "bread" or the "food" of Yahweh (Leviticus 21-22). When Israel offered a sacrifice, they were engaging in a food rite. A portion of the offering was given to the Lord on the altar, and the Lord "ate" it in fire, consumed the animal or grain offering into the cloud of smoke and fire above the altar. Salt makes sense in this context. Salt seasons Yahweh's food. Salt makes the food of Yahweh savory. He makes it tasty, so He doesn't spew it from His mouth (Revelation 3:16).

Leviticus 2 describes the salt on the grain offering as the "salt of the covenant" (Leviticus 2:13). Salt symbolizes the perpetual character of the covenant (Numbers 18:19; 2 Chronicles 13:5). In Numbers 18, Yahweh gives over the firstborn to the priests as their livelihood. This is their due from the sacrifices, because of the service they perform in standing guard around the tabernacle and keeping Israel from being destroyed by the Lord's wrath when it breaks out from before Him. In giving these gifts to the priest, Yahweh says He's making a covenant of salt with the priests (vv.

15-19). In some ancient cultures, two people making a covenant would eat a bit of salt as a way of symbolizing the perpetual character of their agreement. In a world without refrigeration, salt was used as a preservative, and so the salt of the covenant points to the fact that salt symbolizes the continuation and preservation of a covenant agreement.

Jesus speaks of people being "salted with fire" (Mark 9:49), and the whole plain around Sodom and Gomorrah, which had been like the garden of God, becomes a salt waste after Yahweh destroys the cities (Genesis 19:26; cf. Jeremiah 17:6). Because salt inhibits the fertility of land, a conquering nation sometimes sowed a land with salt to keep the conquered people from recovering (Judges 9:45). Because of this, salt could also symbolize a break with the past and a new beginning. This is part of the symbolism of salt on a sacrifice. A sacrifice meant a break with the sins of the past and a new beginning, a new Passover, a new Exodus.

In Jesus' image here, He emphasizes the use of salt for flavor. That's what Jesus goes on to say in the rest of verse 13: If the salt becomes "tasteless" or "foolish," then it is no good and will be trampled underfoot. You can't salt salt and make salt salty again. When it loses its flavor, it becomes useless. Jesus' persecuted people are like the salt on an offering, spread over the earth to make the earth a pleasing sacrifice to the Father. Wherever the Spirit-filled people of God go, they salt the land with fire. Jesus' disciples bring the fiery, saving judgment of God wherever they go, and they turn the world into a holocaust.

But there is a warning here to those who refuse to hear Jesus' teaching. Those who hear Jesus, take up their cross, and follow the persecuted Messiah, will be the salt of the earth. Those who do not listen to Jesus will be trampled underfoot. This is not a generic warning. It's a warning to Israel about their subjection to Rome. If they don't listen to Jesus, they, their sacrifices, and their temple and their city will be "tasteless" and foolish and be trampled under the feet of the Gentiles.

Jesus moves from the salt of the altar into the Holy Place, where seven lamps burned on the menorah. This image is easier to grasp. Jesus is the light who has come to the darkened lands to the north, the land of Zebulun and Naphtali. The people are in gloom, fear of death, despised and marginal. Jesus comes to bring light and life and joy and glory. And Jesus says that we are to be the same. God's light has shone into the world in Jesus. And as long as Jesus was in the world, He was the light of the world. But now Jesus is removed from the world. He sends His Spirit to be with His people, and through the oil of the Spirit the church becomes a lampstand to shine the light of God into the world. Jesus' people are like Him, lights in dark places. The world is conceived as a temple, and we are the lampstand of the temple, shining to light up the whole house. The image of light merges into the image of a city—a lighted city raised up to bring the nations to glorify the Father (v. 16). Jerusalem was supposed to be that city (cf. Isaiah 2:1-4). Jesus says that His disciples will take over that ancient Israelite role. The city that is going to be raised up as the chief city is not Jerusalem but the new Jerusalem, the Jerusalem above, the Jerusalem that is the church.

That point is reinforced when we look at the two images together. Salt is low, on the earth. Light is lifted up on a lampstand, or on a hill, and becomes like the sun or the stars in heaven. The promise to Abraham was that his descendants would be the sand on the seashore and the stars of the heaven. Jesus says salt, not sand; and He says light, not stars. But it's the same promise. The persecuted, oppressed disciples of Jesus are the heirs of the Abrahamic promise. The disciples of Jesus are the salt/earth, and the light/stars are the true Israel. And the church takes over the function that Israel was supposed to have, giving flavor to the holocaust of the world, shining the light of God into the dark places of the earth.[9]

---

9. I believe I picked up most of the ideas in this paragraph from James Jordan in personal communication. It sure sounds like Jordan, and far too smart to be me.

In verse 16, Jesus tells literally what He means by salt and light. We are salt and light when we do good works, men see our good works, and they direct their worship and love and desires to God. If we cease to do good works, we become tasteless and are trampled underfoot. If we cease to do good works, we are placing a bushel basket over the lamp and the world becomes dark. The world is to be sacrificed to God, everything offered to Him. And what makes that offering tasty to God is the presence of Jesus' disciples doing good works. The world is to be lighted, like the first day of creation, and what floods the world with light is the presence of Jesus' disciples doing good works.

There is no alternative source of flavor or light. If the disciples of Jesus are un-salty, the world is without its flavor. If the disciples of Jesus put a bushel over their lampstand, the world is in darkness. It is objectively the case that we are the salt and light of the world. The world cannot realize its purposes without us. It will not join in cosmic worship, glorifying the Father in heaven, unless the church does good works that are evident to men.

Jesus goes on to explain His relation to and teaching concerning the law. The fact that He's preaching the coming of the kingdom, and that He says His people are the renewed Israel might lead to the conclusion that Jesus is destroying everything that went before. He says that His message, His teaching, His life and work "fulfill" the Law and the prophets. We want to understand what Jesus means by this, but we do need to see first what He's denying. He says that He has not come to destroy the law and the prophets, and He goes on to emphasize that the details of the law and the prophets are not left behind. Whatever He means, He does not mean that the Old Testament can just be chucked and ignored and dismissed.

But what *does* He mean by "fulfill"? Some have suggested that it means "establish" or "bring into full effect," and have emphasized the continuity between the law and Christian ethics.[10]

---

10. Greg L. Bahnsen, *Theonomy in Christian Ethics* (Covenant Media Press, 2002).

But "fulfill" isn't the word Matthew would have used in that case. The word Jesus does use emphasizes both continuity between the Law and Prophets and Jesus, and it also points to discontinuity. The word has a dynamic ring to it.

We can get some idea of what the word means by looking at the uses of the word earlier in Matthew. Matthew has already used the word "fulfill" a number of times (2:15, 17-18, 23; 3:15), and we can say that Matthew has already begun to develop a theology of fulfillment. In every case that Matthew has used the word, "fulfill" describes something surprising. Fulfillment brings a twist. Who would have thought that "Out of Egypt I called My Son" (Hosea 11:1) would be fulfilled in Jesus' escape from Herod? Who would have thought that Jeremiah was talking about the slaughter of infants at Bethlehem when he spoke of weeping in Ramah? We can't even find the prophetic statement "He shall be called a Nazarene," and yet Matthew says Jesus fulfilled that. In all these passages, the fulfillment is surprising. Fulfillment does not destroy the past, but it does bring in something new. Fulfillment brings the prophecy to its completion, but the completion is not what one might have expected. If Torah and prophets tell a story, the final chapter has a surprise ending. When we reach the end of the story, we can see that this is where the Law and Prophets were leading from the beginning. But that wasn't where we thought we were headed.

This is the pattern with Jesus' fulfillment of prophecy in general. To read the Old Testament prophecies about the Messiah, we can sympathize with Jews who expected a military Messiah. Many of the prophecies about the Messiah read like prophecies about a great conquest of the nations. Yet, when Jesus comes, He conquers by the cross. That is a conquest. It's the most complete conquest ever. But it's not the conquest that we might have expected from reading the Old Testament. The deepest story that Hosea told was the one he didn't know—the story of Jesus. The deepest story that Jeremiah was telling was about the slaughter of infants. The deepest meaning of the law is the righteousness that Jesus goes on to describe in the remainder of the sermon—the redemptive righteousness that scribes and Pharisees didn't grasp.

This is true at several levels. Jesus personally fulfills the law and prophets in this surprising way in His own life and ministry. He never breaks the commandments of God, but His obedience is not like the obedience of scribes and Pharisees. He eats with publicans and sinners; that's not prohibited by Torah, and in fact Jesus would insist that the Torah *requires* such table fellowship. But the scribes and Pharisees saw the law as prohibiting such table fellowship. Jesus fulfills the commandments of God by doing mercy, justice, and truth, which are the weightier matters of the law. Jesus fulfills the commandments of God by giving Himself to death on the cross.

Not only in His personal life, but also in His *teaching*, Jesus "fulfills" rather than "destroys" the law. He teaches us to keep the law not in the way the scribes and Pharisees do, but to keep the law in the paradoxical and redemptive way that He does. This is keeping the law; the law is brought forward, in all its jots and tittles. Doing what Jesus tells us means doing what the law always required; it is the righteousness that the law was aiming at and didn't achieve. This is fulfilling the righteous requirement of the law. But we fulfill the righteous requirement of the law by following Jesus' example and teaching that includes this unexpected element of surprise. He keeps the law like an adult, the first grown-up in human history.

Jesus is the standard of life for Christians. Torah is fulfilled in Him. It is all brought forward into the new covenant. We don't lose any of the law or the prophets, not a single jot or tittle; He embodies and keeps it all. We need to study the law and the prophets as diligently as any Jew, and pay attention to the details with all the attentiveness of a Pharisee. But we need to read the law and prophets through the lens of Jesus. We need to understand the law in the light of Jesus' example, and learn to obey the law as

He did. We need to understand the law through the lens of Jesus' teaching, and learn to follow His commandments as the way of following the commandments of His Father.

Jesus is the living Torah, the Torah in flesh, the Torah walking and talking and breathing and acting. Not a jot or tittle is lost, but we can keep the law—retain it and obey it—only if we follow the living Torah. Following Jesus is following Torah. Following the law means keeping company with the living Torah, Jesus Christ, the Word of the Father, the Instruction of the Father, the Word of the Father, made flesh to be light to the world. Walk in that light and you fulfill the righteous requirement of the law.

Anger and Lust
Matthew 5:21-30

> You have heard that the ancients were told, 'You shall not commit murder' and 'Whoever commits murder shall be liable to the court.' [22] But I say to you that everyone who is angry with his brother shall be guilty before the court; and whoever says to his brother, 'You good-for-nothing,' shall be guilty before the supreme court; and whoever says, 'You fool,' shall be guilty enough to go into the fiery hell. [23] Therefore if you are presenting your offering at the altar, and there remember that your brother has something against you, [24] leave your offering there before the altar and go; first be reconciled to your brother, and then come and present your offering. [25] Make friends quickly with your opponent at law while you are with him on the way, so that your opponent may not hand you over to the judge, and the judge to the officer, and you be thrown into prison. [26] Truly I say to you, you will not come out of there until you have paid up the last cent. [27] You have heard that it was said, 'You shall not commit adultery'; [28] but I say to you that everyone who looks at a woman with lust for her has already committed adultery with her in his heart. [29] If your right eye makes you stumble, tear it out and throw it from you; for it is better for you to lose one of the parts of your body, than for your whole body to be thrown into hell. [30] If your right

> hand makes you stumble, cut it off and throw it from you; for it is better for you to lose one of the parts of your body, than for your whole body to go into hell. – Matthew 5:21-30

Blessed are the meek, for they shall inherit the earth, Jesus said. Blessed are the peacemakers, for they shall be called the sons of God. Blessed are the pure in heart, for they shall see God. Jesus pronounces blessings to His disciples as they display a character that conforms to Jesus' own character. But Jesus doesn't leave it at that. He doesn't leave His instruction at this general level—be meek, be a peacemaker, be pure. His instructions in the remainder of the Sermon on the Mount explain in detail how we can achieve these virtues, how we can imitate Jesus.

Keep in mind three things as we go through this next section of the Sermon on the Mount. First, remember that Jesus came proclaiming the kingdom of heaven. That's His central message. In the Sermon on the Mount, He explains how we, His disciples, can be part of that Kingdom. But the kingdom is not just a static entity that we join. It's not like a club. It's a powerful movement, the movement of God in the earth, and being part of that kingdom means getting swept up in that movement. The kingdom means God taking His throne and beginning to set the world right, and being in His kingdom means that God works through us to set things right. These instructions are not just membership qualifications. They are redemptive commandments, and Jesus is laying out the specifics of the redemptive righteousness that surpasses the righteousness of the scribes and Pharisees.

Second, remember that these are not antitheses. Jesus isn't contrasting the old law that gave external commands with the new law that gives internal commands. The structure of this passage is not dual but triadic. Jesus cites something said to the ancients; then he describes the deeper dynamics that lead to this sin; then He gives commandments that not only enable us to avoid the overt sin, but also to redeem situations that might lead to sin. Jesus' specific commandments come in the third section of each triad. These are the commandments that we are to do and teach.[11] He does not say, "You heard it said, avoid external sins; but I say, you need to avoid internal sins, too." He doesn't give us impossible commandments. He's not laying out only the most extreme possibilities. He's dealing with everyday situations, and He's giving instructions about how we are to actually behave. His demands are demanding, but He expects His disciples to obey them.

It's often said that Jesus is implicitly pointing to the Pharisaical interpretations of the law. In fact, Jesus quotes from the law itself. Jesus quotes directly from the Ten Words (Exodus 20:12). The warning about judgment on the murderer comes from the Law (Exodus 21:12; Numbers 35:12; Deuteronomy 17:8-13). The phrase "it was said to the ancients" implies that God is the one speaking (cf. Romans 9:12). Jesus introduces these instructions with a reference to Sinai: You have heard that it was said to your forefathers in old times. Jesus begins each of these with a specific reference to the law. This is not because He is contradicting the Torah. He has said already that He doesn't come to annul or destroy the law. Everything He says could be reasoned out from the Law and Prophets. But He is teaching what it means to "fulfill" the law with a righteousness that goes beyond the scribes and Pharisees.

Jesus assumes a very high authority in relation to the law. He refers to God's deliverance at Sinai: You have heard it was said to the ancients. Then he says "I say to you." In saying that, Jesus puts Himself in the place of God: God spoke before, but now God speaks His final word. Through Moses, the Lord laid out the way of righteousness for His people in that time; but now in the new covenant, with the coming of the Son, the Lord is laying out a surpassing righteousness.

Jesus begins with anger, citing the sixth commandment, and then moves on to the seventh commandment that condemns adultery. Anger is not inherently wrong. God gets angry, and very occasionally the Bible refers to justified human anger. In Exodus

---

11. See Glen Stassen, "Fourteen Triads."

11, Moses confronts Pharaoh with the news that the Lord is going to kill the firstborn of Egypt, and he goes out from Pharaoh in "hot anger" (v. 8). Later, Moses comes from the mountain and breaks the tables of the law and grinds the golden calf to powder. The text doesn't say that he was angry, but Moses' actions indicate that he was angry. Nothing in Exodus suggests that this was wrong. When the high priest orders one of his guards to strike Paul, Paul responds with anger: "God is going to strike you, you whitewashed wall! And do you sit in judgment to try me according to the Law, and in violation of the Law order me to be struck?" (Acts 23:3) Paul apologizes for this, but what he apologizes for is not his anger but the fact that he spoke out against the priest, a leader of the people. Jesus Himself gets angry on several occasions. He asks the Pharisees if he should heal a man with a withered hand on the Sabbath, and they refuse to respond; He looks at them "with anger, grieved at their hardness of heart" and then heals the man (Mark 3:5). Jesus gets angry when He throws around the tables of the money-changers at the temple, and He calls His enemies fools (Matthew 23:17), using the same word that he warns about here in the Sermon on the Mount.

Like other emotions, anger motivates action, and indignation with evil impels us to oppose it. Emotions are judgments about a situation that can be fitting or unsuitable.[12] Anger can be motivated by a sense of justice and motivate us to combat injustice and evil. And Jesus' statement is not at odds with this biblical teaching. He doesn't say "Don't get angry." Instead, he does two things.

First, He describes what anger leads to. He describes two levels of anger. The first is the mere emotion of anger, and the last two involve anger expressed in words of insult—calling someone an idiot or a fool. He warns that these sorts of responses lead to judgment, and the judgments are ascending in intensity. A man who is angry is in danger of being dragged before the local court; a man who says "Raca" (blockhead or empty-head) is in danger of

---

12. Robert Solomon, *The Passions: Emotions and the Meaning of Life* (Hackett, 1993).

being brought before the national Jewish court of the Sanhedrin. But the one who says "You fool" is in greater danger, the danger of hell.

This seems absurd. How can anyone be punished by a court just for being angry, especially when anger is not always wrong? How can one be sent to hell for saying "fool" when Jesus Himself calls people fools? Jesus draws on a biblical theme that links anger with strife and murder. Proverbs 15:18 says "A hot-tempered man stirs up strife, but the slow to anger pacifies contention." This doesn't forbid anger, any more than Jesus does. But it says that we should be like our Father, slow to anger. Similarly, in Proverbs 29:8 we read, "Scorners set a city aflame, but wise men turn away anger" and in Proverbs 30:33, Agur tells us that 'The churning of milk produces butter, and pressing the nose brings forth blood, so the churning of anger produces strife." In the deep background, Jesus is alluding to the story of Cain and Abel. Jesus uses the word "brother" four times and also mentions an altar.[13] Cain was angry with his brother, envious because his brother's offering was accepted and his wasn't. That anger eventually boiled up in murder.

All these passages show that anger doesn't stay put. Especially when it's nurtured and cultivated in our hearts, it won't stay inside. It will express itself in word or action. Jesus is saying, "If you let anger go and don't deal with it, you're going to end up in court or worse. If you don't get anger under control, somebody's going to call the cops someday. There's going to be a fight, a blow up, perhaps a murder, and you're going to be hauled before the judge."

How do we solve the problem of anger? Jesus doesn't say, "Don't be angry." But He does give commands that are designed to show how we can avoid the consequences of anger that He's described, and that the Proverbs describe. How can we be angry and not end up in court? More importantly, Jesus shows us how

---

13. William David Davies and Dale C. Allison, *Matthew 1-7* (Continuum, 2004), p. 510.

we can turn our anger into action that overcomes injustice and evil. He shows how the occasion of offense and anger can be turned in a redemptive direction. How can we reverse the situation and bring peace, justice, and hope rather than strife and escalating violence? How can we be peacemakers?

One of the things Jesus says here is that we should defuse anger before it escalates to strife and murder. When we have a conflict, we shouldn't let the anger churn and bubble inside us. We shouldn't just let things go and turn our backs on brothers either. Neither of these are options for Jesus' disciples. Jesus tells us to intervene to restore the situation, and to advance it. We should seek out our brother and reconcile. This means asking for forgiveness, but it also means making whatever restitution is necessary. If you have stolen from your brother, repay; if you have insulted him or gossiped about him, tell the truth and undo the gossip; if you have struck out against a brother, do whatever is necessary to make it good.

The situations Jesus describes are situations where the person who is being commanded has done the wrong. Jesus commands the angry person, or the person who might be angry, not the one who is the object of anger. The situation with the man at the altar is based on the story of Cain, and Cain is the angry man. The phrase "your brother has something against you" means that *you* are the one who has done wrong, given offense, acted wrongly toward your brother, and your brother has a case against you. *You* have done the wrong, so restore it. Elsewhere, we learn that the obligation is also on us if our brother sins against us—go and seek to restore him, Jesus says (Matthew 18:15). The situation is one in which *you* bring a case, and are on your way to court. Jesus says, break off your suit. Don't pursue it. In both cases, Jesus says it's incumbent on the brother who is angry to deal with his anger by seeking out his brother or by renouncing the court case. If his efforts at reconciliation don't work, then we're in a situation of Matthew 18.

Practically, this means that you are not escalating the conflict. You're putting your anger aside. Instead of seeking vengeance to restore your honor, you're seeking reconciliation. But more than that, you are acting *redemptively*. Here's a situation where anger could escalate to insult or worse. Murder might take place, where insults might escalate into slander and libel and into a court case. Instead of adding to that situation of violence, which would add to the turmoil of God's creation, you have brought a little piece/peace of the kingdom, a bit of *shalom*, into the world. You have advanced the kingdom by taking the initiative to reconcile with your brother and break off your suit.

In the ancient world, defending your honor was a high demand. If you were insulted, the honorable thing to do was to restore your honor by punishing the one who insulted you. To put your anger aside and seek reconciliation was a sign of weakness. To initiate a suit and then stop the suit on the way to court would bring considerable shame. Following these instructions requires us to share in the shame of Jesus, which is the shame of God. God has a quarrel with His people, with Israel. To restore His honor, He should punish them and make them pay for the dishonor. Instead, God reverses the dynamics of honor and shame. Instead of destroying Israel, He comes to be reconciled, and *He* bears the burden of that reconciliation. He has a case against Israel, an airtight one, and instead of pressing His case to the court He breaks off the case and takes the punishment on Himself. This is how the kingdom comes, when God and God's people invert honor and shame.

Jesus moves from the sixth to the seventh commandment, teaching about adultery and lust. The pattern of Jesus' teaching is very similar in verses 27-30. He quotes from the law, then describes the dynamics and desires that express themselves in adultery, and finally gives a command that enables us to avoid setting out on the path of adultery. What exactly is Jesus saying is equivalent to committing adultery? Is he saying that sexual desire or attraction is adultery? That indeed would be a hard saying. Not only would this be a virtually impossible command to keep—since we cannot avoid sexual attraction entirely—it would go against the grain of the rest of Scripture. God created us male and female. God created us sexual beings, with sexual desires. Sex and sexual desire are good. The world must be peopled, and the peopling of the world depends on sexual desire. The Bible does not teach that sexual desire is evil and doesn't forbid sexual attraction. Jesus doesn't say, don't have sexual desires. Jesus doesn't say "if you look at a woman with lust" but rather "if you look at a woman *in order to* lust" or "*with the purpose* of lusting." If you look at a woman in order to arouse and to cultivate and to nurture sexual desire, then you are committing adultery with her. Sexual attraction isn't sin; but gazing at a woman other than your wife to arouse sexual desire *is*. There's a difference between noticing beauty and "checking her out." That's what Jesus is forbidding—staring at a woman to arouse lust. The paradigm case of gazing to arouse lust is pornography. That is the gaze that is adultery in the heart, because that is the gaze we indulge to awaken and nurture sexual desire. He is talking about sexual desire that we nurture in our hearts so that we can begin to act on it.

How does Jesus say we should handle this? Radically. Notice first the consequences of not taking steps to deal with this habit. Twice Jesus describes the whole body being thrown into hell. And Paul says the same: Those who are sexually immoral have no place in the kingdom of heaven. The first step in dealing with sexual sin is to recognize, as Paul says, that this sin is a sin against your own body in a way that other sins aren't. Sexual immorality is not the only sin. But it is a serious sin. More specifically, He tells us that we need to do a radical kind of surgery to avoid this sin. This is a sin against our own body, Paul says, and the avoidance should register on the body. If you are in the habit of gazing at women to make them tools to excite your sexual imagination, then pluck out the eye. If you think it enhances your honor as a man to make sexual conquests, then disfigure your body and shame yourself rather than continue.

Jesus is not talking about literal mutilation. He is using hyperbole to reinforce how seriously we need to take these sins. He's saying that we should remove whatever it is that leads us into illicit sexual desire, because that sexual desire is going to lead to sexual sin. Whatever leads into the temptation to gaze or touch for the purposes of sexual arousal, stop it. Cut it out. If it means getting rid of the internet, get rid of the internet. If it means avoiding certain people or settings, avoid those people and settings.

One thing to notice here is that Jesus frames the command as a command to men. Many ancients, and many medievals, thought that sexual attraction was mainly the woman's fault. Her beauty shot out penetrating rays that a man couldn't resist, and it wounded him with the wound of love. Jesus doesn't see things that way. The Bible clearly does teach modesty for women, but Jesus doesn't say we avoid lust by covering the woman's body but by plucking out the man's eye. He condemns the aggressive gaze of the man.

Jesus' words are especially applicable to young men and women who are full of hormones and attractions and potential drama. Jesus is saying, don't let it get started. Don't toy with lust. Don't act like you can handle it. Jesus says, Pluck it out, deal with it, cast it away from you. Get help if you need it, but whatever you do don't let it go. Because, as Jesus says, Blessed are the pure in heart, for they shall see God.

Marriage and Speech
Matthew 5:30-37

> If your right hand makes you stumble, cut it off and throw it from you; for it is better for you to lose one of the parts of your body, than for your whole body to go into hell. [31]It was said, 'whoever sends his wife away, let him give her a certificate of divorce'; [32]but I say to you that everyone who divorces his wife, except for the reason of unchastity, makes her commit adultery; and whoever marries a divorced woman commits

> adultery. ³³ Again, you have heard that the ancients were told, 'you shall not make false vows, but you shall fulfill your vows to the Lord.' ³⁴ But I say to you, make no oath at all, either by heaven, for it is the throne of God, ³⁵or by the earth, for it is the footstool of His feet, or by Jerusalem, for it is the city of the great King. ³⁶ Nor shall you make an oath by your head, for you cannot make one hair white or black. ³⁷ But let your statement be, 'Yes, yes' or 'No, no'; anything beyond these is of evil.
> – Matthew 5:30-37

Later in Matthew, the Pharisees and scribes come to Jesus with a question, "Is it lawful for a man to divorce his wife for any cause at all?" Instead of getting into a discussion about the rules of divorce, Jesus points the Pharisees back to God's original design for marriage. In the beginning, it was not so. God made man male and female, and said that a man should leave father and mother and cleave to His wife and be one flesh. Jesus draws the conclusion: "they are no longer two, but one flesh. What therefore God has joined together, let no man separate." Jesus goes on to talk about divorce and its legitimacy, as he also does in the Sermon on the Mount. But we need to keep the fundamental perspective of Genesis 1-2 before us when we think about marriage and divorce. And we have to think about what Jesus teaches about marriage and divorce in the light of His entire mission.

In the Sermon on the Mount, Jesus is instructing us in a righteousness that surpasses the righteousness of the scribes and Pharisees. Our righteousness should be a redemptive righteousness. It's not merely a righteousness that avoids doing evil, or simply does good. It's a righteousness that, like God's own righteousness, intervenes in the evil patterns of fallen human life, a righteousness that takes flesh in the midst of all the perverse habits and cycles that shape the way we live and breaks them up from the inside. This redemptive righteousness leads to a restoration of Eden. It's never going to be a perfect restoration prior to Jesus' return in glory at the end, the final judgment, the resurrection, and the consummation of the new heavens and new earth. But it's a real restoration. When we live out the righteousness that Jesus teaches, we are not simply living as mankind was intended to live; we are spreading that truly human life into the world. As we live out the righteousness that Jesus teaches and empowers by His Spirit, the kingdom comes, and God's will is done on earth as it is in heaven.

One area where this takes place is in marriage. When we obey Jesus' commandments, our marriages should become like the marriage in the garden, like the marriage of Jesus to His bride. When we obey Jesus' commandments, we really are not two but one flesh, and we don't tear apart what God has joined together. When we obey Jesus' commandments in the power of the Spirit, our marriages become zones of new creation in the midst of the old, our homes little Edens dotting the landscape and spreading to encompass the earth.

Before we start trying to find where the escape hatch is, we need to get settled on what marriage itself is. Marriage is a creation of God, a covenanted partnering of a man and a woman for a lifetime. Marriage is a creation of God because God established the institution of marriage in general. It was not good that man should be alone, and so God made a helper corresponding, suitable to him. God created marriage as an institution in the garden. Each individual marriage is also a creation of God. That's what Jesus' words in Matthew 19 imply: What God has joined together is a particular man and a particular woman. Marriage is not a voluntary association that lasts as long as it makes you happy. Your marriage is something God made, and that means that you have to treat it with the respect you should show a divine creation.

Marriage is a solution to Adam's weakness, helplessness, and isolation. It's not good for man to be alone, the Lord said, and so He made a helper from Adam's side. It's not good for man to be alone, so the Lord separated Adam and then told him to be reunited in one flesh with the rib-turned-woman He had made. It's not good for man to be alone, so God made a helper that is like yet gloriously unlike Adam—a helper corresponding to him.

Not an identical helper, but a helper that co-responds to him. Marriage is designed so that husband and wife can fulfill their callings more effectively and faithfully than they could alone.

Whatever we go on to say about divorce has to be a tragic addendum to that original vision of marriage. Marriage isn't a temporary alliance, a "pure relationship."[14] It was created to be a lifelong covenanted partnership, two made into one flesh, two people living out a single life story together, two people united in such proximity that their lives—waking and sleeping, working and resting, raising children and making love—are simply impossible to disentangle from one another.

Like most of the Jewish teachers of his day, Jesus comments on divorce and talks about the circumstances in which divorce is legitimate. He teaches that marriage was intended to be lifelong, but in the law God accommodated to Israel's hardness of heart (Matthew 19:1-9). This is the cause of divorce—hardness of heart. Hardness of heart shown in resentment and bitterness that cannot be resolved. Hardness of heart shown in adultery. Hardness of heart shown in an unwillingness to forgive and move on. Whatever the particulars, when there's a divorce, you can be sure that there is hardness of heart. Because of the fact of human hardness, God permits marriages to end. It is better for some marriages to be torn in pieces than for them to go on.

According to Deuteronomy 24, a man divorcing his wife had to provide a certificate of divorce. But this passing reference in Deuteronomy had become a large loophole in Jewish thought. According to Glen Stassen and David Gushee:

> The 'conservative' approach, as reflected in the teaching of Shammai, viewed divorce as morally legitimate ('lawful') only in cases of a wife's 'indecency'; that is, some form of inappropriate sexual behavior (probably, though not necessarily, unchaste behavior short of adultery, which was

---

14. This phrase comes from Anthony Giddens, *The Transformation of Intimacy: Sexuality, Love, and Eroticism in Modern Societies* (Stanford University Press, 1993), esp. ch. 4.

officially punishable by death). The prevailing opinion, however—and, apparently, the prevailing practice—appeared to be that of Hillel, who interpreted the phrase broadly to mean 'anything displeasing.' . . . Thus women could be divorced for failing to measure up to the beauty of a rival (Akiba), for failures in the kitchen (Hillel) or for any reason whatsoever.[15]

Jesus also calls attention to the clause about "indecency" in Deuteronomy 24. But he interprets it differently from many of his contemporaries. The man seeks divorce because he finds some "thing of nakedness" in his wife (Deuteronomy 24:1). Jesus takes this as a pre-requisite for a legitimate divorce: "except for πορνεια" (Matthew 5:32). The Greek word can refer to a range of sexual sins —adultery, incest, fornication, prostitution. Paul interprets Jesus' teaching to include abandonment of marriage by an unbelieving spouse (1 Corinthians 7:12-15). Divorce is permissible (not required) when one spouse has broken the marriage covenant in a fundamental way.

But Jesus also makes the somewhat cryptic comment that anyone who divorces for another reason than πορνεια "makes her commit adultery." This might be interpreted in the light of Matthew 19, where Jesus says that a man who divorces his wife for any other reason *and then remarries* commits adultery. That is, he's still considered married because his supposed divorce was not actually permissible. He is still obligated to his first wife. So, if he divorces because of bad cooking or because he finds another woman more attractive, and then marries another woman, he is committing adultery. Perhaps in chapter 5, Jesus is saying that a woman who is divorced for the wrong reasons *and remarries* commits adultery. Perhaps. But that's not what Jesus says. He says that adultery is the result of an illegitimate divorce without saying anything about remarriage. The point seems to be that easy divorce encourages adultery. If I can divorce my wife when I find a new, more attractive woman, then the divorce rules encourage

---

15. Stassen and Gushee, *Kingdom Ethics: Following Jesus in Contemporary Context* (Downers Grove, IL: InterVarsity, 2003), p. 279.

adultery. Jesus may be talking about the cycle of marriage, divorce, remarriage, divorce, remarriage that so often follows from a first divorce. Once the trust of a first marriage is broken, once we've found an escape route, what's to prevent us from doing the same with another? Divorce produces a cycle of adultery, more adultery, and family damage. It's a fact that divorce and adultery commonly cross generations. Parents who commit adultery and/or are divorced leave a wasteland for their children, one that is often filled with adultery and divorce on the part of the children.

However we interpret this comment, it is clear from experience that divorces are not smooth, happy breaks. Broken marriages leave damaged lives in their wake—damaged husband and wife, damaged children, damaged friends and family. There is no such thing as a happy divorce. A divorce always means the tearing apart of something that God has put together. Sometimes this radical surgery is the best solution. But it should not be celebrated, and it should be prevented. We are called to live together in marriage in a way that keeps divorce from happening. Jesus doesn't give instructions about how to arrest the destruction of a marriage, but Paul does. Speaking to wives, he says that a woman who leaves her husband should remain unmarried or seek reconciliation (1 Corinthians 7:11). To save a marriage that's headed for disaster, both wife and husband should humble themselves, confess their sins, and be reconciled. This requires humility and a willingness to accept shame. Just as importantly, husbands and wives should live together with mutual love and respect so that their marriage never gets to the point where divorce is contemplated. Divorce is linked to the seventh commandment, obviously, since it deals with sexuality and adultery. But in Deuteronomy, the divorce legislation is in the eighth Commandment section. Jesus likewise treats divorce as an eighth-commandment issue, then moves on to the ninth commandment, forbidding false witness. Jesus again summarizes the teaching of the law, which permits oaths and requires truthfulness (cf. Leviticus 19:12; Numbers 30:2; Deuteronomy 23:21-23). Technically, there's a difference between vows and oaths. Vows are contingent promises. In vowing, you make a promise to God that's contingent on Him doing something for you. If you help me out here, I'll give up whiskey for the rest of my life. An oath calls God as witness to the truth of what you say. In court, we take oaths, asserting that what we say is true and calling on God to bear witness that what we say is actually the case.

Jesus is talking about oaths here. And he's talking about oath practices that were common among Jews. Here I think Jesus has in view particularly the Jewish practice of finding escape routes for oaths. The Jews had introduced a system that winked at oaths that were not directly oaths in the name of God (Matthew 23:16-22). Other Jewish writers around this time also commented on how common oaths were. Philo notes that "There are some who without even any gain in prospect have an evil habit of swearing incessantly and thoughtlessly about ordinary matters where there is nothing at all in dispute, filling up the gaps in their talk with oaths, forgetting that it were better to submit to have their words cut short or rather to be silenced altogether." Some apparently think "that the continual repetition of a string of oaths will secure them their object."[16] Philo's comments give us some insight into why someone would do this. It's a form of verbal bullying and intimidation and bluster. We are in a disagreement with someone. We know we have a weak case, or we are lying. We can't win our case on the evidence. So we have to bluster and fume and swear that what we are saying is true. We want to win the argument, and so we use verbal forms of bullying to do it.

Despite the apparently absolute statement in verse 34, Jesus does not annul all oaths. The Lord Himself takes oaths to keep covenant (Luke 1:73; Hebrews 6). Paul sometimes adopts oath formulas to reinforce a point that he's making. "I assure you before God I am not lying," he writes in Galatians (see also Romans 1:9; 2 Corinthians 1:23; Galatians 1:20; Philippians 1:8; Hebrews 6:13-20; Revelation 10:6). Jesus Himself submits to an oath in His trial, and

---

16. Quoted in Jerome H. Neyrey, *Honor and Shame in the Gospel of Matthew* (Louisville: Westminster/John Knox, 1998), p. 202.

He uses the oath formula "Truly, truly I say to you; Amen Amen, I say to you." Jesus doesn't forbid oath-taking in its appropriate setting. Oaths settle disputes, the Bible says, and Jesus does not disagree with that. Instead, he's saying three things.

Oaths are all oaths before God, in God's presence, in the name of God. The escape routes that the Jews constructed are false escape routes. They are still oaths in the name of God, even if God's name is not invoked. Changing the words doesn't mean that you've escaped the responsibility. Jesus also commands us not to bluster and swear as a way of bullying people into accepting the truth of what we say. If you've got to yell and swear to be heard, you've got problems already. Let your Yes be Yes and your No be No. Most importantly, Jesus also emphasizes that we are to be a truth-telling people. In place of the casuistry that gave allowance to false oaths, Jesus insists that our words should be truthful and straightforward. We should not have to buttress the truth of what we say by swearing in God's name, or confuse our listeners with convoluted explanations and sub-explanations. The practice of swearing that Jesus condemns is "of the evil one," from Satan, who is the father of the lie. James picks up this theme as well, talking about the hellish origin of evil speech (James 3:6).

Truth is in short supply, and perhaps always has been. We are surrounded by spin and hype and verbal legerdemain and bluster that are designed to prevent us from seeing the truth. We have it in politics, in media, in popular culture, in the church. We are not straightforwardly telling the truth but persuade by all sorts of indirect and irrelevant means. Becoming a truth-telling people is very difficult. It swims against the tide. But this is what Jesus calls us to. He is the Truth incarnate, and we are called to follow truth and speak truth. Let your Yes be Yes and your No be No.

Resisting Evil
Matthew 5:38-48

"You have heard that it was said, 'an eye for an eye, and a tooth for a tooth.' ³⁹ But I say to you, do not resist an evil person; but whoever slaps you on your right cheek, turn the other to him also. ⁴⁰ If anyone wants to sue you and take your shirt, let him have your coat also. ⁴¹ Whoever forces you to go one mile, go with him two. ⁴² Give to him who asks of you, and do not turn away from him who wants to borrow from you. ⁴³ You have heard that it was said, 'you shall love your neighbor and hate your enemy.' ⁴⁴ But I say to you, love your enemies and pray for those who persecute you, ⁴⁵ so that you may be sons of your Father who is in heaven; for He causes His sun to rise on the evil and the good, and sends rain on the righteous and the unrighteous. ⁴⁶ For if you love those who love you, what reward do you have? Do not even the tax collectors do the same? ⁴⁷ If you greet only your brothers, what more are you doing than others? Do not even the Gentiles do the same? ⁴⁸ Therefore you are to be perfect, as your heavenly Father is perfect."
– Matthew 5:38-48

These verses more than any other in the Sermon on the Mount have been the source of confusion and misinterpretation. Some have taken these verses to mean that Jesus teaches pacifism and anarchism, that he's doing away with government and the coercion that is inherent in any form of political order, or at least forbidding Christians from participating in such political orders. At the opposite end is an interpretation more common among Reformed teachers, which is to limit what Jesus is saying to private, personal ethics. According to this view, Jesus is not talking about public or social ethics, but only about what we do in personal private life. And the implication is that public life operates by different ethical standards. Man is moral in private, as an individual; society operates by rules that, by Jesus' standards, are "immoral." It doesn't make historical sense to think that Jesus is distinguishing in this way between moral man and immoral society, between public and private. Scripture doesn't acknowledge any kind of bright line between public and private, which is a modern invention.

Jesus intends for His instructions to be followed by all His disciples, in all their spheres of life. If you are a Christian judge or a policeman, Jesus intends you to be His disciple as policeman or judge. If you're the President of the United States, you have to follow Jesus as a President and not just in your private life. And that means obeying His commandments about resistance and love for enemies in your *public* duties as well as in your private personal and family relations. We should also note that Jesus' command to love enemies doesn't eliminate the category of "enemy." When Jesus says, "Love your enemies," many understand this to mean, "Don't have any enemies." But that's not what He says. He tells us how to deal with enemies, which is to love them and do good to them.

Some misinterpretations arise from a mistranslation of the opening instruction of verse 39. According to many translations, Jesus instructs His disciples, "do not resist him who is evil" (Matthew 5:39, NASB) or "do not resist evil." Strictly grammatically, these are possible translations. But do they make sense in the whole context of the gospel story? Not much. Does Jesus refrain from resisting evil? Of course not: He resists the devil in the wilderness; He resists the Pharisees and scribes; He resists all the evil of the world in His death and resurrection. Jesus spends His entire ministry resisting evil, and since His main instruction to disciples is to follow Him and His example, we can't possibly be instructed to non-resistance to evil. The Greek can equally be translated as "do not resist by evil means."[17] And that, I think, gets at the heart of Jesus' instructions. Jesus did not refrain from resistance. Jesus resisted evil, but He resisted evil by doing good. He calls us to the same kind of resistance.

---

17. N. T. Wright, *Jesus and the Victory of God* (Minneapolis: Fortress, 1996), pp. 290-291.

Jesus quotes from the Old Testament *lex talionis*, the "law of retribution" (v. 38; cf. Exodus 21:24; Leviticus 24:20). This was a principle of civil justice in the Old Testament. If one damaged person or property, he had to restore what he had damaged or suffer a similar damage to himself. Since murder takes life, it had to be punished with the death penalty, life-for-life. Jesus doesn't deny the justice of this principle, and He sometimes appeals to it as a principle of divine justice. Whoever is ashamed of the Son of man, of him shall the Son of man be ashamed, Jesus says (Mark 8:38). Paul says whoever destroys the temple of God will be destroyed (1 Corinthians 3:17).

In the Old Testament, the *lex talionis* limited violence and retribution. Lamech said he would take seventy-sevenfold vengeance on anyone who mistreated him. The Law allows only this limited vengeance. But this principle can be applied in ways that perpetuate violence rather than arrest it. Jesus warns that applying this principle in many settings leads to cycles of violence, insult and return insult, vengeance. Throughout human history, this has been a great tragedy. An insult would lead to a response, and that would lead to a response, and the vendettas would persist until they exhausted themselves. Like a revenge tragedy, they would not end until everyone was dead on the floor, or somebody just stopped. These kinds of vendettas are still common in parts of the world—gang warfare in our inner cities, the Middle East, Kosovo during the late 1990s. These examples show that Jesus' words are not only relevant to personal ethics. How many wars are the result of defenses of honor, attempts to apply some version of eye-for-eye. For Serbs and Croats, for Tutsis and Hutus, all the evil that's been done over centuries has to be avenged, but when the vengeance has happened, it just initiates a new cycle.

We're fooling ourselves if we think that our world is free from these primitive instincts and patterns of response. Don't think, "I've never been involved in a family feud. I've never been tempted to be a vigilante. This doesn't apply to me." We still act out of vengeance, in our marriages, in our friendships, in our dealings with difficult people at work or difficult leaders in the church. A friend insults us, and we want to pay back. Someone makes us look stupid in class, and we want to do something to humble them. Our husband or wife does something embarrassing, and we look for a chance to even the score.

Jesus is telling His disciples not to get caught up in those cycles of honor and violence. Don't even step into that circle, because it won't stop. Yet He doesn't annul the principle of *lex talionis*. Instead, He describes a paradoxical, surprising fulfillment of the law, a fulfillment that surpasses the fulfillment of the law by the scribes and Pharisees, a fulfillment that participates in the coming of the kingdom of God that restores harmony and peace and justice in the world. The first example illustrates His point.

Jesus is not describing a situation in which our lives are imperiled, nor is He prohibiting self-defense. He's not saying that a person is coming at you with deadly force. The law provides for self-defense and defense of your house, family and property if someone is breaking in. Jesus is not eliminating that. He's talking about honor and dishonor, insult and shame. If I receive a slap on the right cheek, either the slapper has slapped me with his left hand or he is slapping me with his backhand. Either would be insulting. In Israel, the left hand was reserved for dirty work—using the bathroom and such. So, getting slapped with the left hand would be insulting. But a slap on the right cheek with the right hand is a backhanded slap, an insulting slap rather than a danger to life and limb. The person who slaps you with the back of his hand is treating you as a slave, as an underling. He's not treating you as an equal. How does Jesus tell us to respond? Instead of carrying out retribution by returning a slap for a slap, instead of returning insult for insult, Jesus calls His disciples to bear the burden of retribution and offer to receive a second slap. If you applied the *lex talionis*, it would be to return a slap for a slap. Jesus says, apply the *lex talionis* in this redemptive, surprising way—*accept* the second slap rather than giving it. The "double restitution" comes back on the disciple, who bears the punishment on behalf of the one who assaults him.

The other commands that Jesus gives are applications of the same principle. They all have specific application to Jews under the rule of the Romans. Roman soldiers could requisition a Jew, for instance, to carry his baggage for a certain distance. The Jews, understandably, were irritated, and you can imagine that the Romans took advantage of this to insult the Jews and shame them. Instead of trying to return the injustice back on the person making the unjust and oppressive demand, Jesus commands us to double the injustice on ourselves, to accept the burden of bearing the *lex talionis*. If someone sues for your coat—which was forbidden by the law, an act of oppression—don't look for an opportunity to get back at him and take his coat. Throw off your shirt too, and stand naked before him. Take the vengeance on yourself, rather than throwing it on him. If a Roman soldier demands that you carry his baggage for a mile, don't pay him back by looking for a chance to bring the oppression back on his head; go a second mile. If an oppressive tax collector demands that you pay, don't grab your money and run. Give it to him.

Many have taken these instructions to be about "non-resistance," but that's inaccurate. Jesus is forbidding us to enter into the cycle of vengeance and counter-strike, but He's also forbidding us from doing nothing. Jesus doesn't want us simply to accept evil and not resist at all. Jesus is not telling us to "take it," glowering resentfully as we get beaten to a pulp. Jesus is not talking about a situation where you simply grudgingly trudge along beside the Roman soldier, burning bitterly the whole time. He's not talking about just gritting your teeth and taking it when someone takes your cloak from you. Scribes and Pharisees could do that; often they had no choice. That's not redemptive righteousness. That's not righteousness at all. That's just realism, Stoicism, accepting oppression and evil, and doing nothing because you can't do anything about it. Doing nothing is not redemptive righteousness; taking the blow, or going a mile, or giving up your cloak doesn't do anything to redeem and reverse oppression.

Jesus says we *can* do something about oppression. We can act, and we can act in ways that arrest oppression and undo it. In other words, Jesus is teaching a form of resistance, but a form of resistance in which good triumphs over evil. Instead of perpetuating insults and blows, Jesus teaches His disciples to act in a surprising way that brings an end to the cycle. Instead of a series of slaps and return slaps, there are at most two slaps, both on the cheeks of the disciple, and then it's over. Instead of a cycle of vengeance and retribution, it's all over after two miles, after the disciple strips down to nothing. No more to be done.

Following these instructions also, subtly, restores the dignity of the person under assault. Instead of being a victim of an unwanted blow, instead of being merely a victim of oppression, the disciple takes initiative into his own hands—he offers his cheek, he removes his undershirt, he goes a second mile, he gives to whoever demands (vv. 40-42). The slapper wants to treat the slappee as a victim, the object of his oppression. The slappee has no choice, no dignity; he's nothing more than the thing my hand lands on. But then he turns and offers his other check, and *I* am suddenly put on the spot. I've got to decide whether to slap him again. He's wrested initiative out of my hands. In doing so, the disciple might also expose the bully for the brute that he is, turning the tables in a way that might bring shame on the oppressor. Slapping might make the slapper look virile, manly, in control. Slapping someone who's willing to be slapped makes the slapper look cruel (think of the attack dogs of the Civil Rights Movement).

Ultimately, Jesus doesn't endorse turning the cheek because it's pragmatic, because it works. It is pragmatic, and it is pragmatic because it advances the kingdom by undoing cycles of violence and anger and revenge and moving toward restoration. He's urging this behavior on us because it's the way we follow Him. There are a number of parallels between this passage and the description of the suffering servant in Isaiah 50.

> The Lord God has given Me the tongue of the learned, that I should know how to speak a word in season to him who is weary. He awakens Me morning by morning, he awakens My ear to hear as the learned. The Lord God has opened My ear; and I was not rebellious, nor did I turn away. I gave My back to those who struck Me, and My cheeks to those who plucked out the beard; I did not hide My face from shame and spitting. For the Lord God will help Me; therefore I will not be disgraced; therefore I have set My face like a flint, and I know that I will not be ashamed (vv. 4-7).

This is the story of Jesus as well. Nearly everything that Jesus mentions here happens to Him in His passion. As Davies and Allison say, "Jesus Himself was struck and slapped (26:67), and his garments (27:35) were taken from him. If his followers then turn the other cheek and let the enemy have their clothes, will they not be remembering their Lord, especially in his passion?"[18]

Beginning in verse 43, Jesus begins to deal with the question of enemies. He doesn't quote the Old Testament itself, but instead summarizes a view that was held by some Jews. The Old Testament doesn't endorse the view that we are free to hate enemies. The law tells us that we are to do good even to enemies —caring for his animals (Exodus 23:4). Proverbs tells us to feed and give a drink to our enemy (25:21-22). The stories of the Bible include many examples of people doing good to those who are persecuting them: Joseph doesn't take vengeance on his brothers, but feeds them and robes them in glory. David has more than one opportunity to pay back Saul, but refuses. The prophets suffer for doing good and don't strike out in vengeance.

Jesus particularly challenges the perversion of loving only those who love you (vv. 46-47). We are to love those near to us (cf. Galatians 6:10), but if our love is restricted by blood, race, kinship, church membership, or whatever, it is no better than the love of Gentiles and tax-collectors. It is not the righteous love that surpasses that of the scribes and Pharisees. Jesus doesn't tell us

---

18. Davies and Allison, *Matthew 1-7*, p. 546.

to leave our enemies alone. He's not talking about non-resistance or non-intervention. He's talking about resistance that takes the form of doing good. Instead of doing nothing when our enemies persecute us, we are to pray for them (cf. Romans 12:14-21).

These instructions have been read as shrewd tactics for an oppressed people. They are that, but Jesus doesn't justify them in a pragmatic way. When he instructs us to love our enemies, He appeals instead to the example of our Father, who gives sunshine and rain to His enemies (v. 45). He ends this portion of the sermon with a restatement of the Old Testament demand, "Be perfect as I am perfect" (v. 48, cf. Leviticus 19:2). Jesus has redefined "perfection" in terms of love for enemies and doing good to those who abuse us.

In Scripture, "perfection" doesn't necessarily mean sinlessness. Instead, it often means maturity. Love for enemies is mature righteousness. Praying for and doing good for those who persecute us is mature obedience and discipleship. It is the sort of righteousness that surpasses the righteousness of the scribes and Pharisees, and the sort of righteousness that undoes the knots of evil that tie up the human race so that God's will is done on earth as it is in heaven.

Righteousness before God
Matthew 6:1-18

> Beware of practicing your righteousness before men to be noticed by them; otherwise you have no reward with your Father who is in heaven. ² So when you give to the poor, do not sound a trumpet before you, as the hypocrites do in the synagogues and in the streets, so that they may be honored by men. Truly I say to you, they have their reward in full. ³ But when you give to the poor, do not let your left hand know what your right hand is doing, ⁴ so that your giving will be in secret; and your Father who sees what is done in secret will reward you. ⁵ When you pray, you are not to be like the hypocrites; for they love to stand and pray in the synagogues and on the street corners so that they may be seen by men. Truly I say to you,

they have their reward in full. ⁶ But you, when you pray, go into your inner room, close your door and pray to your Father who is in secret, and your Father who sees what is done in secret will reward you. ⁷ And when you are praying, do not use meaningless repetition as the Gentiles do, for they suppose that they will be heard for their many words. ⁸ So do not be like them; for your Father knows what you need before you ask Him. ⁹ Pray, then, in this way: 'Our Father who is in heaven, Hallowed be Your name. ¹⁰ 'Your kingdom come Your will be done, On earth as it is in heaven. ¹¹ 'Give us this day our daily bread. ¹² 'And forgive us our debts, as we also have forgiven our debtors. ¹³ 'And do not lead us into temptation, but deliver us from evil. For Yours is the kingdom and the power and the glory forever. Amen.' ¹⁴ For if you forgive others for their transgressions, your heavenly Father will also forgive you. ¹⁵ But if you do not forgive others, then your Father will not forgive your transgressions. ¹⁶ Whenever you fast, do not put on a gloomy face as the hypocrites do, for they neglect their appearance so that they will be noticed by men when they are fasting. Truly I say to you, they have their reward in full. ¹⁷ But you, when you fast, anoint your head and wash your face ¹⁸ so that your fasting will not be noticed by men, but by your Father who is in secret; and your Father who sees what is done in secret will reward you. – Matthew 6:1-18

In Apuleius's Latin novel, *The Golden Ass*, the traveller Lucius has the misfortune of being transformed into a donkey after rubbing himself down with a witch's ointment. Lucius suffers through all the trials and torments of life as a donkey, only to be transformed back into a man, at which point he—rather curiously—becomes a chaste and virtuous devotee of Isis. Apuleius himself was once accused of sorcery by his avaricious in-laws, though he was able to rebuff the charges. At the beginning of Book 11, Lucius returns to his human shape by prayer. As David Garland points out, the prayer is a good illustration of the kind of pagan prayers Jesus condemns in the Sermon on the Mount. He doesn't know exactly whom he is addressing, and since there are many different gods, he's got to be careful about offending one or another. He's worried that if he prays only to Proserpina, Venus might be upset and take it out on him. He's worried that if he prays only to the queen of heaven, then Proserpina might get angry.[19] This is called covering your bases—or something more vulgar.

This is the kind of prayer that Jesus condemns here in this portion of the Sermon on the Mount. He condemns the "Gentiles" who "suppose that they will be heard for their many words." They believed that God had to be awakened to action, had to be cajoled and provoked to respond, had to be flattered and seduced into paying attention, much less showing favor.

In an earlier section, Jesus teaches that our good works are light in a dark world (Matthew 5:14-16). He wants there to be a discernible difference in the way we live as His disciples before men. People should be able to look at how we deal with conflicts, look at our sexual practices and our marriages, look at our truthfulness, look at how we respond to our enemies, and be able to say, "These people are different. It's obvious." The goal of that is not to bring praise to ourselves, but to let our light shine so that they can see our good works and glorify our Father in heaven.

At the center of the sermon, however, He describes acts of righteousness that are not to be done before men but before God alone. These secret acts are crucial to pursuing a righteousness that surpasses that of the scribes and Pharisees, and they are crucial to the coming of the kingdom. The central underlying question about these secret practices of righteousness is the question of what God we are serving. Who is watching us, which is to say, who is our judge? What kind of God is it that we are serving when we give alms, when we pray, when we fast? Jesus highlights this point by repeating the name "Father" ten times in the first 18 verses of this passage. We give alms not before men but before our Father; we pray not to an indifferent deity who has to be bribed to respond, but to our Father; we fast not before men but before our Father. And the way we do these things is all determined by the God we are serving.

---

19. David E. Garland, *Reading Matthew: A Literary and Theological Commentary on the First Gospel* (Smyth & Helwys, 1999), p. 78.

Disciples and hypocrites, then, differ not only in practice but in *theology*. Our piety should manifest what God we're serving. This is not to say there is no difference in practice. There is. Three times in this passage Jesus describes the activity of "hypocrites" (vv. 2, 5, 16). In each case, they perform traditional duties of Jewish piety in order to be seen by men. They call attention to their generosity to the poor, pray long and flowery prayers, and put on a face to make sure everyone knows how much they are fasting. Jesus does instruct disciples to *behave* differently. Even when we are doing the same thing as the hypocrites, we are to do it with different *motives*. They do it to be honored by men. We do it to seek honor from our Father who sees in secret. There is also a difference in *manner*. Because the hypocrites are doing it to receive honor from men, they have to make sure that men are watching. They perform these actions to draw attention to themselves—by announcing their generosity with an apocalyptic trumpet, by praying at length and repetitively, by putting on long faces as they fast.

It's important to notice what Jesus teaches His disciples here. Jesus doesn't tell us to give up these practices. Jesus wants us to perform these actions. He wants us to give alms generously, to pray to our Father, to fast. Also it's important to see that although Jesus is addressing issues of motivation, His actual instructions are not in the realm of motivation. When He condemns the hypocrites for doing righteousness to be seen by men, He doesn't command His disciples: Don't have bad motives. We saw earlier in the sermon that Jesus is concerned about the heart—anger and lust, for instance—but that His instructions are always about actions that we perform—reconciliation and plucking out the eye. The same is true here. What He tells us to do is very specific, concrete, active. He doesn't tell us to stop thinking how we look before others. He tells us a different mode for performing these acts of righteousness. And the accent is on secrecy. We are to change motivations; but motivations are being challenged here by changes in practice.

So, instead of announcing our generosity, we shouldn't even let ourselves know how generous we are. Don't let the left hand know what the right hand is doing. Instead of offering long prayers in the synagogue, we should seek a quiet, secret place to offer our prayers. Instead of fasting with a gloomy face, we should anoint and wash and act as if we're headed to a wedding. This involves a change of motivation—we're seeking the favor of our Father who sees in secret. But we do it by changing how we behave.

The word "hypocrite" occasions some confusion here. It has come to be associated with doing something insincerely, with a divergence between outward behavior and inward motivation. Here, the "hypocrite" is one who pretends to be pious but isn't really interested in God, but only in his own reputation for piety. He gives alms, but he does it neither to help the poor nor to honor God, but because it gives him a reputation for generosity. The problem with this understanding of "hypocrisy" comes out in verses 16-18. Jesus condemns the hypocrites for fasting in a way that calls attention to their fasting. But Jesus' instructions are that we are to fast in a way that covers up the fact that we're fasting. There's a discrepancy between outward action and inner motive. Anointing the head and washing the face is a kind of disguise to make it appear that we are not fasting. This looks like hypocrisy of an inverse kind: We cover up our acts of piety. The hypocrites seem much more straightforward here.

The word "hypocrite" in Greek refers to actors, but in the LXX the word came to mean simply "ungodly." Here, the ungodly manifest their ungodliness in misdirected acts of piety, acts of piety that are designed to be seen by men. But the thing that makes them hypocrites is the fact that they are ungodly, that they are acting as if there were a different God than a kind, generous, all-seeing Father. Their basic error is to consider men their judges. They receive honor and glory, but only from men. That is the extent of their reward, and it's paltry. Jesus instructs His disciples to avoid this kind of honor-seeking from men by doing our acts of righteousness in secret, before our Father, who is our true

Judge (vv. 4, 6, 18). Jesus doesn't say that disciples shouldn't be concerned with rewards. Instead, they should seek reward from the right place—from God.

The longest section deals with prayer, and this section raises some questions. Is Jesus condemning the practice of public prayer? That's impossible, since Jesus Himself took part in services at the synagogue and temple. He shows us, though, how we are to regard our public worship: We are not gathered here to impress one another. We are here, "in secret," to stand together before our Father. This is our inner room, and we call on the God who sees in secret to hear us. Is he necessarily condemning spending a long time in prayer? Again, that's impossible, because He spends whole nights in prayer at times. He is not condemning the length but the setting. His instruction is not, "Cut it short" but "do it in secret."

Jesus also gives a model prayer that avoids the "meaningless repetition" of the Gentiles (v. 7). It is short and direct. The prayer begins with petitions about the kingdom of God; it is a "kingdom prayer" first and foremost, a prayer that God would take charge and establish justice and harmony in creation. The petitions for bread, forgiveness, and deliverance from evil (vv. 11-13) should be seen in this light. We ask for daily bread so that we can participate in the coming of the kingdom. We ask God to care for us, so that we can expend ourselves in serving Him. Each part of the prayer picks up on things that Jesus has said earlier in the sermon or anticipates things he will say later. The prayer is structurally at the center of the sermon, and it gathers together much of what Jesus says elsewhere in the sermon.

He tells us to pray as an address to our Father, and this again highlights the centrality of knowing whom we are praying to. The Father that we address in prayer is the one who knows what we need before we ask and doesn't need to be told or cajoled into responding to us. He is the one who gives sun and rain to the just and unjust. He is the one who, Jesus later says, feeds the birds of the air and clothes grass with glory greater than Solomon's. When we pray, we are to remember who it is we're approaching.

We ask that the Father's name be hallowed, that it be sanctified, held in reverence, worshiped by all men. We pray that the Father would fulfill his and our vocation in us. According to Jesus' earlier teaching, we are to do good works so that men may see and turn to God in prayer. That is, we are to live in a way that sanctifies God's name, and we are to pray also that this happens, so that others will invoke His Name too.

We are to pray for the coming of the kingdom. This is partly a request that the kingdom and its blessings would be ours. We are praying that the Father would realize the Beatitudes in us. We pray for the advance of God's saving, redemptive, restoring righteousness. We pray that the Father would take His throne and would set things in order. We pray that the kingdom would come, as Jesus says in the next part of the prayer, by causing His will to be done on earth as in heaven. We're praying for the restoration of the original created harmony between heaven and earth. And we're praying that we would be part of that restoration, so that as we hear and do what Jesus says, our lives will be set on a rock rather than on sand and that we will bring heaven to earth.

In the final petitions, we are asking for our needs to be met. Again, these pick up on other parts of the sermon. Jesus will go on to assure us that our Father will care for all our needs and that we need not be anxious about any necessities, because the Father will provide for us. Jesus has already spoken about forgiving enemies, and He goes on to reinforce the point about forgiving those who trespass. He has Himself overcome the tempter, and He assures us that our Father will deliver us as well. We are asking for bread to support our lives, for forgiveness of our sins, and for deliverance from the temptations of the evil one. But these need to be set in the context of Jesus' overall message and teaching. We ask for bread so that we can carry out our vocation to do good works that bring glory to our Father.

After giving this model prayer, Jesus focuses on the petition for forgiveness, and He emphasizes the connection between our willingness to forgive others and our Father's forgiveness of us. He says that the Father's forgiveness is dependent on our forgiveness of others (both verses 14 and 15 are phrased as "if . . . then" statements). Jesus later tells a dramatic and convicting parable about a servant whose master re-imposes a forgiven debt because the servant has been harsh toward his fellow-servant (Matthew 18:21-35). We have all kinds of pseudo-pious ways of avoiding this kind of teaching. We are saved by grace, not by our works; forgiveness is a work; therefore, Jesus can't be serious about the Father withholding forgiveness or withdrawing forgiveness from those whom He has forgiven. But He is serious. We shouldn't soften this. Of course, we are acceptable to God because of His grace, because of what Jesus has done for us. But that works itself out in a life of forgiveness, and this *has* to be our disposition, if we want to be forgiven. God oversees all history and every moment of our salvation. God is the initiator. But God also works within time, within history, and in that context He really does respond to what *we* do. He responds to our forgiveness as much as He responds to our prayers. The if-then statements mean what they say. If you are not willing to forgive those who have offended you, then God will not forgive you. You will be judged with the standard by which you judge.

Do not be anxious
Matthew 6:19-34

Do not store up for yourselves treasures on earth, where moth and rust destroy, and where thieves break in and steal. [20] But store up for yourselves treasures in heaven, where neither moth nor rust destroys, and where thieves do not break in or steal; [21] for where your treasure is, there your heart will be also. [22] The eye is the lamp of the body; so then if your eye is clear, your whole body will be full of light. [23] But if your eye is bad, your whole body will be full of darkness. If then the light that is in you is darkness, how great is the darkness! [24] No one can serve two masters; for either he will hate the one and love the other, or he will be devoted to one and despise the other. You cannot serve God and wealth. [25] For this reason I say to you, do not be worried about your life, as to what you will eat or what you will drink; nor for your body, as to what you will put on. Is not life more than food, and the body more than clothing? [26] Look at the birds of the air, that they do not sow, nor reap nor gather into barns, and yet your heavenly Father feeds them. Are you not worth much more than they? [27] And who of you by being worried can add a single hour to his life? [28] And why are you worried about clothing? Observe how the lilies of the field grow; they do not toil nor do they spin, [29] yet I say to you that not even Solomon in all his glory clothed himself like one of these. [30] But if God so clothes the grass of the field, which is alive today and tomorrow is thrown into the furnace, will He not much more clothe you? You of little faith! [31] Do not worry then, saying, 'What will we eat?' or 'What will we drink?' or 'What will we wear for clothing?' [32] For the Gentiles eagerly seek all these things; for your heavenly Father knows that you need all these things. [33] But seek first His kingdom and His righteousness, and all these things will be added to you. [34] So do not worry about tomorrow; for tomorrow will care for itself. Each day has enough trouble of its own.   – Matthew 6:19-34

Jesus announces the new law from the mountain; He is Moses on a new Sinai. But in this passage, Jesus assumes another role for a few moments—the role of Solomon the sage. This section of the Sermon on the Mount, more than any other, resembles the wisdom literature, especially the book of Proverbs. Like Solomon, He points us to the natural world to teach us about God and our responsibilities before God. "Go to the ant; observe his ways and be wise," Solomon had said. There are three things that are stately—the lion, the strutting cock, and a king with his army. Jesus the greater Solomon says, "Go to the birds and grass. Learn a lesson from the world around you." Like Solomon too, Jesus presents "two ways," two paths in life, one a path of foolishness and frustration, the other a path of life and wisdom. Solomon presents this at the beginning of Proverbs as a choice between the Lady Wisdom and the Lady Folly, and he urges the Son to seek Wisdom and choose Wisdom. Jesus the greater Solomon also puts a choice before His listeners: You cannot serve two masters; you have to choose which way you are going to go.

Like Solomon, Jesus is very concerned with the way we regard and use the things of the world. Proverbs is full of practical wisdom for making our way in the world, and it deals a good deal with money and wealth. Jesus the greater Solomon is concerned with our attitude toward and use of food, drink, clothing, and money.

We miss the point of this passage if we just classify it as wisdom literature, a neat little bit of natural theology, and shelve it there. The whole sermon was prefaced by the announcement of the coming of God's kingdom, and that is reintroduced here in v. 33, where Jesus tells us to seek not "wisdom" but the "kingdom of God and his righteousness." Notice the way Jesus describes his hearers at the end. He distinguishes between His hearers and the "Gentiles." Jesus' band of disciples is the true Israel, and those outside are "Gentiles." The Gentiles are obsessed with earthly success, treasure, and power. But Jesus' disciples are supposed to be different, obsessed instead with the kingdom of God and His righteousness. These instructions are addressed to disciples, to those who have been redeemed from Egypt, to those who have been called from their nets, to those who have been healed by the power of the Spirit that flows through Jesus.

The wisdom that Jesus speaks here is wisdom only to disciples. The wisdom that the greater Solomon talks about here is foolishness to the Greeks, and would be foolishness to many Jews too. Jesus is not making arguments that everyone can follow, nor offering assurance that anyone can find helpful. His wisdom is wisdom only to those who follow the Son, who have a heavenly Father, and who are citizens of the kingdom that Jesus announces and commences. What Jesus is teaching is directed to disciples, and it assumes the reality of what Jesus calls the kingdom. This is wisdom only in the new world of the kingdom.

What Jesus says here is *not* wisdom from most perspectives. Don't be anxious. Think about birds. Look at the grass. No wonder so many have read the gospel as the story of a first-century flower child, an ancient hippy, a Cynic. He seems to be telling us to get out of the rat race and spend our time chasing butterflies. And He does seem to be doing a bit of that. His instructions depend on the fact that a new world has erupted in the midst of the old. A new kingdom and a new king are being heralded in the midst of the corruptions of worldly kingdoms, a new city in the midst of the old cities. The Old City is a city of anxiety. For Jesus, anxiety is not just a feeling or emotion that we privately experience. It is that. But it is also the organizing principle of a world, a structure and a regime, a master and a power. Anxiety is the ether of the world outside the kingdom of God. Anxiety keeps the stores open 24/7. Anxiety keeps the highways busy until the wee hours of the morning. Anxiety keeps people working late at the office. Anxiety is what builds the skyscrapers. Anxiety is what drives consumer spending.

Anxiety is driven by a very simple insight, the insight that we are limited creatures, and the particular fact that the future sets the boundary of our limitations. We cannot see past the next moment, much less the next day or next month. Yet we want to be able to manage things. We want to secure our future. We want to be able to know something about what we will eat, drink, wear, do next year, five years, ten years. We want to know that our portfolio will still be expanding, our children will still be living nearby, we will still have a spouse. *And we can't.* If you know that you can't manage the future, and yet you *try* to manage the future, there can be only one result: *anxiety*. This is the way of the world, and it's what drives the Gentiles to "eagerly seek" food, clothing, drink, success, and all the rest.

Jesus invites us into a new world. Jesus announces the kingdom, which, in essence, means announcing God's future, and the future of God. Jesus comes announcing that the future is arriving. God intends to rule over all things, and He is beginning to rule over all things *now*. He intends to set Jesus on the throne over the whole cosmos, and He's beginning to do that *now*. He's going to defeat evil and put His world back together, and He's beginning to do that *now*. The future is arriving, and the future is secure in God's hands. He is the God of the future, and He is establishing His future in the present. And the kingdom which is

God's future world arriving in the present is *not* driven by anxiety but by trust, because within this kingdom we know that the future is secure. We know that God has everything under control. We know that God is our heavenly Father who will care for us. Jesus' wisdom is wisdom *only if* that is true.

Jesus begins by contrasting laying up heavenly treasures with laying up earthly treasures. We lay up heavenly treasures by doing what Jesus said. Verse 19 reaches back to chapters 5-6. When we give alms to the poor in secret, pray in secret, and fast in secret, we are laying up treasures in heaven. When we keep Jesus' commandments as laid out in chapter 5, we are laying up treasure in heaven. In contrast, Jesus says that we should not lay up earthly treasure. We do this by doing good works before men to gain reputation and power among men. We also do this when we accumulate money and lands and gold and silver. Jesus describes this process graphically, using the same word twice—the Greek says that we should not "treasure up treasures." Jesus is not just telling us that we should be oriented to doing our works toward God rather than toward men. He is also insisting on a particular attitude toward earthly wealth, and He is warning about the great harm done by greed.

Warnings against greed are not rare in Jesus' teaching. This is a regular theme of his teaching and ministry. He accuses the Jews and especially the Jewish leaders of being motivated by greed. The Pharisees are full of "greed and wickedness" and "full of greed and self-indulgence." Jesus wants His disciples to avoid this evil. He warns that greed leads to a certain kind of life, a life of uncaring luxury and pleasure, with no regard for the poor and the needy. This is the attitude of the rich man, who indulges himself while Lazarus lies on his doorstep with only dogs to nurse him. This is what He is saying at the end of Matthew's gospel when He puts the goats on the left side because they have not done kindness to the least of the brothers. They have not clothed the naked, fed the hungry, cared for those in need—and because of this *they are heading to hell*. Greed is a deadly sin.

It is deadly in the life to come because it is already deadly in this life. In His encounter with the rich young ruler, Jesus tells the man who boasts that he has kept the law that all he has to do is to give up all his wealth and give it all to the poor. He turns away sorrowing because he was very wealthy, and because he was wealthy he was unwilling to give up his wealth to follow Jesus. His love for money, his greed, leads him to abandon Jesus and cling instead to the wealth. Some of the seed sown by the sower goes into the ground and is quickly choked out because of the concerns and anxieties of this world, because desire for riches chokes out faith.

Jesus says here that the spiritual damage that wealth can cause is enormous, and that it all arises from a false valuation of the security and value of earthly treasure. Ironically, some people treasure up treasures on earth, spending all their time and energy and ingenuity to make sure that they make money. But this is treasure that moth can destroy, that rust can tarnish, that thieves can steal. There is *no way* to ensure that this wealth will be preserved. Put it in the stock market, or in the housing market —you can make a bundle for a time, but there is *no guarantee* that the wealth will still be there when you need it. Treasuring up treasures on earth is *bound* to lead to anxiety because we *know* we cannot guarantee the future.

Jesus follows up with the simple reminder that we will die. You won't be around to enjoy all the wealth you accumulate. Like the rich fool who accumulated treasure and kept building barn after barn, but then found that his soul was required, if you spend your life accumulating money, you're going to be disappointed. You can't keep it. You won't be here.

Jesus asserts that it's impossible to seek both earthly and heavenly treasures. He describes this in terms of the direction and orientation of our heart. In the Bible, the heart is not the center of emotion as it is for us. Instead, it's the center of thought, and more deeply the heart is the center of our basic orientation in life. Our lives go in the direction of our hearts. We have one heart, and it is directed toward either heaven or earth (v. 21). It can't go in both directions at once. It cannot be directed toward heavenly treasure *and* earthly treasure. There's only one of them, so it has to be facing in one direction or another, not both at once.

Jesus also describes our wealth in terms of our eyes. Eyes in Scripture are organs of judgment and evaluation. If our eyes value earthly things, our whole body is in darkness; to be full of light, our eyes must be open to heavenly treasures (vv. 22-23). Or Jesus might have in mind the fact that we are to have our eyes open to the coming of the kingdom, and that we are to value the kingdom above all.

Jesus describes mammon, wealth, as a master. That sounds metaphorical but it isn't.[20] Money becomes a master; wanting to make it big becomes the over-arching and dominating power of our lives. Wealth can become our master, dictating how we spend our time, talents, leisure, energy, etc. Wealth can become so dominant that it becomes an obsession. We want the new thing all the time, the latest thing, and we have to make just one more dollar, just one more big deal. Money is a master, and it is a fearful master. If we are servants of Mammon, we cannot be servants of God (v. 24).

---

20 See Philip Goodchild, *Theology of Money* (Durham: Duke University Press, 2009), pp. 6-7: "God and wealth are set in competition; for time, in terms of 'storing up treasures'; for attention, in terms of the health of the eye; and for devotion, in terms of service. Our evaluations are primarily expressed not by what we say or simply by what we do, but by how we pray – the determination of our time, attention, and devotion." Money's power is seen "not simply in the worship or accumulation of wealth for its own sake, but in the way time, attention, and devotion are shaped by the demands of the social institution of money." The opposition of God and money comes to this: "wealth contains its own principles according to which time, attention, and devotion are allocated. In a society organized primarily for the pursuit of wealth, nothing could seem more evident and unquestionable than that time, attention, and devotion should be allocated to the pursuit of wealth. It is the very obligation to do so that constitutes the spiritual power of money." Economic theory examines the "outcome of economic activity" and involves "the investigation of the powers and principles by which time, attention, and devotion are distributed." Theology can't be content with this, but must be "an exploration of the nature and effects of money's mysterious power."

"But, but," we say. "But we're not Gnostics, so earthly things are good, right?" Yes, earthly things are good. Jesus doesn't deny that earthly things are good. God made them. Of course they are good. Heavenly things, though, are better and more secure. Earthly treasures are always at risk in a way heavenly treasures are not (v. 20). If you want a guaranteed investment, an investment that is completely free from the danger of moth, rust, or thieves, then you need to invest in heaven, not on earth. You need to do the righteousness of the kingdom, which includes *giving money away* rather than hoarding it. Another objection comes: "But we've got to live!" Yes, and Jesus assures us that the way to be sure that we will have enough is to put worry aside and trust our Father. Jesus makes several points. He doesn't simply say "don't worry." He does say that. But that's not all that he says. He points us to disciplines, lines of thinking, and actions that will keep us from anxiety and worry. He emphasizes that life is greater than food and clothing (v. 25). Isn't it pitiful when our lives become about having the latest fashion, or the newest video game? Isn't it pitiful when we expend our energies at work and never enjoy the fruits of our work? Isn't life more than that? We can become so anxious about how we're going to live that we never live. The Father feeds the birds who don't spend a second planning or gathering for the future, and He loves us more than birds (v. 26). He clothes the grass that lasts only a day with glory like Solomon's (vv. 30-31). So the objection that we need to live is true, but it's beside the point. Our Father knows that we need to live. He demonstrates His extravagant mercy and generosity every day, if we would but open our eyes to see it. Part of the setting in Jesus' teaching is the formation of a community of disciples who trust and serve the Father. Individual disciples can be anxiety-free because we know that our brothers and sisters provide a safety net that will catch us. That is one of the ways our Father cares for us.

Jesus gives a command here. Do you really think about the birds and the grass? Have you ever looked at the gnats or mosquitoes that bug you in the summer and wonder at a God who keeps such things alive? Have you ever glanced at the fish in the pet store that are no more than swimming gnats, and considered the fact that they are sustained by the heavenly Father? Who do you think feeds the coyotes or the wolves or the elk or the moose? You don't. Our Father takes care of it all, and Jesus *commands* us to *think about that*.

Finally, He points out the folly of anxiety. We can add nothing to life by being anxious about it (v. 27). Worrying about the bad things that might happen tomorrow doesn't keep them from happening (v. 34). Besides, we've got plenty to deal with today. Above all, "your heavenly Father knows that you need all these things" (v. 32). Do you trust Him?

Jesus' wisdom is a paradoxical wisdom, the wisdom of the kingdom of God. In this kingdom, we can only be guaranteed sufficient goods if we renounce hoarding and greed. In this kingdom, we know we can have food and clothing if we seek something else than food and clothing. In this kingdom, we cling to a master who is despised and rejected and ultimately crucified. In this kingdom, we can only find life if we first lose it. That is the wisdom of the kingdom, the wisdom of Jesus, the greater Solomon.

Logs, Dogs, and Pigs
Matthew 7:1-12

"Do not judge so that you will not be judged. ² "For in the way you judge, you will be judged; and by your standard of measure, it will be measured to you. ³ "Why do you look at the speck that is in your brother's eye, but do not notice the log that is in your own eye? ⁴ "Or how can you say to your brother, 'Let me take the speck out of your eye,' and behold, the log is in your own eye? ⁵ "You hypocrite, first take the log out of your own eye, and then you will see clearly to take the speck out of your brother's eye. ⁶ "Do not give what is holy to dogs, and do not throw your pearls before swine, or they will trample them under their feet, and turn and tear you to pieces. ⁷ "Ask, and it will be given to you; seek, and you will find; knock, and it will be opened to you. ⁸ "For everyone who asks receives, and he

> who seeks finds, and to him who knocks it will be opened. [9] "Or what man is there among you who, when his son asks for a loaf, will give him a stone? [10] "Or if he asks for a fish, he will not give him a snake, will he? [11] "If you then, being evil, know how to give good gifts to your children, how much more will your Father who is in heaven give what is good to those who ask Him! [12] "In everything, therefore, treat people the same way you want them to treat you, for this is the Law and the Prophets."
> – Matthew 7:1-12

The sermon begins with beatitudes to those who have entered the kingdom and displayed the virtues of the kingdom. General statements follow about the role of the disciples in the world—the disciples are to be salt and light and a city—and also about the relationship between Jesus, His teaching, and the Old Testament Law and Prophets. He addresses the true Israel, the sons of the Father, who have been redeemed from the Egypt of Herod's Israel and have entered the kingdom and become subjects of King Jesus. From 5:21 on, Jesus gives instructions in detail about how His disciples are to live out a righteousness that surpasses the righteousness of the scribes and Pharisees. Jesus talks about anger and murder and reconciliation with brothers; adultery and lust and divorce and marriage; swearing and taking vows; how to respond to hatred and opposition and how to treat our enemies; how we give alms and pray and fast; how we should regard our material wealth and money. He ends this section of the sermon with instruction about judgment and about our relation with power.

Through it all, Jesus emphasizes again and again that this righteousness grows out of trust in our heavenly Father and involves imitation of our heavenly Father. Our works bring glory to our Father who is in heaven. We are to treat our enemies the way our Father treats His enemies, since He sends rain and sunshine to the just and unjust. We are supposed to give alms and fast and pray in secret before our Father who sees in secret. Our attitude toward money and toward the future is shaped by our trust in our heavenly Father, who controls the future and who values us above the birds of the air and the grass of the field. In this passage again, Jesus says that our relation to our Father is the central concern in our relation to power.

Verse 12 matches the beginning of this section of the sermon. Jesus again refers to the "law and prophets" and says that His instruction in verse 12 summarizes the justice and righteousness of the law and prophets. Those two references to "law and prophets" act as a frame around this part of the sermon, bookends that mark the beginning and end of Jesus' teaching. After this section, further, Jesus ends the sermon with instructions about entering the right gate into life, about the temptations that would draw us from following Jesus, and about the danger of hearing but not doing His words. He began the sermon with promises of blessing; He ends the sermon with threats of cursing if we hear but turn aside. Verse 12 sums up Jesus' teaching on the law and the prophets. This is the way the law and prophets are to be obeyed. This is the kind of redemptive righteousness that the law and prophets always aimed for.

To make sense of verses 1-12, we have to examine the internal structure of those verses. Few sections of the sermon have been as puzzling as verse 6, but a bit of structural analysis will help clarify some of the issues. Verse 6 starts a new section. Frequently, this verse is seen as balancing the instruction about judgment in verses 1-5. Jesus says don't judge, but then immediately instructs us about how to deal with dogs and pigs; and to determine who is a dog and a pig, we have to make judgments about them. That in itself is true enough. Jesus does not prohibit judging. After all, determining that someone is a dog or pig is a judgment that we have to form.

Basically, verse 6 is a new statement, the beginning of a new section. It's not a balancing statement for verses 1-5, or an illustration of those verses. Both verses 1 and 6 begin with a command, and in this respect, these verses are similar to the warnings of chapter 6. Jesus has said, "beware of practicing righteousness before men" and "do not lay up treasures on earth" and "do not be anxious." Now He says "do not judge" and "do not give what is holy to dogs." Verses 1 and 6 each begin a new section. Within these sections—verses 1-5 and 6-12—Jesus follows the same triadic pattern that He has followed elsewhere in the sermon. Jesus summarizes traditional practice or teaching (vv. 1-2, 6a; cf. 6:1, 5, 16). He warns in verses 1-2 against hypocritical judgment and that the way we judge will come back on us. In verse 6, He warns against giving holy things to pigs and dogs. Then he describes the consequences of mishandling that traditional teaching (vv. 3-5, 6b). If you judge without dealing with your own blindness first, then you won't see clearly to help your brother. You won't be any help to anyone. And if you give holy things to pigs and dogs, you'll find that they turn on you. A comment on the internal structure of verse 6 is useful. It appears to warn that pigs are going to turn and tear you to pieces. Those would be some vicious pigs. The key to understanding this is to recognize that the verse is structured chiastically. Don't give the holy to dogs matches "they will turn and tear you in pieces"; don't give pearls to swine matches "they will trample you under their feet." Dogs tear to pieces, and pigs trample underfoot—a porcine stampede.[21] He gives a command that describes the redemptive righteousness that His disciples must enact (vv. 5-6, 7-11). He gives instructions on how to judge rightly, how to avoid hypocritical judgment. In verses 7-11 He tells us what we should do with our holy things and pearls—not entrust them to pigs and dogs, but entrust them to our Father.

Jesus has condemned the way some Jews gave alms, prayed, and fasted (6:1-18), and here He condemns the Jews for judging hypocritically (cf. Romans 2:1-16). Paul did the same, saying that at the same time the Jews haughtily judged the Gentiles, they were doing the same evil that the Gentiles did. They were trying to pick out the speck in the Gentiles' eyes while having a log in their own eye (Romans 2:17-24). Jesus and Paul are both addressing a habit of first-century Jews, but this habit has been picked up by many

---

21. John Breck, *The Shape of Biblical Language: Chiasmus in the Scriptures and Beyond* (Crestwood, NY: St. Vladimir's Seminary Press, 1994), p. 29.

Christians. It's a universal temptation to judge others more strictly than we judge ourselves, to worry more about the tiny specks in our brother's eye while ignoring the log or two-by-four in our own eye.

Jesus warns that if we judge our brothers harshly or unmercifully, we are going to be judged in the same way; we receive in the same measure that we give (v. 2). We will be judged harshly or mercifully by God. The passive is a "divine passive," with God as the understood subject of the judgment. It's not that other people are going to give it to us in the same intensity that we give it to them. That might happen. But the more important issue is that God judges us according to our standard of judgment. God applies the *lex talionis*, the law of retribution: Judge strictly and unmercifully, and you will be judged the same way. That's what we found back in chapter 6 as well: If we forgive, then our Father forgives us; if we don't forgive, then our Father will not forgive us. As in chapter 6, Jesus means what He says. He is not qualifying by saying "Oh well, you know that your ultimate standing with God has nothing to do with your actions. It's all about imputed righteousness." He says that we will be judged as we judge. If we treat our brothers harshly, we should expect the same treatment from Him.

This is a key to relationships in family, at school, at work, all the places where this principle has to be worked out in detail. Ask yourself, are you judging your husband's or wife's behavior by a stricter standard than you judge your own? Do you pile up accusations against your wife or husband, all the while excusing your own conduct? Are you picking at a speck in your husband's eye while ignoring the log in your own? What would it be like for you to be judged with the same standard that you use for your children? Your boss? Or your roommate? Are you OK with being judged in the way that you judge?

If we judge hypocritically, with logs sticking out of our eyes, we won't be able to help our brother learn wisdom and prudent judgment. Eyes are organs of judgment, and the hypocrite has a huge obstruction in his eye that prevents him from removing the much smaller speck in his brother's eye (vv. 3-4). The end result of what Jesus teaches here is that both we and our brother have clear eyes so that we can judge rightly.

Jesus does not tell us to ignore our brothers' faults. Jesus does not teach tolerance for sin anywhere in the sermon. Jesus is not telling us to leave things alone, to just go along, to take it easy about sin, to let injustice go on its merry way. He's not telling us that moral specks don't matter because they are only specks. He's not saying that we should avoid doing anything. When an enemy abuses us, Jesus doesn't tell us that it's all OK, that we should just ignore it. We don't ignore it; but we act in a way that will bring redemption, that will extend the kingdom. Throughout the sermon, this is Jesus' instruction—that we act in a way that will bring real justice in places where there is injustice and evil. We do this *not* by refusing to resist evil, but refusing to resist *by evil means*. We participate in the advance of the kingdom of heaven when we overcome evil with good.

He says that "first" we should remove the log from our own eye, that is, repent of our own blindness, so that we can see clearly to help our brothers. Self-correction is the beginning of the redemptive righteousness of Jesus' disciples. First, we acknowledge our own sins, confess them, turn from them, clear our own eyes. Once that step is made, *then* we go back to our brother to help him with that speck. That's what it means to love our brothers. We don't want specks floating in our own eyes, and if we really love our brother we want to remove specks from his eye too.

To understand what Jesus is saying in verse 6, we need to recognize that he is beginning a new section here. Verse 6 is not a continuation of the discussion of judgment but a new commandment. But what does it mean? We get a clue from Jesus' reference to "pigs," which appear elsewhere in the gospels, and in first-century Jewish writings, as an epithet for the Roman empire (e.g., the "Legion" of demons and the pigs in Mark 5:1-20).[22]

---

22. Garland, *Reading Matthew*, p. 85.

"Pigs" and "dogs" are Gentiles. Pigs are those who are outside the community of the clean, who wallow in the miasma of the world. Dogs are scavengers who attack and destroy.

Jesus warns against entrusting the care and protection of holy things to Gentile powers. Israel and Judah frequently turned to Gentiles to help them in crisis moments. When Assyria threatened, they tried to protect their holy things by allying with the Arameans. When the Arameans threatened, they appealed over the heads of the Arameans and tried to get the Assyrians to attack from the other side. When Babylon threatened, they turned to Egypt for help. Israel and Judah were constantly trying to play power politics with their Gentile neighbors, and they often actually took holy things from the temple and gave them to the dogs and swine.

Jesus is a shrewd reader of Israel's history. He knows that allying with Gentiles is always playing with fire. When Israel tries to ally with Gentiles, and seek the patronage of power, the Gentiles often turn on them and trample them. The Gentiles help for a while, but then they see an opportunity to subdue Israel. Jesus is also a shrewd observer of His own times. Israel is in danger of again entrusting their holy things to the patronage of Rome. They want protection from Rome rather than Yahweh. The danger is that the Gentile dogs will turn and devour, and the pigs will trample Israel underfoot (cf. Luke 21:24). Jesus is the Holy One, and in His trial the Jews turn over their Most Holy One to the pigs and dogs. They will soon be trampled.

This is a traditional practice, but it is not the righteousness of the kingdom. Jesus does not want His disciples to be seeking protection from pigs and dogs. It doesn't work, and Jesus' disciples don't need this kind of protection. This is the danger that any Constantine, no matter how sincere, will pose to the church. Jesus' disciples already have a patron, a patron more powerful, more wholly good than any earthly patron. You ask a pig for bread, and he might give you a stone; ask a dog for fish, and you're likely to end up with a serpent instead. But the heavenly Patron doesn't do that. Our heavenly Patron gives good gifts to His children.

Instead of seeking the patronage of Gentile powers, Jesus says that we should seek the patronage of our heavenly Father (vv. 7-11). Do not trust in princes, Jesus says, but in the Lord our God.

This was a particular temptation for the early Christians, persecuted by the Jews and later by the Romans. We see in the New Testament that they make appeals to the Roman authorities, and that is legitimate. They use their rights to protect themselves and their ministry, but there is always a subtle temptation for persecuted Christians to think that they will be safe if they could get the right people in power, or at least if they could get the people in power to defend them. We should vote, and we should vote for the right people. But what we must *never* do is trust that any government, no matter how favorable, will be our Patron and Provider.

Jesus concludes the substance of His sermon with a summary of His teaching. The whole law and prophets—and remember that Jesus does not annul the law—is about doing the good to others that we want them to do to us. This is so familiar to us that we don't see just how radical Jesus is being here. He has been talking throughout the sermon about the righteousness that surpasses the righteousness of the scribes and Pharisees. He's been talking about the justice of the kingdom throughout the chapter. And He's still talking about justice here. But this doesn't look like justice. Justice, we think, means giving people what they deserve, paying what people are owed. Justice is about giving in return what people have done. But this is not the justice of Jesus. That justice doesn't restore the world. That kind of justice might bring the world back to where it started. But it doesn't move the world to something new. Jesus' justice is a restorative justice, a redemptive justice that advances the kingdom and brings humanity and the world closer to the consummation.

Again, this golden rule has to be worked out in all our relationships. Do you treat your children the way you want to be treated? Do you respect your parents the way they respect you, or the way you *want* to be respected? Do you treat your husband and wife as you'd like to be treated?

Jesus' justice is the justice of the golden rule, the justice of doing to others what we would have them do to us. We don't act toward others as they deserve; we act as we want them to act toward us. That is the justice of Jesus, the righteousness that surpasses the righteousness of the scribes and Pharisees.

Standing and Falling
Matthew 7:13-29

"Enter through the narrow gate; for the gate is wide and the way is broad that leads to destruction, and there are many who enter through it. [14] "For the gate is small and the way is narrow that leads to life, and there are few who find it. [15] "Beware of the false prophets, who come to you in sheep's clothing, but inwardly are ravenous wolves. [16] "You will know them by their fruits. Grapes are not gathered from thorn bushes nor figs from thistles, are they? [17] "So every good tree bears good fruit, but the bad tree bears bad fruit. [18] "A good tree cannot produce bad fruit, nor can a bad tree produce good fruit. [19] "Every tree that does not bear good fruit is cut down and thrown into the fire. [20] "So then, you will know them by their fruits. [21] "Not everyone who says to Me, 'Lord, Lord,' will enter the kingdom of heaven, but he who does the will of My Father who is in heaven will enter. [22] "Many will say to Me on that day, 'Lord, Lord, did we not prophesy in Your name, and in Your name cast out demons, and in Your name perform many miracles?' [23] "And then I will declare to them, 'I never knew you; depart from me, you who practice lawlessness.' [24] "Therefore everyone who hears these words of Mine and acts on them, may be compared to a wise man who built his house on the rock. [25] "And the rain fell, and the floods came, and the winds blew and slammed against that house; and yet it did not fall, for it had been founded on the rock. [26] "Everyone who hears these words of Mine and does not act on them, will be like a foolish man who built his house on the sand. [27] "The rain fell, and the floods came, and the winds blew and slammed against that house; and it fell--and great was its fall." [28] When Jesus had finished these words, the crowds were amazed at His teaching; [29] for He was teaching them as one having authority, and not as their scribes. – Matthew 7:13-29

The Schmalkald Articles, written in 1538 to summarize the Protestant case against Roman Catholicism, evaluates Roman Catholic theology and practice by the standard of the "first and chief article," which is the article on Christ and faith. Everything turns on getting the first article right, on getting Christ and faith right. "On this article rests all that we teach and practice against the pope, the devil, and the world." Luther did not use the phrase "standing and falling" in the Schmalkald Articles, but his emphasis on Christ and justification as the "first and chief article" anticipates what he says elsewhere: "if this article stands, the Church stands; if it falls, the Church falls."

Jesus too is talking about standing and falling of the church, of the house. He is talking about what ensures that our house will stand. He is talking about standing and falling articles. Jesus is also talking about righteousness, a righteousness that surpasses that of the scribes and Pharisees. That is the theme of the whole sermon: Jesus is teaching His disciples about the righteousness that He demands from His disciples. But Jesus' teaching is a corrective to various misunderstandings of the Reformation. Jesus, after all, is not teaching about an imputed righteousness. He is not talking about His own righteousness that we receive as a gift. He is not talking about the righteousness that is counted to us. He is talking instead about our actual, daily practice of righteousness. He is talking about being righteous in the way we deal with anger, in our sexual lives, in our marriages, in our speech, in our response to opponents and enemies, in our alms-giving, our prayer, and our fasting, in our attitudes toward money, in the way we judge, in our relation to power. Jesus is not teaching that we can achieve this righteousness by our own efforts. Nor is he talking obedience that has nothing to do with faith. He emphasizes the necessity of trust in the heavenly Father throughout the sermon. He is speaking to disciples who have been called and multitudes that have been healed. And he repeatedly emphasizes that His disciples can fulfill the righteousness He demands only by trusting their Father who is in heaven.

But Jesus makes it quite clear here that *this* righteousness, this righteousness in action, is what determines the standing or falling of the house. It is not enough to hear the words of Jesus. It is not enough even to admire and believe the words of Jesus. It's not enough to mouth the slogans of Paul or the Reformation. Jesus says that we must "do" what He says: "Everyone who hears these words of Mine, and does them," that is the man who builds on a rock (v. 24). Anyone who "hears these words of Mine, and does not do them" is a fool.

To understand what Jesus is saying in this final section of the Sermon on the Mount, we have to see this section in the context of the entire sermon and in the context of Jesus' ministry. Jesus comes announcing the kingdom of heaven. That is the central thrust of His ministry. God is going to take the throne, and He is going to put His disrupted world back in order. He's going to establish righteousness and peace wherever evil and violence reign. He is going to vindicate His pronouncement at the beginning: The creation is very good. This is an announcement to Israel in particular. Jesus comes to the lost sheep of the house of Israel, and He calls them to repentance. He calls them to bow before their Lord, who is taking His throne and asserting His power. This announcement is good news for those who turn to God in repentance. Those who bow before God and acknowledge His reign will be blessed.

That's how Jesus opens the sermon. He promises a share in the kingdom, comfort, satisfaction, the earth, seeing God, the name sons of God, to those who repent and bring forth the fruits of the kingdom. Those who are poor in spirit, meek, who hunger and thirst for righteousness, who are merciful and pure and peaceable —these will receive the blessings of the reign of God. They will receive the blessings of the kingdom. It's important to see that Jesus' sermon is part of that good news of the kingdom. The good news is that God is coming to reign and to establish peace and righteousness. And Jesus' teaching in the sermon gives specific instruction about how God's reign and righteousness takes form on earth. Jesus is giving instructions about how His disciples can avoid the vicious cycles of sin that hold humanity enslaved.

When Jesus says not to nurture anger at a brother but be reconciled, He's announcing good news. You don't have to end up before the judge or in hell; by the power of God, you can deal with your anger. When he tells us not to worry about what we eat, drink, or wear, but to trust our Father, He's not giving law; He's preaching gospel. This is good news. You don't have to live in constant anxiety about the future. The Father knows what you need, and He loves you.

But Jesus ends His sermon on a note of warning and threat. Those who respond to the announcement that God is coming to be King will receive a share in that kingdom, with all the benefits and blessings that entails. But those who resist and refuse to follow Jesus are not going to receive the blessings of the kingdom. As John the Baptist already said, the trees that do not bear good fruit will be cut down and cast into the fire. Again, Jesus' warnings are specifically given to the Jews of the first century. He has given them a program not just for national survival, but for national renewal and blessing. He's told them how they can flourish even when they are surrounded by Roman enemies. And he warns that if Israel fails to follow His program, Israel is doomed.

Israel has two ways set before them: the opening, the gate to one of the ways is narrow, small, hard to discover. Jesus is teaching in out of the way Galilee; He is not preaching in king's houses. To find the gate to this path, you need to search. The other way is obvious and the gate is wide. The other way is for Israel to continue on her idolatrous course, her course of foolish resistance to Rome, her course that will end with her destruction. This is why Jesus' final exhortations anticipate the eschatological discourse of chapters 24-25. He is warning Israel ahead of time about what they are going to face in the future if they don't repent. And repentance means leaving the big gate and the broad way they've been following and searching out the narrow gate of Jesus.

One of the links with Jesus' later eschatological discourses is His warning against false prophets. There are enticements to enter the wrong gate, which come from false prophets. In the Old Testament, false prophets appear in abundance when Israel is under threat, and Jesus later warns that the same will happen after His departure to the Father (cf. Matthew 24:11, 14). Jesus warns His disciples to be prepared for false teaching, which could mislead them from the narrow gate to the broad gate of destruction. Jesus tells His disciples to follow a way of peace with enemies, loving enemies and those who persecute them. But there will be false prophets and false Christs who encourage Israel to confront Rome, who tell Israel they can take Rome down. Jesus says that those false prophets are wolves, predators rather than shepherds, who eat up the sheep.

False prophets may try to demonstrate their credentials by miracles, but this doesn't prove anything (vv. 21-23; cf. Deuteronomy 13). They can try to make their case before the judge: We did all this stuff in your name. But Jesus will treat them as enemies. Verse 23 quotes from Psalm 6, and the "workers of iniquity" are not merely bad people but enemies of the Psalmist. Jesus will treat false prophets, who prey on the sheep while pretending to do God's will, as enemies, and they will be cast out. The test is not miraculous powers but fruit. Fruits that demonstrate that someone is a true prophet are the fruits of a life according to the words of Jesus. If they don't live as Jesus commands, they know nothing about the "law and the prophets" (7:12). Israel is compared to a vine and a fig tree, and Jesus is telling His disciples how to distinguish the true Israel from the false. A tree that bears no fruit is nothing more than a thistle, which springs up because of God's curse on the ground (cf. Genesis 3:18).

Jesus also has the situation of Israel in mind when He warns about the house standing or falling. In the context of Jesus' ministry, the "house" that he talks about in verses 24-27 must be the temple and/or the house of Israel.[23] Jesus is giving Israel a way

---

23. Wright, *Jesus and the Victory of God*, p. 416.

of survival rather than destruction. If Israel continues to pursue her traditional patterns of life, she will end up surrounded by Roman armies; Rome is the "flood" that comes crashing against the house built on sand and destroys it. Jesus is speaking like one of the prophets, like Ezekiel, who warned Israel in similar words (Ezekiel 13:8-14).

By the time we get to the end of the gospel, the Jews have made their choice. They have decided to go through the wide gate and follow the broad way. They have rejected the way of peace. They have listened to false prophets, and they have heard but not done Jesus' words. They are doomed, and so Jesus comes back to the image of the falling house. Only this time, in Matthew 24, it is not a warning but a prediction. Israel has chosen to build on sand, and the wind and rain and flood of God's judgment will come, the axe will be laid at the root of the fruitless trees, and Israel will perish in fire.

Jesus is warning Israel specifically, but Jesus' words have rightly been taken more broadly. The temple can serve as a trope for our lives, our families, our churches, our businesses, our schools. And the same warnings apply. And these warnings apply specifically to the new Israel, the church. And Jesus warns us that it is not enough to parrot the Reformation creeds and slogans. A church can memorize the Westminster Catechism from now until judgment day, and that will not keep the church stable and strong. That will not hold her up in the day when the rain and wind and rivers beat against it. She will stand only if she hears the words of Jesus and *does* them.

And, closer to home, it doesn't cut it for us to do great things in Jesus' name. When we are brought before the judge, it won't do any good to say: Lord, Lord, did we not establish schools in your name? Didn't we publish books in your name? Didn't we plant churches in your name? Didn't we reform the church in your name? That will not impress the judge. And if that's all we've got to say for ourselves, then Jesus will say what He said to the Jews who heard Him but didn't do what He taught: I never knew you; depart from me, you who practice lawlessness.

The thing that keeps a church standing, the thing that ensures that all our projects are really successful—the *only* thing that ensures this—is hearing *and doing* the words of Jesus. The only thing that prevents us from being cut down and cast into the fire is to be a good tree that produces good fruit. It's not the one who says "Lord Lord" who enters the kingdom of heaven, but "he who does the will of My Father who is in heaven."

4

To the Lost Sheep

Bearing Our Infirmities
Matthew 8:1-17

When Jesus came down from the mountain, large crowds followed Him. ² And a leper came to Him and bowed down before Him, and said, "Lord, if You are willing, You can make me clean." ³ Jesus stretched out His hand and touched him, saying, "I am willing; be cleansed." And immediately his leprosy was cleansed. ⁴ And Jesus said to him, "See that you tell no one; but go, show yourself to the priest and present the offering that Moses commanded, as a testimony to them." ⁵ And when Jesus entered Capernaum, a centurion came to Him, imploring Him, ⁶ and saying, "Lord, my servant is lying paralyzed at home, fearfully tormented." ⁷ Jesus said to him, "I will come and heal him." ⁸ But the centurion said, "Lord, I am not worthy for You to come under my roof, but just say the word, and my servant will be healed. ⁹ "For I also am a man under authority, with soldiers under me; and I say to this one, 'Go!' and he goes, and to another, 'Come!' and he comes, and to my slave, 'Do this!' and he does it." ¹⁰ Now when Jesus heard this, He marveled and said to those who were following, "Truly I say to you, I have not found such great faith with anyone in Israel. ¹¹ "I say to you that many will come from east and west, and recline at the table with Abraham, Isaac and Jacob in the kingdom of heaven; ¹² but the sons of the kingdom will be cast out into the outer darkness; in that place there will be weeping and gnashing of teeth." ¹³ And Jesus said to the centurion, "Go; it shall be done for you as you have believed." And the servant was healed that very moment. ¹⁴ When Jesus came into Peter's home, He saw his mother-in-law lying sick in bed with a fever. ¹⁵ He touched her hand, and the fever left her; and she got up and waited on Him. ¹⁶ When evening came, they brought to Him many who were demon-possessed; and He cast out the spirits with a word, and healed all who were ill. ¹⁷ This was to fulfill what was spoken through Isaiah the prophet: "He Himself took our infirmities and carried away our diseases." – Matthew 8:1-17

There are seven mountains in Matthew.[1] All the mountains recapitulate Eden. When Jesus is tempted on the mountain in the wilderness, he is the new Adam who was tempted on the mountain of Eden. When He delivers the law to His disciples on the mountain, He is Yahweh delivering the commandment to Adam. When He pronounces curses on Israel, He is Yahweh delivering the judgment against the sinful Adam. When He sends His disciples out into the world to make disciples of the nations, He is Yahweh commanding His new Adamic people to be fruitful and multiply and fill the earth.

The first and last mountains match. At the beginning Satan takes Jesus to a mountain to show him "all the kingdoms of the world" and to offer them to Jesus: "All these things will I give You, if you fall down and worship me." Jesus remains obedient to His Father, obeying even to death, and as a result, on another mountain at the end of the gospel, He can announce "I have been given all authority in heaven and on earth." The second mountain also has a matching mountain at the end of the book. In Matthew

---

1. See the unpublished paper of Warren Gage, "The Theme of Matthew: Jesus, the True Moses" (1998).

5, Jesus ascends to the mountain from which he delivers the Sermon on the Mount. That sermon begins with the Beatitudes, pronouncements of blessings to those who display the character of Jesus. Later in the gospel, he ascends the Mount of Olives to prophesy concerning the approaching destruction of Jerusalem, a prophecy preceded by a series of curses against the scribes and Pharisees for their hypocrisy. Jesus stands on a mountain to pronounce blessings; Jesus later stands on the mountain to pronounce curses. Blessings and curses echo across the gospel the way the blessings and curses echoed across the valley between Ebal and Gerizim (Deuteronomy 27).

The mountain of the Sermon on the Mount is a new Sinai, where the new Moses delivers a new law. And the symbolism of Jesus as Moses continues in chapters 8-10. Matthew records ten miracles in these chapters, and it's possible that there is some reference to the ten plagues of Egypt. Jesus as the greater Moses brings miracles of revival, not miracles of destruction, but the numerical connection links it with the plagues. This is the new Moses acting in power to bring His people out of the Egypt of Herodian Israel. In the Pentateuch, Moses came down from the mountain and led Israel through a wilderness of rebellion and judgment. According to Numbers 14:22, Israel committed ten acts of rebellion against Yahweh in the wilderness. They rebelled "these ten times." In Numbers, the ten rebellions ironically refer back to the ten plagues: Yahweh had stretched out His arm to perform ten miraculous acts of deliverance, and instead of obeying in gratitude and faith, Israel rebels against Yahweh ten times. Jesus, the new Moses, comes down from the mountain at the head of a great multitude (8:1). But his journey is a journey of healing, not judgment. In Matthew 8-9, Jesus performs ten powerful acts (cleanse leper, heal paralytic, heal fever, calm storm, cast out demons, heal paralytic, raise dead girl, heal woman with blood, give two blind men sight, cast out demon from a dumb man). These match, and invert, the ten rebellions of Israel in the wilderness (Numbers 14:22). Jesus, the true Israel, reverses the ten rebellions of the wilderness.

Coming down from the mountain of the sermon, Jesus is followed by a great crowd. Jesus and His company flow down like Eden's river from the mountain, bringing life and refreshment and healing to the surrounding land. Jesus comes down from the mountain and meets an unclean leper; He cleanses him and flows on. A centurion comes to Him asking for help for his paralyzed servant; He raises him from his bed and flows on. He flows into the house of Peter's mother-in-law, and He raises her from a bed of fever and then settles in to cast out demons and heal any who are ill. Wherever Jesus goes, life and health break out. As He says in chapter 9, He is the physician who has come to heal those who are sick. He is the flowing river of Eden, which comes to renew the dry and thirsty land where there is no water.

There is another pattern here that will help us see the logic of what appears to be a fairly random list of miracle stories. The works are arranged in a rhythm that is somewhat reminiscent of the pattern of the plagues of Egypt. Jesus does three miraculous acts, mostly miracles of healing. In 8:1-15, he cleanses the leper, heals the centurion's servant, and delivers Peter's mother-in-law from a fever. In 8:23-9:8, he calms a storm on the Sea of Galilee, casts demons out of the Gadarene demoniacs, and heals a paralytic. In 9:18-34, he raises the synagogue official's daughter and cleanses a woman with a flow of blood, gives sight to blind men, and makes a dumb man speak. Each of these sections, further, includes some explanation of Jesus' ministry. In 8:16-17, Matthew quotes from Isaiah's prophecy to explain what Jesus is doing in His healings. In 9:10-17, Jesus explains why he eats with tax gatherers and sinners and why His disciples do not fast. In 9:35-38, He is the Good Shepherd who comes to guide those who are without a shepherd. Each of these sections concludes with a call to discipleship.[2] After healing Peter's mother-in-law, two come to Jesus wanting to be disciples, and Jesus tells them about the nature of discipleship. After healing the paralytic, Jesus

---

2. The word "follow" is used ten times in chapters 8-10, climactically in 10:38, where Jesus warns that those who follow Him must take the cross.

calls Matthew from his tax booth. After healing the dumb demon-possessed man, Jesus sends out the Twelve with authority to carry out His mission.

The rhythm is first healing, then a description of ministry, and finally an exhortation to discipleship. The accent falls on the last sequence, where the discipleship section is expanded into an entire chapter. The passage points to an important demand of following Jesus. As Jesus performs these works, there is growing opposition from the Pharisees. As Moses took the people through the wilderness to the promised land, there was opposition from various people and groups within Israel. Jesus the new Moses is the same. There is no opposition in the first cycle (8:1-17), but when Jesus casts demons from the Gadarene demoniacs, people start getting upset (8:34; 9:3, 10-17, 34). Already, we see the kingdom's reversal: Centurions and tax collectors are coming into the kingdom, while the Pharisees attack Jesus. This climaxes in 9:34 when the Jews charge that Jesus casts out demons by the power of the devil.[3]

In the first cycle, Jesus overthrows death in various forms. Leprosy was not a deadly disease, but a form of uncleanness. But it was a state of exclusion, a state of living death. The servant of the centurion is paralyzed, unable to move, and Peter's mother-in-law is in bed. Later, we see Jesus cast the demons from the Gadarene demoniacs who live among the tombs. Many of those whom Jesus heals and helps are in a state of death. He is the life-bringing water from Eden. We can also see Jesus restoring full human beings. He restores the faculties of sight and hearing and speech and thus restores a full man. Jesus brings life in its fullest sense, which includes restoration of communion among men.

In contrast to the other gospels, Matthew puts the cleansing of the leper first, front and center. Leprosy was not a deadly disease; it didn't lead to physical death. But it was socially deadly. According to Leviticus 13:45-46, once the priest found the leper to

---

3. Austin Farrer emphasizes the cyclical pattern of this section of Matthew in *St Matthew and St Mark* (Dacre Press, 1954).

be unclean, he had to adopt the life of an outsider, an untouchable: "As for the leper who has the infection, his clothes shall be torn, and the hair of his head shall be uncovered, and he shall cover his mustache and cry, 'Unclean! Unclean!' He shall remain unclean all the days during which he has the infection; he is unclean. He shall live alone; his dwelling shall be outside the camp." That's the state this leper is in: unkempt, living outside the community, avoiding human contact. Yet, remarkably, he comes to Jesus.[4] He approaches Jesus. He's heard about Jesus' power, and He knows that Jesus is capable of cleansing him. And Jesus touches him. For the Jews, touching a leper was like digging your fingers into a rotting corpse. It was repulsive; they would instinctively avoid the leper in the way we step past something icky on the sidewalk. But Jesus doesn't. He touches and heals him. Jesus does tell him to go to the temple and go through the rites of cleansing for lepers. That would integrate him back into normal Israelite life. But Jesus has already brought him into fellowship with a new community. By touching the leper, He makes the leper part of his community.

We often feel like outcasts. Less often, we actually are outcasts. But Jesus knows no outcasts. Those who come to Him for healing and cleansing and health and salvation can be confident He will accept them. If you go to Jesus seeking help and health, He won't step back in repulsion. He won't say "Ick." He is willing. He will touch you; He will heal you.

Jesus is immediately greeted by another outcast from the communion of Jews, a Gentile, who is not only a Gentile, but a Roman centurion, another of the occupying force that has conquered and rules Israel. Like Naaman the Syrian, he is a captain of the army that has been fighting and oppressing Jews. Yet, the Gentile centurion also approaches Jesus. He knows that

---

4. In the LXX, "coming-to" ($\pi\rho\sigma\epsilon\rho\chi\omega\mu\alpha\iota$) means a liturgical approach, Aaron's approach to the altar (Leviticus 9:7) or the unauthorized "coming-to" holy things by an unclean person (Leviticus 22:3). Coming-to a holy thing while suffering from skin disease was enough to get one cut off from before Yahweh (Leviticus 22:4-6). Jesus doesn't cut off the leper who comes to worship him, but instead heals.

Jesus won't stand back in revulsion. He asks for Jesus to heal the boy, and Jesus heals him at a distance with an authoritative word (vv. 8-9, 13).

Jesus is amazed at the faith of the centurion, and He says that this is a sign of what is coming. The sons of the kingdom, the Jews who ought to be in the feast of the kingdom, who were given all the privileges of being the people of God, are going to be cast out, while Gentiles are going to feast with Abraham, Isaac, and Jacob. If you want to know why the Jews began to oppose and hate Jesus, you can see it here. How dare He say that the Messianic banquet is going to include unclean Gentiles, that they are going to be there at the table, not merely eating a few crumbs. And the Jews are going to be cast out. How dare Jesus say this! He's a traitor to His race.[5]

The exchange with the centurion has to do with authority of the word. The centurion can speak a word and make things happen. He can tell soldiers to go, and they go; to come, and they come. So, he knows that Jesus has even greater authority in His word. Jesus speaks without ever seeing the boy, and the boy is healed. This is a sign of Jesus' authority. It is also a sign of Jesus being "under authority," like the centurion. The centurion knows that his words have no effect in themselves. The reason soldiers obey his words is because he's got the authority of his commanding officer, and the officer above him, and ultimately of the emperor backing him up. Jesus has authority in the same way: Jesus' words have authority because Jesus is a man under authority, because He acts under the authority of His Father.

There's a Trinitarian hint there, but we also see that Jesus has authority in Himself. As Jesus says in John 5, the Father has given Him to have life in Himself and has given Him to pass judgment. We can see this if we compare Jesus' miracles to the similar miracles of Elijah and Elisha in Kings. In each case, Jesus heals on His own authority. He cleanses the leper because He is

---

5. The point is emphasized by R. T. France in *The Gospel of Matthew* (NICNT; Grand Rapids: Eerdmans, 2007), p. 317.

willing (v. 2); the centurion comes asking Jesus for help; Jesus has power over demons and sicknesses (v. 16). Jesus doesn't pray, as Elijah and Elisha did when they healed. He doesn't do a spell. He simply touches and speaks. The leper has it right: "If you are willing, you can cleanse me." And Jesus says, "I am willing." The only pre-requisite for Jesus to heal is that He be willing to heal.

Life, health, and cleansing flow from Jesus to the sick and the unclean. But in addition to that outflow, there's an inflow. When Jesus touches the leper, He cleanses him, but Matthew tells us that Jesus also receives the leprosy. When He touches Peter's mother-in-law with a fever, health flows out, but He also takes on the fever. Matthew explains these healings with a reference to Isaiah 53. We normally think of Isaiah 53 as a passage about the death of Jesus for our sins, and it is certainly that. But Matthew (translating from the Hebrew) emphasizes that Jesus takes not only sins but infirmities, weakness, and disease upon Himself so that He can bear them away. He not only bears our sins on the cross, but throughout His life He bears disease and weakness, as the great High Priest.[6]

Each of these sections ends with a call to discipleship. A scribe wants to follow Jesus, but Jesus warns him that He is not going to have a comfortable life. Disciples find no place in the ground (foxes) and no place in the trees (birds), but are suspended between earth and heaven, which is where the Son of Man is. Having come from heaven to earth, He doesn't have any place to lay His head. The second exchange is even more challenging. It's likely that the man is not talking about burying a recently deceased father. If his father had just died, he would be home making preparations for the funeral. He's talking about seeing his father through the latter part of his life, caring for his elderly father until his death and seeing him buried. After that, he

---

6. The fact that Jesus bears sins shows that He is the temple. Jacob Milgrom says that the tabernacle is Israel's "picture of Dorian Gray," the magnet where the uncleanness and sin of Israel registers. Jesus is the new picture of Dorian Gray. As temple, "He became sin who knew no sin, that we might become the righteousness of God in Him."

will follow Jesus.⁷ Still, Jesus' words are shocking. Few obligations are more settled and demanding in Judaism than obligations to parents. If we think about it simply as a demand that the man neglect his duty to bury his father, it is a shocking statement. But the specific way Jesus says this is also shocking: He is saying that the man's family is among the dead. The old family is dead, and life is found in following Jesus. According to Jesus, the man lives in a tomb, surrounded by zombies.

Matthew shows us something important about the nature of discipleship. We often think of being a disciple as a matter of being healed. And that's true. The centurion whose servant is healed is a follower of Jesus. But being a disciple is not just about being healed. It's about healing. So, what sick people have you been helping recently? How have you been acting as a healer? What if the equivalent of a leper comes to you and seeks cleansing? What if a leper wants to be reincorporated into communion with others? What happens when we are approached by people who need our help? Do we back off in horror, sickened by the festering wounds? Or do we do what Jesus does? Touch the sick, receive the outcasts, bind up the broken-hearted and wounded. Discipleship also means participating in the healing ministry of Jesus. Being a disciple is not just about being saved; it's about being Jesus' instrument to bring health.

What Manner of Man?
Matthew 8:23-9:17

When He got into the boat, His disciples followed Him. ²⁴ And behold, there arose a great storm on the sea, so that the boat was being covered with the waves; but Jesus Himself was asleep. ²⁵ And they came to Him and woke Him, saying, "Save us, Lord; we are perishing!" ²⁶ He said to them, "Why are you

---

7. Kenneth A. B Bailey, *Poet and Peasant and Through Peasant Eyes: A literary-Cultural Approach to the Parables in Luke* (Grand Rapids: Eerdmans, 1983), pp. 268-271.

afraid, you men of little faith?" Then He got up and rebuked the winds and the sea, and it became perfectly calm. ²⁷ The men were amazed, and said, "What kind of a man is this, that even the winds and the sea obey Him?" ²⁸ When He came to the other side into the country of the Gadarenes, two men who were demon-possessed met Him as they were coming out of the tombs. They were so extremely violent that no one could pass by that way. ²⁹ And they cried out, saying, "What business do we have with each other, Son of God? Have You come here to torment us before the time?" ³⁰ Now there was a herd of many swine feeding at a distance from them. ³¹ The demons began to entreat Him, saying, "If You are going to cast us out, send us into the herd of swine." ³² And He said to them, "Go!" And they came out and went into the swine, and the whole herd rushed down the steep bank into the sea and perished in the waters. ³³ The herdsmen ran away, and went to the city and reported everything, including what had happened to the demoniacs. ³⁴ And behold, the whole city came out to meet Jesus; and when they saw Him, they implored Him to leave their region. ⁹:¹ Getting into a boat, Jesus crossed over the sea and came to His own city. ² And they brought to Him a paralytic lying on a bed. Seeing their faith, Jesus said to the paralytic, "Take courage, son; your sins are forgiven." ³ And some of the scribes said to themselves, "This fellow blasphemes." ⁴ And Jesus knowing their thoughts said, "Why are you thinking evil in your hearts? ⁵ "Which is easier, to say, 'Your sins are forgiven,' or to say, 'Get up, and walk'? ⁶ "But so that you may know that the Son of Man has authority on earth to forgive sins"—then He said to the paralytic, "Get up, pick up your bed and go home." ⁷ And he got up and went home. ⁸ But when the crowds saw this, they were awestruck, and glorified God, who had given such authority to men. 9 As Jesus went on from there, He saw a man called Matthew, sitting in the tax collector's booth; and He said to him, "Follow Me!" And he got up and followed Him. ¹⁰ Then it happened that as Jesus was reclining at the table in the house, behold, many tax collectors and sinners came and were dining with Jesus and His disciples. ¹¹ When the Pharisees saw this, they said to His disciples, "Why is your Teacher eating with the tax collectors and sinners?" ¹² But when Jesus heard this, He said, "It is not those who are healthy who need a physician, but those who are sick. ¹³ "But go and learn what this means: 'I desire compassion, and not sacrifice,' for I did not come to call the righteous, but sinners." [14] Then the disciples of John came to Him, asking, "Why do we and the Pharisees fast, but Your disciples do not fast?" [15] And Jesus said to them, "The attendants of the bridegroom cannot mourn as long as the bridegroom is with them, can they? But the days will come when the bridegroom is taken away from them, and then they will fast. 16 "But no one puts a patch of unshrunk cloth on an old garment; for the patch pulls away from the garment, and a worse tear results. 17 "Nor do people put new wine into old wineskins; otherwise the wineskins burst, and the wine pours out and the wineskins are ruined; but they put new wine into fresh wineskins, and both are preserved." – Matthew 8:23-9:17

Once again Matthew records a series of three miracles. First Jesus sleeps in a boat during a storm at sea, but proves Himself greater than Jonah by waking up and calming the storm with a word. Then He confronts two demoniacs who have been terrorizing a city and harassing travelers. David calmed evil spirits with his music, but Jesus the son of David drives the demons to the sea with a word. The demons address Him by the royal title "Son of God," and recognize Him as a conqueror. Then Jesus plays the role of a priest by forgiving the sins of a paralytic, and He demonstrates His authority to forgive by raising the paralytic from his bed. Jesus is greater than the prophet Jonah; Jesus is more powerful than King David; Jesus forgives sins on His own authority, without sacrifice. Jesus shows His power over the sea, His power over Satan, His power over sin. No matter what power is arrayed against Jesus, He overcomes it with the word of His power. In each case, He manifests divine power. God has the power to dispel the demons, and the Pharisees are correct that only God has authority to forgive sins. Perhaps the most dramatic demonstration of Jesus' divine authority is the first story, Jesus calming the sea. Men don't have the power to calm the sea. That is God's prerogative (Job 38:8-11; Psalm 29:3-4; 65:5-7; 89:8-10; 107: 23-29). Yahweh alone is the master of the sea. He formed the world from water with the wind of His Spirit. He alone can bring peace and calm to the roaring sea or to the roaring of the nations. Jesus stills the sea with a rebuke. He speaks to the sea and wind and storm as a subordinate. No wonder the disciples react as they do, marveling at Jesus. They know that only Yahweh can do this, and yet Jesus does it without appealing to any authority but His own.

The first story not only demonstrates Jesus' divine authority and power, but also teaches us some important things about following Jesus. Verse 23 is only the second reference to disciples in Matthew's gospel. The first is at the beginning of the Sermon on the Mount, when Jesus' disciples gather to hear him teach. Discipleship means listening to Jesus. Here discipleship is described as "following" Jesus, which is what the disciples do: They follow Him aboard the boat to cross to the other side of the sea. And immediately, there's a storm at sea. The Greek word is not "storm" but "quaking"—the same word used elsewhere for earthquakes. There are two other earthquakes in Matthew's gospel—the quaking at the crucifixion of Jesus and the quaking at His resurrection. This quaking of the sea foreshadows those events. The disciples follow Jesus, and they find immediately that they have followed Him into danger, into mortal danger. And having followed Jesus into danger, the disciples watch Jesus seeming to check out. He's asleep in the boat, and when the other earthquakes occur in the gospel, Jesus is asleep in death. This is what discipleship is about. Following Jesus doesn't lead us into safe havens. It leads us into danger, if we are really following Him. If we follow Jesus, we will find ourselves in the midst of quaking; our world will heave in turmoil beneath our feet. It will seem as if Jesus is absent, as if Jesus has checked out, as if Jesus is sleeping.[8]

---

8. In the sequence, the shaking of the sea parallels the violence of the demoniacs, and both in turn parallel the objection of the scribes. The demons object to Jesus coming to deliver before the time, while the scribes object to Jesus claiming power to forgive. Scribal objections to Jesus are another form of diabolical violence, another shaking of the sea. Frederick Dale Bruner points out that there are three "quakes" (σεισμος) in Matthew: The quake of the sea, an earthquake at the cross, and another at the resurrection of Jesus. The three are related: Jesus sleeps and awakes to calm the quaking sea is parallel to Jesus going

The disciples are frantic. They panic—"Save! Lord! We die!" They turn to Jesus, to be sure, but they turn to Jesus in panic, not in courage. Jesus rebukes them as "cowards," and calls them "Little faiths." Faith means confidence in Jesus in all circumstances. Faith means courage. Faith is the opposite of panic. Faith is not courage that arises from self-confidence. Faith is courage that comes from confidence that Jesus is with us, and that He is equal to every danger. Jesus responds. He rebukes the disciples as cowards and chides them for their little faith, but He doesn't stay asleep. He responds to their fears. They shouldn't have feared, but they did turn to Him, and turning to Him is an act of faith, even if it expresses little faith. Followers of Jesus can be assured that He does respond. Even if our faith is little, even if our faith is mixed with fear, even if our faith is not the deep courageous faith it should be, Jesus wakes up and calms our seas. Don't wait for your faith to grow and become courageous before turning to Jesus. Turn with your tiny faith to Jesus. The cry of little faith can wake Him.

In contrast to the last sequence of miracles, this sequence focuses our attention to people's reaction to Jesus. In the miracles in the previous section, we know nothing about their reaction. Jesus tells the leper to go to the priests and go through the rites of cleansing as a testimony to them, but we never hear how the priests reacted. We learn that the servant of the centurion was healed at the very hour that Jesus spoke, but we near nothing about anyone's response. But in this series of miracles, we hear about reactions from everyone. This is the climax of every story. Jesus calms the sea, but the climax of the story comes when the disciples marvel at how Jesus has calmed the sea, and they wonder what sort of man He must be. The climax of the story of the Gadarene demoniacs comes in the last two verses. Jesus sends

---

into the sleep of death on the cross but rising to calm the sea of the nations, to rebuke the winds and sea and to make them calm at His resurrection (Bruner, *Matthew: A Commentary: Volume 1: The Christbook, Matthew 1-12* [Grand Rapids: Eerdmans, 2007], pp. 397-398).

the demons into the herd of pigs, and they go stampeding into the sea and drown. The whole city comes to see Jesus, and we expect some kind of respect shown to Him. After all, He's just opened up the road past the tombs, which had been blocked by the demoniacs. Instead, they have come out to entreat Him to leave their area. Jesus is a danger to their way of life, which depends on pig-herding and perhaps depends on the demoniacs. Most dramatically, in the final miracle, the conflict with the Pharisees and scribes comes to the forefront. They are described as "scribes" in 9:3, and then there are complaints from Pharisees later on in the chapter. This is the beginning of Jesus' conflicts with the Jewish leadership, and here it focuses on Jesus' claim to be able to forgive sins without any recourse to the normal channels of forgiveness, without any appeal to God as the one who forgives sins.

Opposition continues. Jesus passes a tax booth and calls Matthew from the tax booth to become His disciple. Tax collectors were despised by the Jews. They were Jews who cooperated with the Romans, who collected taxes on behalf of the empire. And the opposition to them was at once religious and political. Politically, they were cooperating with the enemy, collecting taxes for the Gentile empire that many Jews considered an oppressive power. Religiously, they cooperated and hob-knobbed with unclean Gentiles. These two objections are tied together. Many Jews opposed the Roman presence in Palestine for the same reason Osama bin Laden opposed the infidel US troops in Saudi Arabia. This is holy ground, and the defiled infidels have no business being on holy ground. In fact, for many of the Jews, the whole future of Israel depended on faithful Jews keeping their distance from the unclean Gentiles and their collaborators. So long as Israel was muddled and confused, so long as clean and unclean were mixed up together, then Yahweh was never going to come and deliver them from the Gentiles. The Pharisees especially held to a program of national redemption through national holiness. If they can be holy and clean, they will be redeemed.

And national holiness means national separation from the sources of uncleanness, the Romans and other Gentiles who infected the land and Jews who spend time with them.[9]

These concerns come to particular focus in issues of table fellowship. The Pharisees were a table-fellowship movement.[10] Table fellowship was one of the central expressions of their separateness, of their holiness code, of the program the Pharisees had for the redemption of Israel. They had to make sure that their tables were not defiled by the presence of Gentiles, nor their food defiled by the possible presence of unclean or untithed foods. Table purity was central to their hope for the future of Israel. So the Pharisees object, as we would expect them to, to Jesus' table practices. He not only calls Matthew as a disciple, but then goes into a house where tax gatherers and sinners gather to eat with Jesus and the disciples. The Pharisees demand an explanation, and Jesus' response is twofold.

Jesus responds by calling attention to the nature of His ministry. Jesus' ministry is a ministry of healing, restoration, resurrection, life to the dead and acceptance to the outcasts and release to the prisoners. He comes as a physician to heal the sick, and it doesn't make any sense for a physician to avoid contact with his patients. Notice that Jesus is talking about table fellowship here. That is where the physician meets with the sick, and also the place where the sick can find healing.

Jesus also responds by citing a passage from Hosea 6. Hosea is condemning the sins of Ephraim and Judah. Their faithfulness is like a morning cloud or dew that evaporates as the heat of the day comes. The Lord has sent His prophets to slay them and to judge them. He has shed light on them, but they still break His covenant.

---

9. See N. T. Wright, *The New Testament and the People of God* (Minneapolis: Fortress, 1992).

10. This is from Jacob Neusner, *From Politics to Piety: The Emergence of Pharisaic Judaism* (Englewood Cliffs, NJ: Prentice Hall, 1973); "Two Pictures of the Pharisees: Philosophical Circle or Eating Club," *Anglican Theological Review* 64 (1982), pp. 525-538.

They are bloodthirsty and lie in wait for each other. Priests murder, and Ephraim commits harlotry. They continue their sacrifices, but the Lord says "I delight in loyalty rather than sacrifice, and in the knowledge of God rather than burnt offerings" (Hosea 6:6).[11] Jesus interprets loyalty as "mercy" or "compassion," and He is saying that the Lord prefers compassionate and faithful covenant behavior to the flesh of sacrifices. The issue here is purity in table fellowship, not sacrificial technicalities, but the point is the same. Jesus is not condemning the Pharisees for paying attention to the details of the law. He is an advocate of the "jots and tittles." But He is condemning them for paying so much attention to the jots and tittles that they miss the really important thrust of the law — mercy and compassion and loyalty, expressed in table fellowship.

Jesus' statement here goes back to the Sermon on the Mount. The kind of righteousness Jesus demands surpasses the righteousness of the scribes and Pharisees. It doesn't surpass the righteousness of scribes and Pharisees by being more scrupulous than theirs. It surpasses the righteousness of scribes and Pharisees by being a redemptive righteousness, a righteousness of compassion and healing. Jesus has a different program for Israel's redemption, not holiness by separation but compassion for tax gatherers and sinners. Meals are not occasions for haughtiness toward others. They are occasions for generosity and hospitality. That's the nature of a meal.

Even where there is not opposition, there is confusion about Jesus. There are questions about Jesus. John's disciples question Jesus about fasting. Fasting was one of the main pieties of faithful Jews. For some Jews, fasting was a way of securing forgiveness of sins. Jews also fasted during times of calamity, in hope that Yahweh would deliver them, in hope that Yahweh would turn mourning

---

11. Hosea implies that his prophecy will make the people of God a pleasing sacrifice. Ephraim and Judah have no loyalty (*hesed*), which is what delights Yahweh more than sacrifice. So He sends the prophets who hew and slay Judah and Israel with words. That is to say, Yahweh *makes* a pleasing sacrifice *of his people*; the prophets are priests bringing Yahweh's people to the altar so that their judgments will flash forth like light and burn like fire.

to feasting. With Jesus, the feast has started, and the old patterns no longer hold. The potent kingdom Jesus brings cannot be held in the wineskins of the law. Jews fasted in anticipation. Fasting meant waiting, and specifically waiting for the feast to begin. But once Jesus has come, the time of anticipation is over; the time of waiting has reached its end. With His coming, everything begins to change. He comes as a man who has authority over the wind and the sea. He comes "before the time" to triumph over the demons. He comes to forgive sins. He comes to welcome tax gatherers and sinners, to heal the sick, and to preach that compassion is better than sacrifice. With the coming of Jesus, the feast of the kingdom has begun. He has come to make all things new.

News
Matthew 9:18-38

While He was saying these things to them, a synagogue official came and bowed down before Him, and said, "My daughter has just died; but come and lay Your hand on her, and she will live." [19] Jesus got up and began to follow him, and so did His disciples. [20] And a woman who had been suffering from a hemorrhage for twelve years, came up behind Him and touched the fringe of His cloak; [21] for she was saying to herself, "If I only touch His garment, I will get well." [22] But Jesus turning and seeing her said, "Daughter, take courage; your faith has made you well." At once the woman was made well. [23] When Jesus came into the official's house, and saw the flute-players and the crowd in noisy disorder, [24] He said, "Leave; for the girl has not died, but is asleep." And they began laughing at Him. [25] But when the crowd had been sent out, He entered and took her by the hand, and the girl got up. [26] This news spread throughout all that land. [27] As Jesus went on from there, two blind men followed Him, crying out, "Have mercy on us, Son of David!" [28] When He entered the house, the blind men came up to Him, and Jesus said to them, "Do you believe that I am able to do this?" They said to Him, "Yes, Lord." [29] Then He touched their eyes, saying, "It shall be done to you according to your faith." [30] And their eyes were opened. And Jesus sternly

> warned them: "See that no one knows about this!" ³¹ But they went out and spread the news about Him throughout all that land. ³² As they were going out, a mute, demon-possessed man was brought to Him. ³³ After the demon was cast out, the mute man spoke; and the crowds were amazed, and were saying, "Nothing like this has ever been seen in Israel." ³⁴ But the Pharisees were saying, "He casts out the demons by the ruler of the demons." ³⁵ Jesus was going through all the cities and villages, teaching in their synagogues and proclaiming the gospel of the kingdom, and healing every kind of disease and every kind of sickness. ³⁶ Seeing the people, He felt compassion for them, because they were distressed and dispirited like sheep without a shepherd. ³⁷ Then He said to His disciples, "The harvest is plentiful, but the workers are few. ³⁸ Therefore beseech the Lord of the harvest to send out workers into His harvest." – Matthew 9:18-38

Math is one of the defining disciplines of our world. The natural sciences depend on mathematics, and in the past several decades the social sciences have followed. Ancients were also obsessed with numbers, but in a different way. They thought that numbers revealed the structure of the universe. Numbers were a clue to the meaning of everything. But ancient mathematics tended to be religious and mystical and not scientific in our sense. For some Greeks, number was nearly idolized.

When we look at an ancient text and see a series of similar things, it pays to begin counting. The number of episodes, the number of items in a list, the number of names in a genealogy is often significant, as are the numbers in a census. Matthew records a series of miracles in chapters 8-9, and we should begin counting. We've already done some counting, but as we come to the end of these chapters, it's worth stopping to do some more counting. In this text, there are three episodes, but the first is a double episode, with healing of two unrelated people from two unrelated maladies. Jesus agrees to go and raise the daughter of the ruler from the dead, and on the way the woman with the flow of blood touches Him and is healed. Jesus raises the girl then heals two blind men, and then a demoniac who is also dumb and possibly deaf as well. In this section, Jesus performs four healings and heals five people. This brings the total number of healed individuals in these chapters to eleven, the number of healing miracles to nine. We know that Jesus healed many more, but Matthew is selective. He records only a few specific incidents of healing: the leper, the centurion's servant, Peter's mother-in-law, two demon-possessed men, a paralytic, the daughter of the ruler, the woman with the flow of blood, two blind men, and a dumb demoniac. That makes eleven individuals healed, nine miraculous healings. In total, Jesus performed ten wonders here, but the ten wonders include the calming of the sea. The other nine are healing miracles.

That's a bit odd, we think. If Matthew is going to give us a series of individual healings, it would seem that he would give us some significant number—seven or ten or twelve. Nine and eleven don't seem to fit. They seem like unfinished numbers. We want a tenth healing, or maybe a twelfth. It pays to wait, because a few chapters later, Jesus again heals an individual, the man with the withered hand in the synagogue, whom Jesus heals on the Sabbath day. There's our tenth healing, and that number is a bit more significant, more like what we expect. And it's the twelfth person healed. Fittingly, as soon as the Pharisees see Jesus heal the man with the withered hand on the Sabbath, they "counseled together against Him, as to how they might destroy Him"—on this same Sabbath! Jesus has healed twelve individuals, a full Israel. He heals the full number of the lost sheep of the house of Israel, and then the Pharisees say, "Enough is enough; we need to get rid of Jesus."

Matthew isn't finished even yet. That comment about the "lost sheep of the house of Israel" should alert us. That's what Jesus says to another individual who comes for healing: the Syro-Phoenician woman that Jesus meets in the region of Tyre and Sidon, in Canaanite territory, who appeals to Jesus as the Son of David who can cast a demon from her daughter (Matthew 15). "I was sent only to the lost sheep of the house of Israel," Jesus says. "It is not good to take the children's bread and throw it to the dogs." The woman is quick: "But even the dogs feed on the crumbs that fall from their master's table." That puts things off a bit: now we have eleven healing miracles and thirteen people healed. We expect another one to finish things off. We get one. After Jesus is transfigured in the presence of Peter, James, and John, He goes down from the mountain and heals a demon-possessed boy. Jesus continues healing through the rest of His ministry. Even in the last week of His life, when He goes to the temple, Jesus heals the blind and lame (Matthew 21:14). But this boy is the last of the individual healing miracles, and it brings our total to twelve.

When all is said and done, Jesus performs twelve healing miracles and heals fourteen individuals, since two of the healings are double miracles. Jesus has come to the lost sheep of the house of Israel, and Matthew symbolizes this by recording a series of twelve miracles of healing, which heal fourteen people. Through His healing, Jesus is forming a new Israel. But when we look at who is included in these twelve healings, we see the character of the Israel Jesus forms. It's not like the Israel that the Pharisees wanted. It's not a pure-bred, pure-blood Israel. It includes a centurion's servant, a Gentile, and a member of a Roman house. It includes two demoniacs who live in a territory where they raise pigs, which is not Jewish territory. It includes the daughter of a Syro-Phoenician woman. Matthew records a twelve-fold healing, but the twelve-fold healing extends beyond the bounds of traditional Israel. Jesus' Israel is a new Israel. Jesus' Israel is one where there is no boundary of Jew or Canaanite. The numerological pattern that Matthew gives highlights both that Jesus is forming an Israel, and that Jesus' Israel is different from that envisioned by many Jews. And that points to one of the sources of the conflict between Jesus and the Jewish leaders. That intensifying conflict is one of the themes of the last sequence in Matthew 8-9. Matthew notes the growing rift with his phrase "*their* synagogues" (v. 35); when Jesus teaches in a synagogue, he enters alien territory.

This is actually a threefold conflict. It's not just Jesus versus the Jewish leaders, but Jesus, the crowd and the Jewish leaders. The enthusiasm of the crowd makes the Pharisees suspicious of Jesus. He's gaining a large hearing. He's getting people to follow

Him, listen to Him, and proclaim Him a prophet. The crowd plays a big role here in this passage. Matthew has been noting this all along. When Jesus begins His ministry, "great multitudes followed Him from Galilee and Decapolis" (4:25). When Jesus finishes the Sermon on the Mount, "the multitudes were amazed at His teaching" (7:28). As Jesus descends from the mountain, "great multitudes followed Him" (8:1). And here again Jesus is surrounded by crowds. There is a crowd in the house of the ruler whose daughter Jesus raises from the dead (9:23, 25), and when Jesus casts the demon out of the dumb man, the crowds again marvel at Jesus' unprecedented ministry. This is a threat to the Pharisees. They have been the honored teachers of Israel. They have their own disciples. But now it seems as if Jesus is stealing their sheep. He's taking away the disciples that once followed the Pharisees. Later, Pilate will discern that the Jewish leaders want to kill Jesus because of envy, and their envy begins here. Why is Jesus surrounded by all these amazed crowds? Why don't people listen to us anymore? Jesus is the Son of David; the Pharisees are envious Sauls.

Twice the text tells us that the news of Jesus is spreading throughout the land. After He raises the ruler's daughter, the "voice" or "news" goes throughout the land. When Jesus heals the two blind men, news again travels throughout the land. He is too popular, and He is too loose. But the Pharisees cannot deny what Jesus has done. There is a dead girl walking around, and there are blind men who now see, and there is a demoniac who no longer is possessed by demons. They can't deny the facts, so they interpret them differently. The Pharisees begin their spin, saying that Jesus casts out demons in the power of the devil, a charge they repeat and Jesus rebuts later.

This is the way the Pharisees respond to Jesus throughout the gospel story. They cannot avoid the realities. They cannot deny that Jesus is a wonder-worker. They cannot even deny that the body of Jesus is missing on the third day after His death. Instead, they attempt to spin the story, giving their own interpretation, and making Jesus out to be a wonder-worker who is in league with the devil. As Jesus says in the gospel of John, they are the ones in league with the devil (John 8:44). They are liars and murderers, like their father the devil, who was a liar and murderer from the beginning. But this is a neat ploy of Satan and satanic men: They accuse the godly of the very demonism they practice.

The first double miracle reminds us of the first cycle of miracles (8:1-13). The first two healings in these chapters were a leper and the centurion's servant, and the double healing in chapter 9 resembles it. Like the centurion, the ruler appeals to Jesus on behalf of another (9:18) and like the leper, the woman with the flow of blood is cleansed from defilement (9:20; cf. Leviticus 15:25-30). Matthew has not only given us a neat numerological pattern but also framed off these miracles with similar episodes. The woman with the flow of blood does not have a life-threatening illness but has been in a state of Levitical impurity for twelve years (v. 20; cf. Leviticus 15:25-28). For twelve years, she has been excluded from worship and from feasts. She has been infecting every bed and chair, and she has been passing on uncleanness, ceremonial death, for twelve years. She has been in a state of exile from God's presence for twelve years. And now, in confidence that Jesus can and will help her, she reaches out to Jesus to touch His garment. Jesus again defies purity regulations, allowing Himself to be touched by the woman and taking the dead girl by the hand (v. 25). In this series of miracles, Jesus delivers from several of the major forms of impurity—leprosy, blood, death. These are all forms of death, literal and ceremonial. In doing so, he raises the woman from ceremonial death and the girl from literal death. Jesus' hand is the "hand" of God, the "hand" of Yahweh, which does mighty things, which He can stretch out and lay on people and heal them with a touch.

The length of the woman's impurity (v. 20) hints at the symbolism of the passage. The woman is associated with the number twelve, the number of Israel. And she is a woman who is reaching out to Jesus for healing. She wants to touch the "hem" or the "corner" of his garment. This is a marital image in Scripture. When Ruth wants Boaz to take her as his wife, she asks him to spread the "wing" of his garment over her (Ruth 3:9). When Israel comes into a marital covenant with Yahweh, He spreads the wing of His garment over her (Ezekiel 16:8). The woman is seeking healing, but she is also a representative of the bride who seeks a husband who will cover her with the corner of his robe.

After Jesus has raised the little girl from the dead, He is confronted by two blind men who cry out to him as the Son of David, the greater Solomon. Matthew tells us at the beginning of his gospel that Jesus is the son of David (1:1), but the two blind men are the first to recognize Him as such (9:27). And this points to the symbolism of Jesus' healing of the blind men. When Jesus restores human capacities, He reveals His ability to restore spiritual capacities. There is hope for those who cannot "see" that He is Son of David, if they cry out to Him for healing. The disciples themselves are blind to Jesus. They often fail to "see" who He is. But Jesus comes to open the eyes of the blind. He comes to heal sight, but physical sight and the spiritual insight to see God's work in Him.

We find something similar in the last healing. In fulfillment of the prophecies of Isaiah 35:6, Jesus looses the tongue of a dumb man, whose inability to speak was the result of demon-possession (v. 32). Jesus not only enables the blind to see, but gives the dumb speech to testify about Him. The focus of the story, though, is on the different reactions to Jesus. While the crowds marvel at the unprecedented miracle, the Pharisees grumble that Jesus is in league with the devil (v. 34). When Jesus has healed the blind men, He warns them strongly to keep the story quiet: "See, let no one know." This is an odd thing for Jesus to say. They have been blind, and now they see. Aren't people going to notice? Jesus tells them not to spread the story aggressively. It's impossible that people won't realize they can see now. But they should keep Jesus' identity and His miracle quiet.

Jesus doesn't do stunts. Think about what would happen if someone like Jesus were around today. Some PR firm would be knocking at His door the next day, asking to represent Him, getting Him appearances on Today, Oprah, and Nightline, arranging media interviews. But Jesus doesn't work this way. Jesus' kingdom is like the leaven. Leaven works imperceptibly. You can't see the loaf growing. But if you go away for an hour and come back you'll see that this imperceptible growth has had results. You can't see it happen, but it is happening. More deeply, Jesus knows that He is on a collision course with the Pharisees, and He doesn't want that clash to reach a climax too soon. Jesus will perform a public prophetic act in the temple. He will call attention to Himself. Now is not the time. Timing is all.

As Jesus travels, heals, preaches, and teaches, He sees that Israel is in disarray, as they were in the times of Ahab (cf. 1 Kings 22:17). The analogy is a close one. Israel is ruled by the Herodians, who are very like Ahab. Herod's relationship with John is very much like Ahab's relationship with Elijah. Herod is incited to kill John by a woman, as Ahab is incited against Elijah by his wife Jezebel. Israel really does need a shepherd, a king, a king different from the king they now have. They are like the people of Israel during the days of Saul, when David gathered the downcast and the distressed to himself and formed an Israel-in-exile while he waited for the Lord to give him the kingdom.

In verses 37-38, Jesus changes the imagery from herds to farming. Jesus sees that the people are distressed like lost sheep, wandering and vulnerable and hungry and thirsty. Jesus also sees that this condition of Israel is a moment of opportunity. The people are downcast, and are looking for help and hope. And that means that the field is white to harvest. They are ready to be gathered in. This is the first time that the image of the harvest has been used in Matthew, but it is an important one.

Jesus' parables use the imagery of harvest. He tells the parable of the wheat and tares, where an enemy sows the wheat field with weeds. And the owner of the field says that his workers should wait until the harvest before they do anything; they shouldn't pluck up the tares now because they might pluck wheat by mistake (13:30). Jesus explains that the enemy is the devil, who sows weeds in God's wheat field (13:39). In Matthew 21, Jesus tells the parable of the vineyard, where the harvest of the grapes is the time when the owner sends his servants to collect his share. The tenants of the vineyard instead mistreat the slaves, beat them, and finally kill the son. The harvest is an image of the end, when Yahweh comes to gather His people. But when Jesus talks about the harvest, He talks about it as something that is about to happen, something that is happening. The harvest is plentiful; it's time to send out the laborers to pick the grain and bring it into the barn. The harvest is taking place. Jesus is talking about His own ministry, His own lifetime. But there are other times of harvest as well. And Jesus instructs His disciples to pray the Lord of the harvest to send workers who can gather them in, and this is a permanent prayer for the church. Jesus is going to send out laborers to gather the harvest in the next chapter. And Jesus continues to send out laborers to gather in the lost and scattered sheep, to bring the wheat into the storehouse. Israel's history is coming to a climax, but there are other climaxes in history, other times of harvest, other opportunities to gather.

The Lost Sheep of Israel
Matthew 10:1-15

Jesus summoned His twelve disciples and gave them authority over unclean spirits, to cast them out, and to heal every kind of disease and every kind of sickness. ² Now the names of the twelve apostles are these: The first, Simon, who is called Peter, and Andrew his brother; and James the son of Zebedee, and John his brother; ³ Philip and Bartholomew; Thomas and Matthew the tax collector; James the son of Alphaeus, and Thaddaeus; ⁴ Simon the Zealot, and Judas Iscariot, the one who betrayed Him. ⁵ These twelve Jesus sent out after instructing them: "Do not go in the way of the Gentiles, and do not enter any city of the Samaritans; ⁶ but rather go to the lost sheep of the house of Israel. ⁷ "And as you go, preach, saying, 'The kingdom of heaven is at hand.' ⁸ "Heal the sick, raise the dead, cleanse the lepers, cast out demons. Freely you received, freely give. ⁹ "Do not acquire gold, or silver, or copper for your money belts, ¹⁰ or a bag for your journey, or even two coats,

> or sandals, or a staff; for the worker is worthy of his support. ¹¹"And whatever city or village you enter, inquire who is worthy in it, and stay at his house until you leave that city. ¹² "As you enter the house, give it your greeting. ¹³ "If the house is worthy, give it your blessing of peace. But if it is not worthy, take back your blessing of peace. ¹⁴ "Whoever does not receive you, nor heed your words, as you go out of that house or that city, shake the dust off your feet. ¹⁵ "Truly I say to you, it will be more tolerable for the land of Sodom and Gomorrah in the day of judgment than for that city. – Matthew 10:1-15

The last chapter ended with Jesus observing the condition of Israel and speaking of what it needed. He observed that the people were distressed, downcast, lying down, directionless, wandering like sheep without a shepherd. It was not the first time Israel had been shepherdless. Ezekiel rebuked the shepherds of his day (34:2-6), and through Ezekiel the Lord also promised a new good shepherd who would do everything the false shepherds failed to do (Ezekiel 34:11-16). Jesus is Yahweh incarnate, and when He sees the people scattered and oppressed like sheep, He has compassion and takes action to gather and protect them. Jesus is also the new Moses. Like Moses (Numbers 27:17), Jesus sees that Israel is like sheep without a shepherd (Matthew 9:36), a field white to harvest. Moses gave authority to Joshua to lead Israel in and out in conquest; Jesus gives authority to the Twelve to carry out another conquest (10:1).

A shepherd is a king, and announcing the kingdom of God is telling the lost sheep the good news that the Lord is coming to shepherd His people and to establish a new David as the king at His right hand. Shepherding the people of God means pointing them to their true Shepherd, the heavenly King who comes to assert His reign. But shepherding also means dealing with all the evils that leave Israel wandering and alone, aimless and oppressed. That's what Ezekiel said: The shepherd was going to deliver the sheep from dangerous animals, including their own predatory shepherds. The disciples are going out as shepherds to heal the sick; this is a shepherding task. This is what Jesus comes to do, and what He sends the Twelve to do. Jesus tells the twelve to raise the dead. Jesus comes to combat death in all its forms, and this is what the twelve shepherds do. He tells them to cleanse lepers, to bring the excluded lepers back into the fellowship of the community. This is the task of the shepherd, to bring the wandering lambs back. They are to cast out demons, liberating from the oppressive power of Satan.

There are four tasks of shepherds in 10:8: Heal sick, raise dead, cleanse lepers, exorcise demons. Four is the number of the corners of the earth, the number of geographic, spatial extension. The shepherds have a fourfold mission that extends to the four corners of the land, combating the evils that crowd in against the sheep from every point of the compass. This is how the reign of God comes. This is the gracious reign of heaven on earth. But 9:37-38 uses a different image, the image of the harvest. This is a different image, with different connotations. I mentioned briefly at the end of the last section that the harvest is an event of the end. It is an eschatological symbol. Planting takes place at the beginning of the agricultural year, and harvesting at the end. Harvest is an eschatological image. But Jesus sees that the fields in His own time are ready for harvest. The end has come. It's time to send out laborers to gather in the harvest. Harvest is a joyful occasion, when people begin to enjoy the produce of the earth and the fruit of their labors. As an image of the end, it is also an image of judgment. Jesus uses it this way in the parable of the wheat and tares. The owner of a field sows his field with wheat, but an enemy comes in and sows weeds that mix with the tares. The owner tells his laborers not to harvest yet, since they might pull up the wheat with the tares. But when the harvest comes, the end comes, and the tares and wheat will be separated. The tares are going to be burned and the wheat gathered into barns (Matthew 13). Jesus sees that the harvest is ready *now*, in His own day. That's what the parable of the wheat and tares is about. It's about the Lord sowing Israel back into the land after the exile, and the enemy, Satan, sowing weeds in the wheat field of Israel. That happened centuries before Jesus came, and now that He's arrived, the harvest is about to begin. It is not time for planting. Planting took place long before. Now the harvest is ready.

Jesus says that the harvest needs laborers, and in the very next verse (10:1), Jesus summons the Twelve and sends them out. They are the laborers going out to the harvest, gathering in the wheat. But they are also the laborers going to harvest and beginning the sifting and separation of wheat and tares. The ministry of the Twelve is a ministry of mercy to the lost sheep of the house of Israel. But Jesus says they are going to encounter persecution and opposition and hatred. They are going to encounter some people who are "worthy" (v. 11, 13) and some who are not. Jesus comes to bring a sword, not peace, and He comes to set family members against one another (10:34-36). The very presence of shepherds among the lost sheep, the presence of harvesters in the field of harvest, separates sheep and goats, wheat and chaff. The cities that don't receive them are chaff, like Sodom and Gomorrah ready for burning. Jesus comes announcing and bringing the gracious reign of heaven. He comes as a good Shepherd to heal and gather and protect and feed Israel. But He is a sign of contradiction, a cause of offense, a divisive figure, an instrument of judgment. So are His disciples. As they go into the world in a ministry of mercy, they divide the world.

Jesus has come as *the* Shepherd, healing, cleansing, liberating, raising the dead. He sends out the Twelve as under-shepherds, doing the same work. But He and the Twelve are also laborers in a harvest, and their ministry is beginning to sift Israel. In chapters 11-12, we see the growing opposition of the Jews to Jesus, and by chapter 13 He has begun to speak in parables because the Jews have shut their ears. And this also shows the pattern for the mission of the church throughout the ages. This is inevitable. It happens throughout the history and mission of the church, not just in Jesus' lifetime. We go out on the same mission. We go to announce the kingdom, to heal, to raise the dead, to cleanse, to cast out demons. And the results are going to be the same—division, sifting, a harvest that is also a separation of wheat and chaff. Sometimes the church's mission is to sow. But that sowing eventually leads to harvest, which means both an occasion for joyous gathering and an occasion for separation and judgment. The church's mission always ends with a harvest feast; it also ends with a fire for burning.

For the first time Matthew refers explicitly to the specific group of "twelve disciples" (10:1; cf. 9:37). The number, as always, is significant: Jesus chooses the twelve patriarchs of a new Israel. There are Twelve missionaries to the Twelve tribes. There are Twelve shepherds for the Twelve tribes of lost sheep. They are qualified shepherds because they have a shepherd. They can serve the lost sheep of the house of Israel because they are no longer lost sheep themselves. They have received from Jesus—power to heal, cleanse, raise the dead, deliver from Satan. They have received, and so they have something to give. They are the root of the new tree of Israel, the first spark of the new Israel that will be a light to the nations.

They receive authority, authority captured in the title change that takes place in verses 1-2. "Disciples" are students, and Jesus has many more than twelve students. The Twelve are different because they are given authority over unclean spirits and diseases (10:1) and thereby become "apostles" (10:2). An "apostle" is a representative who acts on behalf of a master, with the full authority of his master. The Twelve are not simply students but bear the authority and carry out the work of Jesus as His delegates. The list of apostles suggests another Old Testament connection. Jesus is Moses giving authority to a set of new Joshuas who are going to carry on His work. But Jesus is also like Moses sending out the twelve spies who looked over the land (Numbers 13).

Jesus and His disciples accomplish this mission. Their goal is the restoration of Israel, and Jesus says that they will continue going through the cities of Israel until the Son of Man comes (v. 23). By that time, by the time of the Son of Man's coming in judgment against Jerusalem, Israel is restored, a new Israel gathered around Jesus, and Israel is the mechanism of world mission. The prophets all predict that salvation will come to the nations once Israel is restored. When Jerusalem is raised up and the exile ended, then the Gentiles will flock to the holy city. Paul says the same thing in his epistles: Salvation is to the Jew first and also to the Greek. Some Jews, especially the Jewish leaders, reject Jesus. Many respond with faith, and are gathered into the new Israel under the oversight of the Twelve Shepherds. This restored Israel becomes the instrument of redeeming the nations.

Jesus instructs His disciples to take neither money nor a change of clothes (vv. 9-10). Instead, they are to depend on the generosity of those whom they serve (vv. 11-13). Those who receive them are going to prosper, but those who reject them are going to be judged more severely than Sodom, because they have been visited by something greater than a couple of angels. The apostles are going to shake the dust from their feet, the cursed dust that the serpent eats, the dust that a Jew would shake off his sandals when leaving a pagan land and entering the holy land. A city that rejects the apostles has become a Gentile land, ripe for judgment.

The apostles' method of mission manifests the nature of the kingdom, the lifestyle of the kingdom. At the center of the Sermon on the Mount, Jesus gives instructions about money. There, He instructs His disciples not to be anxious about their food or clothing, but trust in their heavenly Father to provide. They are to consider the birds and the lilies and not fear. Jesus repeats some of that teaching in this chapter. The apostles are supposed to go out on the mission in a fashion that reflects this confidence in their Father. If they went out with massive funding, with armies of protection, with a large pack of extra clothing, they would be denying in their behavior what they teach. The form of their mission would contradict the content of their mission. Jesus' instructions are also for the people of Israel, the lost sheep, to make their acceptance of Jesus concrete and real. It's not enough to receive the apostles' message; to receive Jesus, people will have to provide concrete aid to His representatives. The towns that don't receive Jesus and His apostles face a judgment more devastating than that of Sodom and Gomorrah (v. 15).

The differences between Jesus' mission instructions and the missionary practices of many contemporary churches are dramatic. We won't send a missionary out until he has hundreds of thousands of dollars in support. We hesitate to send missionaries out into dangerous areas. They need to maintain a lifestyle, but their dependence on foreign money is a massive denial of what they say about their Father, a massive lesson that the Father can be trusted so long as there are large supporting churches in the background, too. This is not the way the monks of the Middle Ages went on mission. Some Irish monks did what they called White Martyrdom. They climbed in a boat, shoved off from shore, and went wherever the waves took them. If they found people who accepted them, they would stay there and build a church. If the people rejected them, they'd shove off and go to the next island, assuming they survived.

The apostles were unique. The mission of the Twelve was unique. It went to the lost sheep of Israel, and they were given unique authority and power to carry on Jesus' mission among His people. But the pattern of our mission is the same. The church still goes out in the authority of Christ. We are not all apostles, but we all have received the Spirit of Jesus, and we are all called to participate in Jesus' shepherding—His ministry of healing, raising the dead, cleansing lepers, casting out demons. This takes a different form today than it did then, but it's the same mission, and we are all called to it in our particular locations. The Twelve were the beginning of a new Israel, gathered around their new Shepherd. They were the foundation of the church. And as the foundation, they show us what the church is supposed to look like. The church is not a community that has a mission; the church is a mission. Disciples of Jesus are not saved people who happen to have a task to fulfill; being saved means being caught up in the mission of Jesus. For us, as for the disciples, Jesus' instructions stand: Freely you have received. Freely give.

To the Lost Sheep

HATED BY ALL
Matthew 10:16-33

Behold, I send you out as sheep in the midst of wolves; so be shrewd as serpents and innocent as doves. [17] But beware of men, for they will hand you over to the courts and scourge you in their synagogues; [18] and you will even be brought before governors and kings for My sake, as a testimony to them and to the Gentiles. [19] But when they hand you over, do not worry about how or what you are to say; for it will be given you in that hour what you are to say. [20] For it is not you who speak, but it is the Spirit of your Father who speaks in you. [21] Brother will betray brother to death, and a father his child; and children will rise up against parents and cause them to be put to death. [22] You will be hated by all because of My name, but it is the one who has endured to the end who will be saved. [23] But whenever they persecute you in one city, flee to the next; for truly I say to you, you will not finish going through the cities of Israel until the Son of Man comes. [24] A disciple is not above his teacher, nor a slave above his master. [25] It is enough for the disciple that he become like his teacher, and the slave like his master. If they have called the head of the house Beelzebul, how much more will they malign the members of his household! [26] Therefore do not fear them, for there is nothing concealed that will not be revealed, or hidden that will not be known. [27] What I tell you in the darkness, speak in the light; and what you hear whispered in your ear, proclaim upon the housetops. [28] Do not fear those who kill the body but are unable to kill the soul; but rather fear Him who is able to destroy both soul and body in hell. [29] Are not two sparrows sold for a cent? And yet not one of them will fall to the ground apart from your Father. [30] But the very hairs of your head are all numbered. [31] So do not fear; you are more valuable than many sparrows. [32] Therefore everyone who confesses Me before men, I will also confess him before My Father who is in heaven. [33] But whoever denies Me before men, I will also deny him before My Father who is in heaven.

– Matthew 10:16-33

Jesus summoned the Twelve to Him and gave them authority and power. He sent them out to the lost sheep of the house of Israel. He told them to proclaim the kingdom of heaven. He said that they would have power to heal, raise the dead, cast out demons, cleanse lepers. They didn't even have to take any staff with them to ward off attackers or wild animals. They didn't need any money; the Father who made the world from nothing could generate support from nothing. They could pronounce peace to a house and a city, and the peace would remain. They could shake the dust from their sandals in a curse against a city, and that city would be judged more severely than Sodom and Gomorrah. The fate of the towns of Judah would turn on what they did to the Twelve and what the Twelve do to them.

Well into Jesus' sermon, the Twelve are thinking, we're going to be unstoppable. Nothing is going to stand before us. We're like Joshua, before whom no enemy can stand. Then the tone of the talk changes. Jesus says "I sent you out as sheep in the midst of wolves." No problem; we can take care of it; we've got power. Jesus says, "They are going to take you to court, and before Gentile governors and kings." A shadow falls across the Twelve's enthusiasm. What happened to our power? they begin to ask, nervously. "Brother will deliver brother to death, and a father his child," Jesus continues. And "don't fear those who kill the body." Who said anything about killing?? the Twelve begin to demand. We've got power, power from Jesus, power over demons, power over sickness, power over death, power over uncleanness. What is Jesus doing talking about wolves, and courts, and kings, murderous Cainite brothers, and death and killing? What did we get ourselves into?

Jesus gives power to the Twelve, power over sickness, uncleanness, death, and the devil. He does *not* give them the power to escape persecution. Persecution is integral to mission. There is no mission without it. Jesus said it already in the Beatitudes: We are blessed if we are persecuted, hated, slandered, and killed, because this is precisely what happened to the prophets. If we want to share in the fullness of the blessing of the kingdom, we're going to have to share in the sufferings of the King. We follow a Crucified Messiah, and there is no way to follow Him or carry out His mission unless we share in the cross, unless we take up the cross and follow Him. Persecution, threat, opposition, and the possibility of death are integral to the mission of the Twelve because of the situation in Israel. The Twelve are sent to the lost sheep of the house of Israel, and they are sent because the sheep are harassed, discouraged, stomped down.

They are sent to be shepherds to those sheep. But Jesus also says that they are not above the sheep. In fact, they are sheep themselves (v. 16), sent out into an Israel full of predators, wolves who want to devour the sheep. Jesus has talked about wolves already in Matthew. At the end of the Sermon on the Mount, He warned the disciples about "false prophets, who come to you in sheep's clothing, but inwardly are ravenous wolves" (7:15). They try to appear as sheep, but they are really sheep-eaters. Jesus goes on to say that we can know the wolves by their fruits. The wolves that act wolfishly are not sheep but wolves. He is talking specifically about false prophets, but the image is broader too. He is talking about false teachers, false leaders, and even false disciples. But He is talking mainly about the false prophets and teachers of Israel. Jesus clearly has Jews in view in chapter 10 when He uses this image. The wolves are the ones who are going to deliver the Twelve to court and scourge them in "their synagogues" (v. 17). The wolves have synagogues. They are going to deliver the Twelve over to Gentile kings and their courts, where they will be called to testify. As the story of the Twelve continues from here and into the book of Acts, we see the Jewish leaders doing exactly this—delivering the disciples to Gentile rulers. The Jewish leaders are the wolves. They've been preying on the sheep of Israel. That's one reason why the sheep are lost and harassed. And the Twelve don't come along to join the wolves. They identify themselves with the sheep, to suffer oppression and harassment alongside the sheep. Though shepherds, they have a shepherd. They are to stand with the oppressed rather than the oppressors.

Too often, the seductions of power have been too much for the church, and she has taken her stand with the wolves. Many in the hierarchy of Russian Orthodoxy lent their imprimatur to the Soviet regime, going along to get along, and many Protestants greeted Hitler like a second Messiah. Christians have joined with some of the most brutal regimes in history and given those regimes a patina of sanctity. The church gives the most pious reasons. If we hang out with the thugs, perhaps we can moderate their thuggishness. Being with the thugs will give us an opportunity to witness to them. Maybe, in some rare cases this works. More often, Christians in these situations become useful idiots, and they aid and abet tyranny. Jesus will have none of this. The fact that liberation theologians say it doesn't make it wrong: When the church enters a society polarized between the wolves and sheep, it is blindingly obvious that her place is with the latter. The church overcomes the wolves as Jesus did, by suffering alongside the sheep.

In this kind of situation, the disciples have to be shrewd. "Be wise as serpents," Jesus says. The first wise serpent in the Bible is a deceiver. Is Jesus encouraging His disciples to use deception to protect themselves? In part, the answer is "Yes." Paul escaped the ethnarch Aretas in a basket let down through a window in the wall of Damascus, and we can be certain that he didn't inform Aretas of his plans beforehand. Deception is a tactic of war, and the apostles were at war. When the disciples leave a town where they've been persecuted, they don't leave a forwarding address. They slip out and go somewhere else. They might wear disguises, as Calvin had to do at times when he traveled. Behind these tactics of deception is an eye-for-eye justice. The serpent deceived Eve, and as a result Adam and Eve were cast from the garden. It's just that Satan the deceiver be deceived. We receive Satan and Satanic oppressors as a strategy of protection, but also as an act of just retribution against Satan.

But there is more to the wisdom of serpents. Solomon observed that one of the four small things that is "exceedingly wise" is the lizard that can be grasped with the hands "yet is in kings' palaces" (Proverbs 30:28). Reptiles are shrewd in their ability to slip into places designed to keep them out. This is the wisdom of Jesus' serpentine disciples. Persecutors lay hands on believers, drag them before kings and governors, and—magically—Christians have slipped into king's palaces, ready to speak a word inspired by the Spirit. Through persecution, the mission to Israel will become a mission to the Gentiles. The Jews will not only "scourge you in their synagogues," but will bring them "before governors and kings" (vv. 17-18). Without persecution, Jesus' disciples would never gain access to Gentile rulers. The Twelve don't have to prepare persuasive speeches; the Spirit will testify to the Gentiles through them (v. 20).

Jesus assures the Twelve that they will be delivered and vindicated when the Son of Man comes (v. 23). This isn't a reference to the end of the world. Jesus is not saying that there will be a mission to the lost sheep of the house of Israel that will last from the first century to His final coming. When Jesus talks about the "coming of the Son of Man" in Matthew, He's talking about something that happens within the lifetime of the apostles (cf. 16:24-28; 23:29-35). Jesus is not just talking about a mission carried out in his own lifetime. He's talking about a mission extending to the end of the *age*, not to the end of time. The mission of Israel has an endpoint, which is the coming of the Son of Man. This is the end-point of the mission to Israel. There will be a great crisis during that mission. The persecution of the Twelve and the other disciples will be a part of the birth pangs of the coming new age. Whoever perseveres with Jesus through that crisis will be saved (v. 22).

The mission to Israel, in other words, continues through the events that we read about in the book of Acts. Peter ministers to the circumcision, and Paul to the uncircumcision. But it's not until the end of Acts that Paul finally turns from the Jews to the Gentiles. His mission among the Gentiles, as he explains in Romans 9-11, is designed to provoke Israel to jealousy. Though he preached the gospel to the Gentiles, his eye was always on Israel, to see how the Jews would respond. He worked among the Gentiles with the hope that all Israel would be saved.

Jesus tells the disciples to expect the same treatment as He received (vv. 24-25). So far, the opposition to Jesus has been fairly mild (9:34), but eventually He will be scourged (v. 17) and turned over to Gentiles (v. 18). Jesus' trial and crucifixion set the pattern of Christian mission. This is scary. The world is a dangerous place, not only in first-century Israel but all around us today. We can't sit safely in our enclaves. That would be unfaithful. We are sent out, as much as the Son and Spirit are sent out. We are not saved and then sent out. Being saved means being caught up in a sending, the sending of the Son and Spirit. But it's dangerous. We will face hatred, opposition, attacks from brothers and family members. So Jesus assures the Twelve that they have nothing to fear. Persecution is an essential aid to mission. Persecution is the mechanism for bringing secret things to light (vv. 26-27). Persecution is not an obstacle to mission but an opportunity for witness. Jesus tells the Twelve things in their ears. He whispers. He doesn't slip into king's palaces. But the Twelve will, and they will announce all that He has spoken. Jesus whispers, but the Twelve will shout.[12] The fact of persecution itself *reveals*—it reveals the character of the persecutors, and it is a test of the character of the persecuted. The persecutors can't do any more than kill the body. The Twelve should fear God's judgment more than human judges (vv. 28). Our ultimate future is not determined by human authorities but by whether we confess or deny Jesus (vv. 32-33). The thought of God judging us seems frightening, but Jesus says it's liberating. Because we fear God's judgment, we have no fear

---

12. Whispers to shouts: This is the history of the church in a nutshell. A Pharisee traveling to Damascus is thrown from his horse and Jesus speaks to Him, and the mission to the Gentiles begins. A wealthy young man hears a sermon about giving up earthly goods, hears the call of Jesus, sells everything, and soon he's surrounded by disciples who devote themselves to humble service in the growing cities of Europe. A lone monk agonizes over the opening chapter of Romans, Jesus whispers to Him, and He shouts out a Reformation.

of human authorities, no matter how vicious. The Father takes care of His children, more than He cares for sparrows (vv. 29-31). "Not a single hair shall fall" is a common expression in the Bible (1 Samuel 14:45; 2 Samuel 14:11; 1 Kings 15:2), but Jesus doesn't promise that. He promises that when our crown of hair falls to the dust, our Father knows it. Hair is glory and a crown, and losing hair means losing glory, being dishonored, being shamed, being driven to the dust. Instead of a crown, we have dust on our heads, the dust of mourning and defeat. None of this happens apart from the Father. He takes care of the birds of the air, and He will take care of us even when our crown is cast down to the ground.

There is a broader point here about the mission of the church. As the church goes about her mission, she doesn't necessarily look powerful. She looks like a flock of sheep, not a pack of wolves. She is vulnerable and not just vulnerable but actually oppressed, attacked, arrested, tried. But Jesus is promising that the Twelve's mission really is unstoppable. What looks like an interruption of mission—arrest and trial—is actually opening a door for mission—the word that the Twelve speak in the power of the Spirit.

What can stop this kind of mission? Arrest and trial? Hardly. That expands the mission to new territory. Execution? Not even that will help, because as Jesus says, the disciples are not to fear the ones who can kill the body but cannot kill the soul. The destiny of believers turns on whether they testify and confess Christ before men. If they do, then they will be confessed before the Father. If they don't, Jesus will deny them. It might seem that Jesus' instructions about persecution undermine the power that He has given the Twelve. But that's not true. He's still talking about power and authority. He's talking about the unstoppable power of the mission of the church, which is the mission of the Crucified.

To the Lost Sheep

Not Peace But A Sword
Matthew 10:34-11:1

"Do not think that I came to bring peace on the earth; I did not come to bring peace, but a sword. ^{35} For I came to set a man against his father, and a daughter against her mother, and a daughter-in-law against her mother-in-law ^{36} and a man's enemies will be the members of his household. ^{37} He who loves father or mother more than Me is not worthy of Me; and he who loves son or daughter more than Me is not worthy of Me. ^{38} And he who does not take his cross and follow after Me is not worthy of Me. ^{39} He who has found his life will lose it, and he who has lost his life for My sake will find it. ^{40} He who receives you receives Me, and he who receives Me receives Him who sent Me. ^{41} He who receives a prophet in the name of a prophet shall receive a prophet's reward; and he who receives a righteous man in the name of a righteous man shall receive a righteous man's reward. ^{42} And whoever in the name of a disciple gives to one of these little ones even a cup of cold water to drink, truly I say to you, he shall not lose his reward." $^{11:1}$ When Jesus had finished giving instructions to His twelve disciples, He departed from there to teach and preach in their cities. – Matthew 10:34-11:1

At several points in His discourse, Jesus specifically speaks of opposition coming from family members. "Brother will deliver up brother to death, and a father his child; and children will rise up against parents, and cause them to be put to death" (v. 21). And again, "I came to set a man against His father, and a daughter against her mother, and a daughter-in-law against her mother-in-law, and a man's enemies will be the members of His own household" (vv. 34-35). Even the most intimate relationships will be disrupted. Jesus says that the Twelve are going to encounter persecution as they carry out the mission He gives them. They have power over sickness, the devil, death, uncleanness, but they do not have power to escape or avoid opposition. Persecution is inherent in mission, unavoidable. But Jesus is more specific. It's not just persecution, but persecution *from family members*.

We have little experience of what Jesus is talking about. Some of us may be slightly estranged from family members because of our Christian faith. At worst, they might avoid us at family reunions, refuse to invite us to their homes, resist letting a conversation drift into religious topics. That is painful, and it is real persecution. It is of the same genus as the persecution that Jesus is talking about. But the effects of becoming estranged from family in first-century Judaism were far more severe. The family was what gave people identity. Jews thought of themselves as "sons of" or "daughters of" their father and mother. James the son of Zebedee – that's how you distinguish one James from another, by his family ties.

Families were also the main social welfare network. Under the Mosaic law, if a man died without a son, his widow didn't turn and apply to some federal program for assistance. There weren't any federal programs. Her brother-in-law or some other relative would be responsible for taking up her support. Families were also the main mechanism for business and personal contacts. Sons benefited from the reputation of their fathers. Family provided for the future by providing an inheritance. In some ancient cultures, the family actually had responsibility for carrying out the death penalty in some circumstances. Families could put individuals to death, sell them into slavery, banish them. And this could be done, in Roman families, not only for attacks against other family members, but for economic offenses "such as destroying the cornerstone of the family lands or menacing the future of the family."[13] There's no protection from state authorities in this kind of system, since the state itself is a union of *gentes*.

What happens when someone in this kind of setting is estranged from his family? He's not just shunned at family reunions. He loses his identifying name—James no-longer-the-

---

13. Carle Clark Zimmerman, *Family and Civilization* (Wilmington: ISI Books, 2008).

son-of-Zebedee. He loses the contacts that he might need to get along economically. He loses the safety net that will keep him from excruciating poverty if disaster strikes. He loses inheritance. It would not be uncommon for estrangement from the family to take a violent form. If you want to imagine what Jesus' disciples might have heard when Jesus tells them they risk losing their family, think of what happens to Muslims who convert, or Jehovah's Witnesses or Mormons. That's what Jesus is telling them to expect.

Persecution is inherent in mission because the nature of mission is to be a "harvest" (9:37-38), an eschatological separation and judgment (cf. 13:30). As they spread out throughout Israel, they separate wheat and tares. The sword of Jesus cuts into families. Normally, the sword is a metonym for warfare. That's part of what Jesus means. In verses 35-36, Jesus quotes a series of phrases from Micah 7, where the prophet describes a time of social and political chaos. Because the wicked "thorns" dominate Israel, the Lord is sending an invader and the Jews can't trust one another (Micah 7:1-6). Jesus' ministry brings a similar crisis. Some family members turn to Jesus, some don't. When later the Romans invade, family divisions become even more intense. Jesus demands that His disciples cling to Him, even if it costs them all the security, affection, and benefits of family life (v. 37).

So there are various dynamics at work here. But it's important to feel the force of what Jesus says, and the way He says it in verses 34-35. He doesn't say that this is an accident, an unfortunate and unintended after-effect of His mission. He says that He came to do this. He came to bring a sword, not peace, and He came to set family members against one another. Jesus says He's the one who comes with a sword. In the background of Jesus' words here are images from the Psalms and Prophets about the Lord coming with a sword to Israel (cf. Psalm 7:12; Isaiah 49:2; Jeremiah 12:12). What is the purpose of the incarnation? Why the God man? The purpose of the incarnation is to bring salvation and health. But Jesus here says that there is another purpose to the incarnation, which is to bring division and hostility. Peace is the ultimate aim, but the way to peace is through division and conflict. Hebrews speaks of the Word as a sword that cuts between joints and marrow, a sword that prepares people for sacrifice by dividing them in pieces. That's another dimension of Jesus' teaching here. He brings a sword of sacrifice, to cut Israel in pieces, to cut families in pieces, so that they can be laid on an altar and ascend to the Father, transfigured in smoke. He is the Prince of Peace, but before He brings in the peace of the kingdom, He brings in a sword.

Jesus has to do this because of the power of the family. Though we don't like to think of it, Jesus sees that He has to bring a sword against families because families are one of the biggest obstacles to the advance of the faith. God can use families to advance His kingdom, of course. The family is one of the main means God uses to fill the world with believers and worshipers. The close ties, the emotional bonds, the loyalties of family life often present tremendous obstacles to discipleship.[14]

The Jews were protective of family, blood ties, loyalties in clans and nation. And this was an obstacle to Jesus' call in the same way that being Iranian today is an obstacle to Jesus' call. Respond to Jesus' call in Iran, and you're in significant danger. It is simply very difficult to respond to the call, and you literally give up your whole social world. If the family is going to flourish,

---

14. After the exile, the natural bonds of Jewish family life were reinforced by the need for maintaining strict marital boundaries between Jews and others. N.T. Wright quotes George Foot Moore: "In the conditions that existed in Judaea in the age of the restoration and afterwards, an urgent part of the task of the religious leaders was to resist the admixture of heathenism and lapses from Judaism through the intimate relations between Jews and the surrounding peoples, and especially through intermarriage." This is not unique to Jews, or to this period, but the Jews "had more reason than others. Under Persian rule, they did not exist as an independent nation. 'They had only a national religion, and in its preservation lay their self-preservation.'" As Moore says, "The separateness of the Jews, their *amixia*, was one of the prime causes of the animosity toward them, especially in the miscellaneous fusion of people and syncretism of religions in the Hellenistic kingdoms and the Roman world; but it accomplished its end in the survival of Judaism, and therein history has vindicated it" (*Jesus and the Victory of God* [Minneapolis: Fortress, 1997], p. 399).

and if Jesus' kingdom is going to be proclaimed, then a sword must be brought against families: Division and destruction, in order to be transfigured and raised again. In this setting, if a man was not willing to give up everything, his whole familial-social network for the sake of Christ, He would not be a worthy disciple.

Matthew 10:38 is Jesus' first reference to the "cross," the first in the New Testament. Significantly, it refers not to Jesus' own cross, but to the cross of the disciples. Christians have often understood Jesus' words about cross-bearing as a general exhortation about suffering. We are to take up our cross in the sense that we have an illness, or we have a difficult husband or boss, or the pipes keep busting, or our car doesn't work right. The generic frustration of life is our cross. I don't want to minimize the importance of that kind of frustration for our spiritual growth. We are tested in all kinds of tiny ways, and if we are faithful in those little things we are being prepared to be faithful in larger things. If we can deal with the frustration of a busted radiator, or a computer program that won't work, we are ready to deal with larger ones.

But that is *not* what Jesus is talking about here in this passage. In the context, it refers to the threats of mission and specifically the threat of being cut off from families. In the chiastic structure of the passage, it links to Jesus' warnings about persecution (vv. 16-23). Jesus is not talking about generic suffering. He's talking about the suffering we endure as a result of opposition in the course of mission. When people hate us as we go about proclaiming the kingdom of Jesus, healing the sick, raising the dead, driving out demons, then we are bearing the cross and following Jesus. When our own fathers and mothers and brothers and sisters and daughters and sons turn against us because we are following Jesus, then we are taking up our cross, because Jesus Himself was opposed by "His own." It's even more specific than that. Jesus doesn't just say that family members will oppose us; He says that they will deliver us up to death. Our closest friends and family members will be willing to deliver us over to death. *That* is the cross Jesus has in mind. Jesus is talking about the real possibility of death, the real threat that the families of the Twelve will turn them over to the Romans for execution.

For the Twelve, the cross that Jesus warns about is literally a cross. The cross has become such a common symbol that we forget both what it was for and what role it played in Jewish and Roman life. The Twelve literally have to be ready to die on Roman crosses, since their families members will deliver them to Gentile governors. The Roman governors are going to put them on crosses. The cross is an instrument of torturous death. It is a method of execution. "Sit in your electric chair and follow Me," Jesus says; take up the lethal injection and follow Me. And the cross was often reserved specifically for Jewish revolutionaries who were opposing Rome. The Romans knew how to send a message of disapproval: If the Jews start fighting, then put a few dozen on crosses around Jerusalem, and they'll get the message. In the midst of this, Jesus assures them that this apparent loss of life is actually the way to life (v. 39). The cross is not a path of failure and destruction. It is an instrument of death, but in giving ourselves to this death for Jesus' sake, we're finding life rather than losing it. Precisely by provoking this kind of opposition, the Twelve will be serving one of the purposes of the kingdom. By provoking opposition, the Twelve will be laborers in the harvest, separating wheat and tares. The Twelve go out bearing Jesus' authority and carrying on His mission. They are His representatives, and therefore receiving them is equivalent to receiving Jesus Himself (v. 40).

There is another level to the chiasm of sending and reception: The Father sent Jesus who sent the Twelve; receiving the Twelve is receiving Jesus and the Father. Jesus is satisfied with minimal reception. The Twelve are "prophets," "righteous men," and "little ones" (vv. 41-42), and whoever gives them as little as a cup of cold water receives a reward. This is a remarkable statement. Jesus promises rewards to people who do no more than show basic human kindness to the Twelve. We should again remember the situation. The Twelve arouse opposition and murderous hostility, and anyone who gives them cold water or a simple meal *in those circumstances* is also risking a lot. They too are risking being cut off from families—"What!? One of those Apostles came, and you let him in the house!? Do you want to be His disciple too? We're disciples of Moses, not this Jesus." So, we shouldn't minimize the courage it would take to do these simple acts of kindness.

At the same time, it's striking that Jesus doesn't expect everyone to join in with the Twelve. He doesn't limit His rewards to those who engage in a dramatic public ministry. He doesn't even limit His rewards to people who give open and active support to the Twelve. A cup of cold water is pretty minimal, and yet Jesus has promises for these too. We are far stingier than Jesus.[15] Before we promise people rewards for serving Jesus, we want to see some *real* commitment. Cup of cold water! Hah! We want sackcloth and ashes and a memorized catechism and dotting the T in the five points of Calvinism, and all that. We want to see someone become a prophet before He can receive a prophet's reward. Jesus' generosity, however, far exceeds anything we're comfortable with. His generosity is so free and overabundant that we find it offensive. How *dare* Jesus give a righteous man's reward to the guy who did nothing but receive me, when I've put in a lot of time and effort to becoming a righteous man! We are like Jonah, offended at the freedom, the prodigality, the waste of God's mercy.

The chapter break here is not a good one. Each of Jesus' discourses in Matthew ends with a statement about Jesus finishing His words. Like the Sermon on the Mount (7:28), this discourse ends with the report that "Jesus finished commanding His twelve disciples" (11:1). The phrase reminds us of Genesis 2:1. God spoke for six days, and then His creative work was "finished." God formed and divided and rearranged things for six days, and then He sat back and saw that His finished world was good. God doesn't face any opposition in creation, but the creation

---

15. Jesus shows Himself to be like David, who shared the plunder of his war with the Amalekites with the men who stayed behind to keep the baggage.

week includes acts of dividing and separating. When God acts to recreate the world after the fall, these creative acts of dividing and separating become acts of violence, but they have the same end – to make the world new. Now, Jesus, the living Word, speaks the word of new creation. He gives instructions to the Twelve, words of new creation, and as the Twelve—and we—carry out these words of new creation, Jesus is bringing His sword to divide and break and destroy. But then, like His Father, His words will finish, and the mission will finish, and the world will be renewed. Then Jesus will sit enthroned on His kingdom, and rest, knowing that all his works are "good."

The Greatest Prophet
Matthew 11:1-19

When Jesus had finished giving instructions to His twelve disciples, He departed from there to teach and preach in their cities. ² Now when John, while imprisoned, heard of the works of Christ, he sent word by his disciples ³ and said to Him, "Are You the Expected One, or shall we look for someone else?" ⁴ Jesus answered and said to them, "Go and report to John what you hear and see: ⁵ the blind receive sight and the lame walk, the lepers are cleansed and the deaf hear, the dead are raised up, and the poor have the gospel preached to them. ⁶ "And blessed is he who (H)does not take offense at Me." ⁷ As these men were going away, Jesus began to speak to the crowds about John, "What did you go out into(I)the wilderness to see? A reed shaken by the wind? ⁸ "But what did you go out to see? A man dressed in soft clothing? Those who wear soft clothing are in kings' palaces! ⁹ "But what did you go out to see? A prophet? Yes, I tell you, and one who is more than a prophet. ¹⁰ "This is the one about whom it is written, 'Behold, I send My messenger ahead of you, who will prepare your way before you.' ¹¹ "Truly I say to you, among those born of women there has not arisen anyone greater than John the Baptist! Yet the one who is least in the kingdom of heaven is greater than he. ¹² "From the days of John the Baptist until now the kingdom of heaven suffers violence, and violent men take it by force. [13] "For all the prophets and the Law prophesied until John. [14] "And if you are willing to accept it, John himself is Elijah who was to come. [15] "He who has ears to hear, let him hear. [16] "But to what shall I compare this generation? It is like children sitting in the market places, who call out to the other children, [17] and say, 'We played the flute for you, and you did not dance; we sang a dirge, and you did not mourn.' [18] "For John came neither eating nor drinking, and they say, 'He has a demon!' [19] "The Son of Man came eating and drinking, and they say, 'Behold, a gluttonous man and a drunkard, a friend of tax collectors and sinners!' Yet wisdom is vindicated by her deeds." – Matthew 11:1-19

Matthew's gospel is a replay of Israel's history, and this replay occurs at two different levels. On the one hand, Jesus relives Israel's history and does it faithfully. He is the Son, the true Israel, called out of Egypt, baptized in the sea, tempted in the wilderness. He is the new Moses, declaring the Lord's law from a mountaintop and sending His apostles out into the land for conquest; He is a new Solomon, teaching in riddles and parables about the character of His kingdom; He is the new Elisha, who comes on the heels of the prophet Elijah; He is the new Jeremiah, announcing the doom on the temple and the scattering of Israel. He is the true Israel, thrown into the grave of exile, and returning from the grave to receive all authority and to send His disciples into the world like a new Cyrus. On the other hand, Israel also lives through her history all over again. She is confronted by Jesus, the New Moses, the new Solomon, the new Elisha, the new Jeremiah. She is put to the test again. She is being called to renew covenant and to repent in the face of the coming of the kingdom.

To understand what Matthew is teaching us, we need to keep our eyes on both of these levels. We need to recognize both that Jesus is the true Israel living through Israel's history but doing it right; we also have to recognize that *Israel* is Israel, confronted with God's messengers and servants and doing it all wrong, again.

That's where we are in the narrative when we begin chapter 11. Jesus comes healing, casting out demons, raising the dead, preaching the good news to the poor. His ministry to Israel started in chapter 4, with His healing and teaching and exorcisms; we have seen Him teaching the people from the mountaintop, telling them how they are to produce a righteousness that surpasses the righteousness of the scribes and Pharisees. Then for two chapters we saw Him at work healing and raising the dead and casting out demons. He enlisted the Twelve to do the same, sending them to carry on His work. Jesus summarizes His own work in His response to John's disciples here in chapter 11: "the blind receive sight and the lame walk, the lepers are cleansed and the deaf hear, and the dead are raised up, and the poor have the gospel preached to them" (v. 5). The question now is, How will Israel respond? *Will* she receive Him? Or will she reject Him as they rejected Moses and the house of David and Elijah and Jeremiah? Chapters 11-12 are about this response, the initial response of Israel to the coming-again of Yahweh's messengers, rulers, and judges.

Chapter 11 is divided into three sections. Verses 1-19 concern the role of John the Baptist; in verses 20-24 Jesus condemns three cities of Galilee for rejecting Him; and in verses 25-30 Jesus praises His Father for withholding the kingdom from the proud and revealing it to babes. Each section begins with a question (vv. 3, 7, 16). John's disciples ask Jesus "Are you the Expected One?" Then after they go away, Jesus asks the crowd about John: "What did you go out into the wilderness to look at?" And then at the end he asks, again to the multitude, "To what shall I compare this generation?" Each section also talks about some "coming." John wants to know if Jesus is the "coming one" (v. 3), and Jesus speaks of John as "Elijah who was to come" (v. 14) and of John and the Son of Man coming, though in different ways (vv. 18-19). The whole section is enclosed by references to "works": the "works of Christ" in v 2 and the "works of wisdom" in v. 19.

The first section has to do with Jesus' identity. John has been in prison since the beginning of Jesus' ministry (4:12), but he has received reports of Jesus' work (11:2). He knows something of Jesus' activities, and Jesus puzzles him. He prophesied an imminent judgment; the "axe is already laid at the root of the trees" (3:10). But instead of cutting down trees, Jesus is restoring them. If Jesus is the Messiah, why is John still languishing in prison? Why haven't the prison doors burst open? Can this be the judgment that John predicted? It doesn't look like judgment. Jesus is restoring rather than judging Israel. John has predicted that Jesus is the one who will "come after me" and who will baptize with Spirit and fire, who has the winnowing fork in his hand and is going to gather wheat and also burn the chaff (3:11). Where's the winnowing fork? Where's the fire?

This is the same odd sequence we find in 1-2 Kings. Elijah goes to Horeb, where Moses delivered the law, and He accuses Israel of abandoning Yahweh and tearing down His altars and persecuting His prophets. Yahweh agrees with Elijah's assessment of things and declares that it's time to act. He's going to do something to end the evils of the house of Ahab through Jehu and Elisha (1 Kings 19:15-18). Jehu does carry out a judgment against the house of Ahab, a massive one that leads to the death of a large number of the members of the royal house. But before Jehu ever appears on the scene, we have the ministry of Elisha, and Elisha doesn't seem to do anything that punishes Israel. Elisha leaves a few dead bodies around—the 42 young men who mock him and are killed by bears. Mostly, though, Elisha is doing good. He heals a Syrian leper, feeds some prophets who are without food, and restores property to widows. He raises the dead and gives advice to the kings of Israel and Judah. Elijah wasn't around to see all this, but we can imagine His reaction: "Where is the sword of Elisha? He's barely killing anyone. Are you the Coming One, or do we look for another?" Later in Matthew 11, Jesus identifies John as "Elijah who was to come," the new Elijah prophesied by Malachi. That means that Jesus is Elisha, carrying on the ministry of Elisha and fulfilling exactly the prophecies of judgment that the new Elijah delivered.

To see how it is judgment, we need to look deeper than Jesus does. We need to recognize that Jesus is dividing and sifting Israel, as people respond to His ministry with either faith or unbelief. Precisely by showing mercy, giving sight to the blind, healing the lame and cleansing lepers, Jesus is bringing a sword to Israel, because Israel is not going to respond. The winnowing fork is the winnowing fork of mercy to Israel. Those who want to be with Jesus form a new community around Him, the true Israel. Those who reject Him are the chaff that is thrown into the fire. Jesus answers John's disciples by quoting a series of phrases from Isaiah (26:19; 29:18; 35:5-6; 42:7; 61:1). These are passages that talk about the restoration of Israel after exile, the Lord's return to Zion, and His resurrection of the people of God. How does this answer the question? Jesus doesn't give any new information to John. If John has heard about His works, he has no doubt heard that Jesus makes the blind to see, the lame to walk, and the deaf to hear, and so on.

This is an answer to the question in several ways. It gives John a context to understand what Jesus is doing. He is doing all these miraculous signs, but what do they mean? Jesus quotes from Isaiah to indicate to John that these are all part of a larger program, the redemption and restoration of Israel. More specifically, Jesus cites only parts of the passages He quotes. He cites those portions of Isaiah that describe His ministry of healing and teaching, but He leaves out portions of the same prophecies that talk about the judgment that Yahweh is bringing on the wicked. He quotes from Isaiah 35:5: "Then the eyes of the blind shall be opened, and the ears of the deaf shall be unstopped." But the previous verse says, "your God will come with vengeance, with the recompense of God." Jesus quotes only positive parts of the prophecy, but by putting His work in the context of Isaiah, He is saying that He is fulfilling the entire prophecy. He does the same thing in His citation of Isaiah 61. He quotes verse 1, which says that the Spirit-anointed Servant of Yahweh will "preach good tidings to the poor," but He doesn't quote from verse 2, which says that the Servant will "proclaim the acceptable year of the Lord, and the day of vengeance of our God." Jesus is telling John that His work is part of a larger design, and that this design does include chopping down the trees and putting the unfruitful trees into the fire. But it's not time for that yet.

Jesus also includes some things in his list that are not included in Isaiah. Isaiah talks about blind and deaf and lame being healed, but Isaiah says nothing about lepers being cleansed or the dead being raised. Jesus says that His ministry actually goes beyond the hopes of Isaiah and the prophets. It includes everything they hoped for but includes something more as well. Jesus ends with a blessing: "blessed is he who is not scandalized by me." That is, blessed is anyone who doesn't stumble at what Jesus is doing. The stumbling block here is Jesus' ministry of mercy rather than judgment. All the Jews who were hoping for redemption were hoping for fire to burn up compromised Jews, Jewish sinners, and the Romans. Jesus brings fire, but not at first. First, He is going to gather the wheat, gather the wheat that doesn't appear very healthy.

The visit from John's disciples gives Jesus the opportunity to describe John's ministry. He asks a series of questions about who John is, about what people were expecting from him. Did they go into the wilderness to see reeds shaken by the wind? Or a man in soft clothing? Or a prophet? The answer to the second is clearly "No." John is not a man in soft clothing; he is not the kind of man found in kings' palaces. And the answer to the first also seems to be "No." John is not a reed shaken by the wind. The last one is the correct answer: John is a prophet, the greatest of the prophets, the last of the prophets before the coming of the kingdom.

Why would anyone think he was a reed or a man in soft clothing? Where would these alternatives come from? The best answer to that, I think, is that Jesus is alluding to various cryptic promises of the coming age, of the Messiah. Reeds aren't found in the wilderness, but by water. Putting together reed and wind and wilderness evokes Israel's exodus experience, when the Lord's wind blew back what Exodus calls the "Sea of Reeds" so that Israel could pass through and out of Egypt. Jesus is asking if the people gathered in the wilderness because John is a new Moses, who will lead them out of Egypt, and out of the wilderness, into the promised land. The reference to men in soft clothing in kings' palaces may be a reference to the promise of a coming Davidic king. Jesus is asking if the people went out to the wilderness in hopes of finding the Messiah.[16] The answer to that is "No." John is not the new Moses, nor a Davidic king. He is the prophet promised by Malachi 3 (v. 10), the prophet "Elijah" (v. 13). He is not the Coming One, but the one who comes to prepare for the Coming One.

John's work is the hinge point of redemptive history. With the "days of John," one phase of history comes to an end and a new one is about to begin. The phase of history that comes to an end is the phase of what Jesus, in an unusual phrase, calls "the prophets and the law," which "prophesy" until John (v. 13). Why does Jesus say that the time of the prophets and the law has come to an end with the "days of John"? Verse 12 gives the answer. Verse 12 is a difficult statement, interpreted in various ways. But the point seems to be about both the powerful progress of the kingdom, which begins with John, and the violent opposition that this progress unleashes. With John, God begins waging war against His enemies, and His enemies violently attack Him (v. 12).

Jews expected that prior to the triumph of the Messiah there would be a time of tribulation and apostasy. The prophets spoke of a time when the law would become ineffective and true prophecy would cease (Lamentations 2:9; Ezekiel 7:25-27; Zephaniah 3:3; Zechariah 7:19). John's ministry marks the beginning of this climactic battle, this cosmic warfare between the kingdom of God and the forces of evil. John's ministry initiates the Messianic tribulation, a time of lawlessness and false prophecy when the prophets and law are silenced. This is the time that Israel is in, the time of the kingdom. The climax of Israel's history has arrived, and yet many of the Jews are tone-deaf to the tune of the times (vv. 16-17).

John called Israel to repentance and mourning, but Israel said he was demon-possessed (v. 18). John did not bring in the kingdom. He did not bring a new Exodus, and he was not the king in the Davidic line. But he was the preparation for all that.

---

16. See Davies and Allison, *Matthew 8-18* (Continuum, 2004), p. 247.

He was the prophet that was going to restore all things before the Lord's coming. But the Jews didn't listen. They wouldn't accept his prophetic warnings. Instead, they put him in prison and eventually killed him. The days of John are the transition, and when the days of John come to an end, especially with his death, then the tribulation will begin in earnest. On the other hand, Jesus comes feasting, but they charge Him with being a rebellious youth (v. 19; cf. Deuteronomy 21:20) and condemn Him for associating with publicans and sinners. Yet Jesus is the Wisdom of God (v. 19), and His works speak for themselves and will vindicate Him.

"This generation" is the generation of John and Jesus. And "this generation" also brings to mind the generation of Israel that came out of Egypt, that rejected the leadership of Moses, and that fell in the wilderness. This generation went out into the wilderness perhaps expecting a new exodus. What they found was a prophet, and the prophet didn't live up to expectations. This generation, like the first generation of the exodus, is going to fall in the wilderness and never enter the promised land. But their children will.

Though John's ministry is unique, and Jesus' of course is also unique, what Jesus says here is permanently relevant. There are times in our individual lives, and times in the life of a church, or of the church as a whole, when a new tune begins to be played. There are times when God calls us to mourn, and times when God calls us to dance. Our response to those times is eternally relevant. Refusing to mourn when God sings a dirge will make us like the generation of Jesus, lost and wandering in the wilderness. Refusing to dance when the Lord plays a wedding song will also leave us in the wilderness. There is no question more crucial than, What time is it? What music is playing? But there is also no more difficult question to answer. Jesus' reference to Wisdom is not gratuitous. Wisdom is insight into the time. There is a time to mourn, and a time to dance; there is a time to laugh, and a time to weep; there is a time to gather, and a time to scatter; a time to give life and a time to kill. Wisdom is knowing what time it is, and this kind of wisdom only comes from the Living Wisdom, the Incarnate Wisdom, who has promised to give us the Spirit of wisdom.

The Yoke of Jesus
Matthew 11:20-30[17]

> Then He began to denounce the cities in which most of His miracles were done, because they did not repent. [21]"Woe to you, Chorazin! Woe to you, Bethsaida! For if the miracles had occurred in Tyre and Sidon which occurred in you, they would have repented long ago in sackcloth and ashes. [22] Nevertheless I say to you, it will be more tolerable for Tyre and Sidon in the day of judgment than for you. [23] And you, Capernaum, will not be exalted to heaven, will you? You will descend to Hades; for if the miracles had occurred in Sodom which occurred in you, it would have remained to this day. [24] Nevertheless I say to you that it will be more tolerable for the land of Sodom in the day of judgment, than for you." [25] At that time Jesus said, "I praise You, Father, Lord of heaven and earth, that You have hidden these things from the wise and intelligent and have revealed them to infants. [26] Yes, Father, for this way was well-pleasing in Your sight. [27] All things have been handed over to Me by My Father; and no one knows the Son except the Father; nor does anyone know the Father except the Son, and anyone to whom the Son wills to reveal Him. [28] Come to Me, all who are weary and heavy-laden, and I will give you rest. [29] Take My yoke upon you and learn from Me, for I am gentle and humble in heart, and you will find rest for your souls. [30] For My yoke is easy and My burden is light." – Matthew 11:20-30

---

17. Matthew 11:25-27 is organized as a modified chiasm:
    A. Father hides and reveals as is well-pleasing, vv 25-26
      B. Father gives all to the Son, v 27a
        C. No one knows Son, v 27b
          D. except the Father, v 27c
          D'. No one knows Father, v 27d
        C'. except the Son, v 27e
   A'. Son reveals as He wills, v 27f

Tyre and Sidon were twin Phoenician cities, north of Israel on the coast of the Mediterranean, two of the greatest trading cities of the ancient world. From these Phoenician ports, ships sailed to establish colonies all over the Mediterranean, most famously at Carthage in North Africa. According to some historians, Phoenician ships sailed past the Strait of Gibraltar and got to the Americas. Because of their trading, Tyre and Sidon became extremely wealthy. In Scripture, Tyre and Sidon were known as Canaanite cities. Sidon was the firstborn of Canaan, and as a result the city of Sidon was the prototypical Canaanite city. Yet it was not always so. During the days of Solomon, Hiram king of Tyre helped Solomon with the temple, sending materials and craftsmen to build Yahweh's house in Jerusalem. When Solomon wrote to Hiram asking for help, Hiram responded by saying, "Blessed be Yahweh today, who has given to David a wise son over this great people" (1 Kings 5:7). Hiram was using the covenant name of the God of Israel, blessing the God of Israel for keeping His promise to set a son of David on his throne. As a result, "there was peace between Hiram and Solomon, and the two of them made a covenant" (5:12). That peace between Tyre/Sidon and Israel, and the faith of Hiram, were not to last. During the monarchy, a Sidonian princess became queen of the Northern kingdom of Israel; her name was Jezebel, and her promotion of Baal worship and persecution of the prophets was characteristic of the Canaanite culture from which she came. Sometime between Hiram and Jezebel, Tyre and Sidon had reverted to their earlier Canaanite ways. They turned from Yahweh and from Israel, and the prophets regularly condemn the cities of Tyre and Sidon for their unfaithfulness.

Tyre and Sidon, along with a dozen other cities and peoples, are going to drink the cup of the wrath of Yahweh, Jeremiah warned, and then they are going to drink and stagger and go mad, and eventually fall (Jeremiah 25). Ezekiel devotes a long chapter (27) to the fall of Tyre, celebrating Tyre's beauty and wealth, wealth gathered from all over the world (cf. vv. 3b-9). Ezekiel also warned that Tyre was going to fall. Judgment day was coming (vv. 27-32). The wealth and glory of Tyre and Sidon were considerable. More, they were Canaanite cities that turned to Yahweh during the reign of Solomon. They turned back to their own gods, rejected Yahweh, and were destroyed. What could be worse? Yet Jesus said that there was something worse.

We all know about Sodom. We know that the wickedness of the cities was so great that its cry rose to the Lord. We know that the men of the city tried to break down Lot's door so that they could get to know the angels whom Lot had welcomed into his house. Ezekiel condemns Sodom for its mistreatment of the poor and needy, and their treatment of the angels is consistent with this. Instead of welcoming the strangers and giving them hospitality, they wanted to gang rape them. This was hospitality, Sodom-style. The cities were destroyed when fire rained down from heaven and burned them and all their inhabitants. The destruction of Sodom became an archetype of Yahweh's judgment of the wicked, and the wickedness of Sodom became an archetype of human wickedness. When the prophets wanted to condemn Israel and Judah in the strongest terms, they could not do worse than address them as Sodom (Isaiah 3:9; Jeremiah 23:14; cf. Jeremiah 49:17-19). Judgment day came to Sodom and Gomorrah, and they were utterly destroyed, without inhabitant, without walls or streets or buildings or anything. What could be worse than the evils of Sodom? What could be worse than fire falling from heaven to destroy the cities? Yet, Jesus said that there was something worse.

The worse thing that Jesus talks about is the sin of the Galilean cities of Chorazin, Bethsaida, and Capernaum. The worse thing is the judgment that is coming on them. These are towns in Jesus' own district, and Matthew has mentioned that Jesus "settled" in Capernaum (4:13). This is His own home town.

"Woe," Jesus says, because these cities of Galilee are more hardened than Tyre, Sidon, and Sodom. If the miracles of Jesus had been done in these cities, they would have responded. But the Galilean cities did not. And Jesus also says that it is worse because of the judgment that is coming. The "day of judgment" here is not the final day of judgment. Sodom, Tyre, Sidon, and the other cities will not appear before the judgment seat of Christ on the last day. Rather, it's talking about moments of judgment in history. The day of Galilee's visitation will be more severe than the day of Sodom's destruction, or the day when Alexander conquered Tyre.

This doesn't look like a greater sin, and can there really be a greater judgment? Sodom committed sodomy; how can the sin of the Galilean cities be worse than that? Tyre and Sidon worshiped Baals; how can Chorazin's sin be worse than that? Jesus says it is. The great sin of Galilee was rejecting or being indifferent to Jesus; because they have been blind to the greatest light, they are more culpable. Hebrews compares the threats of the Mosaic law to the threats of the New Covenant: If those who violated the law received punishment for their transgressions, "how shall we escape if we neglect so great a salvation" (2:2-3; cf. Hebrews 10:28-29). The greater the revelation, the greater the responsibility. Christians have received much more than Israel did, much more even than the cities of Galilee. Greater things have been done than Jesus did, by His apostles and His church, through the Spirit, for 2000 years. If Chorazin, Bethsaida, and Capernaum were worse off in the day of judgment than Tyre, Sidon, and Sodom, what will it be like for us in the day of judgment if we ignore Him?

The condemnation of Capernaum is stated differently than the condemnation of Chorazin and Bethsaida. For the first two, Jesus simply points to the miracles that had been done, and the failure of the cities to repent. In verse 23, though, He describes Capernaum as a city that apparently attempted, without success, to be exalted to heaven. The phrase alludes to the taunt against Babylon in Isaiah 14: "you said in your heart," the taunters will say to the king of Babylon, "I will arise to heaven, I will raise my throne above the stars of God, and I will sit on the mount of assembly, in the recesses of the North" (v. 13). Yet, Babylon's real destiny is quite different: "you will be thrust down to Sheol, to the recesses of the pit" (v. 14). Likewise, Capernaum exalts herself to heaven, but will be thrown down to Hades. Capernaum is the city in which Jesus Himself settled. Heaven came to earth and settled in Capernaum, but instead of being exalted by welcoming the home town boy's disciples, they rejected Jesus and are going to be brought to Hades. They had been exalted like Babylon, but they are going to fall as dramatically as Babylon.

Jesus' reproach of Capernaum sets us up for the following prayer that Jesus addresses to the Father. Reflecting on His reception in Galilee, Jesus turns to the Father in one of the most profound prayers in the New Testament. Jesus addresses the Father, and He addresses Him as the One who hides and reveals. He is not only the "Father," but is "Lord of heaven and earth," and His Lordship is manifest in hiding and revealing. As Lord, He shows "these things" to some people, and He hides "these things" from others. Why do some receive Jesus and some not? Why do some know "these things" and others find them puzzling or offensive? Jesus says that it's because the Father, the Lord of heaven and earth, hides and reveals. The whole is a prayer of praise. Jesus speaks of the Father's Lordship and His sovereign good-pleasure in revealing and hiding, but He doesn't treat it as something to fear, or as a debating point. It is an occasion for praise. When the Father hides and reveals, Jesus is motivated to praise the Father, the Lord of heaven and earth.

Specifically, the Father hides things from the "wise and intelligent" and reveals them to "babes." Jesus is using "wise and intelligent" with some irony. A truly wise response to the gospel of the kingdom would be to embrace it. Wisdom is vindicated by her deeds. Jesus means those who consider themselves wise and intelligent, the learned, the scholars and scribes of the law, the Pharisees and the educated Jews. They are the ones who reject Jesus. And the Father hides the things of the kingdom from them. Babes, on the other hand, are those who don't consider themselves wise and intelligent. They have not received training. They are not intelligent and well-educated by the world's standards. They are ignorant bumpkins. But these are the ones who receive the revelation of the Father, and know "these things."

In context, Jesus is talking about the varying response of the cities of Galilee. The sequence of events is: Jesus comes to Galilee preaching and doing the miracles of the kingdom. Then He sends out the Twelve to do the same. In that sense, the Father reveals Himself and His kingdom to the cities of Galilee. They have seen Jesus and all He does. But the cities of Galilee reject Jesus. They are proud, arrogant, think themselves wise, and so they are passed over. Those who recognize their need and their weakness and their ignorance, those who are humble and receptive, they come to know the kingdom. The Father does this for His own good pleasure, because it delights Him. That is, He reveals and hides by His good pleasure, but more specifically He reveals to babes and hides from the proud and self-inflated for His good pleasure. God delights in reversing the expectations and standards of the world. He takes pleasure is exalting the humble and debasing the proud. This is all set in a Trinitarian context. The Son is the Father's channel of revelation. Jesus claims that He has received "all things" from His Father (cf. Matthew 28:18-20), and that the Father and Son have an exclusive relationship of knowledge and love.

Jesus, like the scribes, has received something "handed over," a "tradition." But His tradition comes directly from the Father. Though the Father and Son have an exclusive relationship with one another, yet through the Son the mutual knowledge of Father and Son is opened up to babes (v. 27). No one knows or comes to the Father except through Jesus, who reveals the Father to whomever He will. This deepens our understanding of what is hidden and revealed. Jesus says "these things" in verse 25, talking about His kingdom and the things that He and His disciples have been doing. The significance of Jesus' work and teaching is revealed and hidden. But "these things" that are revealed and hidden are part of the "all things" that have been handed from the Son to the Father. "These things" are also connected to the mutual, exclusive knowledge of the Father and Son. Jesus focuses on His exclusive relationship with the Father. He alone knows the Father, and the Father alone knows the Son. When the Father reveals "these things" to babes, He is revealing Himself; when the Son reveals the Father to babes, that means that the babes are being brought into the mutual and exclusive relationship of love and knowledge that exists between Father and Son.

Jesus is already alluding to Exodus 33:12-14 in verse 27, and the reference to the "yoke" and "rest" extends the comparison with Moses. "Yoke" is a common image for Mosaic law and for submission to any leader. Kings place yokes on their people, put them into service to them. Jesus is a new Moses who offers Sabbath rest, deliverance from the burdens of Pharisaical "Egypt." Yet, Jesus' claims surpass Moses. Jews spoke of the "yoke of the Torah" but never of the "yoke of Moses." No teacher claimed that the yoke was his own yoke, but Jesus does. He is making a claim beyond any teacher in Israel, identifying His own teaching with the yoke that His disciples wear. This is a claim to be the giver of law, not merely the mediator of law. This is a claim that He is Himself the embodiment of Torah (cf. Jeremiah 6:16).

Contrary to the beliefs of some Christians, Jesus *has* a yoke. His disciples are obligated to obey Him and work for Him. Because Jesus is "meek" (like Moses, Numbers 12:3) though, His yoke is easy and His burden light. There are two errors to avoid here. On the one hand, there is the route of easy faith. Jesus, we might believe, gets rid of the law and doesn't impose any requirements on His disciples. Jesus comes to bring an end to orders and commandments of every kind. Jesus comes to break *every* yoke, every possible yoke. That is not what Jesus says. He does come with a yoke. Work animals wear yokes. Jesus comes to place a yoke on us, so that we can participate in the harvest. Jesus does demand a certain kind of life from His disciples. On the other hand, there is the route of harsh and grinding legalism. Once we say that Jesus brings a yoke, we're tempted to weigh down the yoke. Jesus brings a yoke, but we think Jesus lets people off too easy. In the following chapter, there is a series of debates about the Sabbath. Jesus brings Sabbath rest, but the Jews use the law to oppress and prevent Sabbath.

Jesus issues an invitation. He has spoken of the Father's Lordship in hiding and revealing, but He doesn't see this as incompatible with an open invitation. He invites "all" who wish to come. How can we know that the Father will reveal "these things" to us if we come? How can we know that we are among the "babes" to whom the Son reveals the Father? That's obvious: If we come to Jesus, and receive His yoke, and learn of Him, and imitate and share in His humility, then clearly we are babes. The wise and intelligent refuse the yoke. The wise and intelligent refuse the yoke, especially the yoke of a yokel like Jesus. They refuse to learn from an unlearned man. The invitation is to all who are weary and weighed down. It doesn't matter what is weighing down. He probably has the Jews oppressed by the Pharisaical tradition particularly in mind, but the invitation is broader. What burdens are you carrying around? The burden of guilt for past sin? Come to Jesus: He gives rest. The burden of worry over money or career? Come to Jesus: His yoke is easy. The burden of battered relationships with your siblings, your parents, your wife, your husband, your classmates? Come to Jesus: His load is light. Are you just tired of it all, weary of life and its strains and stresses? Come to Jesus, and "you shall find rest for your souls."

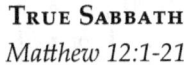

True Sabbath
Matthew 12:1-21

At that time Jesus went through the grainfields on the Sabbath, and His disciples became hungry and began to pick the heads of grain and eat. ²But when the Pharisees saw this, they said to Him, "Look, Your disciples do what is not lawful to do on a Sabbath." ³But He said to them, "Have you not read what David did when he became hungry, he and his companions, ⁴ how he entered the house of God, and they ate the consecrated bread, which was not lawful for him to eat nor for those with him, but for the priests alone? ⁵Or have you not read in the Law, that on the Sabbath the priests in the temple break the Sabbath and are innocent? ⁶But I say to you that something greater than the temple is here. ⁷But if you had known what this means,

'I desire compassion, and not a sacrifice,' you would not have condemned the innocent. ⁸ For the Son of Man is Lord of the Sabbath." ⁹ Departing from there, He went into their synagogue. ¹⁰ And a man was there whose hand was withered. And they questioned Jesus, asking, "Is it lawful to heal on the Sabbath?"—so that they might accuse Him. ¹¹ And He said to them, "What man is there among you who has a sheep, and if it falls into a pit on the Sabbath, will he not take hold of it and lift it out? ¹² "How much more valuable then is a man than a sheep! So then, it is lawful to do good on the Sabbath." ¹³ Then He said to the man, "Stretch out your hand!" He stretched it out, and it was restored to normal, like the other. ¹⁴ But the Pharisees went out and conspired against Him, as to how they might destroy Him. ¹⁵ But Jesus, aware of this, withdrew from there. Many followed Him, and He healed them all, ¹⁶ and warned them not to tell who He was. ¹⁷ This was to fulfill what was spoken through Isaiah the prophet: ¹⁸ "Behold, My Servant whom I have chosen; My Beloved in whom My soul is well-pleased; I will put My Spirit upon Him, and He shall proclaim justice to the Gentiles. ¹⁹ He will not quarrel, nor cry out; nor will anyone hear His voice in the streets, ²⁰ A battered reed He will not break off, and a smoldering wick He will not put out, until He leads justice to victory. ²¹ And in His Name the Gentiles will hope." –Matthew 12:1-12

"Come to Me, all who are weary and heavy-laden, and I will give you rest. Take My yoke upon you and learn from Me, for I am gentle and humble in heart, and *you will find rest for your souls*. For My yoke is easy and My burden is light." Matthew ended chapter 11 with this invitation from Jesus. Jesus is the greater Moses, the One who brings the final rest that Moses prefigured. Moses did not lead Israel into rest in the land, and he himself did not enter into rest. Jesus is greater than Moses; He is the last Joshua, who does lead His new Israel into the land of rest and enters into rest Himself. In the first part of chapter 12, we have stories that illustrate how Jesus is the rest-giver. We see specific examples of how Jesus' yoke—though it is still really a yoke—is an easy yoke and a light burden.

He is the rest-giver because He relieves His disciples of the burdens of Pharisaical rules and regulations, rules and regulations that strangle rest and burden people rather than delivering them. He fights with the Pharisees over the interpretation of the Sabbath and shows that the Sabbath is for doing good and for giving relief, not for burdening. We see the contrast between the way the Pharisees and scribes apply the Torah and the way Jesus does. His yoke is easy and His burden light because of the way He interprets the law, *not* because He gets rid of the law.

The Sabbath was a central institution for first-century Jews. Along with circumcision, food laws, and other visible badges and institutions, the practice of the Sabbath marked the Jews out distinctly from the Gentiles.[18] Practicing the Sabbath was a way of memorializing the exodus, the defining event of Israel's history. In the exodus, Yahweh led Israel out of bondage, out of a situation where they worked with no rest, into rest and celebration. The goal of the Exodus was Sabbath.

This helps to explain why the issue of Sabbath-keeping was such a point of contention, why the Jewish leaders would decide after the second incident in the synagogue that they had to get rid of Jesus. This was a highly charged practice, one that carried a lot of Israel's identity and history with it. Violating the Sabbath was like spitting on your grandmother's grave, like turning traitor and supporting an enemy invader. It was an act of disloyalty, and Jesus, like Jeremiah before Him, had to go. Jesus was a Jew, and

---

18. David Garland writes, "The significance of the Sabbath went beyond the fact that it was one of the two positive commands in the decalogue. It was a sign of the exclusive relationship between Israel and God throughout the generations. . . . Many reveled in the fact that the Creator sanctified only Israel of all the nations to keep the sabbath. . . . The sabbath was therefore considered to be a symbol of what made Israel distinct and special to God, and by observing it Israel celebrated the act of creation and imitated God, who rested on the seventh day. . . . As a kind of national banner, the breach of the sabbath would have been similar to desecration of the flag in modern times; and it triggered similar reactions. Dishonoring the sabbath was viewed as part of Israel's apostasy that resulted in exile, according to Jeremiah" (*Reading Matthew: A Literary and Theological Commentary on the First Gospel* [Smyth & Helwys, 1999], p. 136).

He didn't contest the keeping of Sabbath. What He contested was a Sabbath-keeping, a way of observing and teaching the law, that didn't achieve the aims of the law. He challenged the way the Sabbath laws—and other laws—were twisted so far that they turned into the opposite – laws about rest that kept people restless.

The first incident is complex. Both the Pharisees' criticism of the disciples and Jesus' responses require some careful consideration. As Jesus' disciples walk through a field on the Sabbath, they pluck grain and eat it (12:1). They are hungry, and so they eat. If we walked through a field plucking bits of grain, we'd have the farmer after us with his shotgun. But the Pharisees don't object that the disciples are stealing grain that doesn't belong to them. And they're right not to object. According to the law, the needy and hungry were free to take grain from the corners of fields, though they were not permitted to take a sickle into the field in order to harvest. This is not theft but a form of gleaning, permitted by the law (cf. Leviticus 19:9-10; Deuteronomy 24:20-22). Beyond gleaning, the law permits travelers to eat enough grain or grapes from a neighbor's field to satisfy themselves, a practice known as "scrumping" (Deuteronomy 23:24-25).[19]

The Pharisees' objection is not our objection, which would be that the disciples are violating property rights. The objection has to do with timing. The laws concerning Sabbath-keeping are brief and leave the key term, work, undefined. They prohibit work and punish at least certain forms of Sabbath-breaking with death. But the laws don't define what constitutes work (cf. Exodus 20:8-11). Other parts of the Bible make the definition of work somewhat clearer. Gathering manna and firewood are prohibited, as are plowing and harvest, kindling a fire, trading, and carrying a load —all these qualify as "work."[20] Given the laws and the severe penalty attached to violations, the Jews naturally tried to figure

---

19. See David L. Baker, *Tight Fists or Open Hands?: Wealth and Poverty in Old Testament Law* (Grand Rapids: Eerdmans, 2009), pp. 248-250.

20. See R. T. France, *The Gospel of Matthew* (NICNT; Grand Rapids: Eerdmans, 2007), p. 455.

out the limits of the law. By the first century, the Jews had devoted a lot of attention to laying out the limits of work, how far you could walk on a Sabbath without working, how much you could prepare food without working, how much you could do in a field without working. The Pharisees' objection is that the disciples are working on the Sabbath. Taking grain and rubbing it to get the kernel is a kind of work. Jesus and His disciples are violating the Sabbath rules.

Jesus' response to this accusation is a complex one. He cites Old Testament examples, announces that something greater than the temple has come, quotes again from Hosea 6, and then announces that the Son of Man—Himself—is Lord of the Sabbath. The examples that He gives don't seem to fit very well, and this has been interpreted as Jesus renouncing the law of Sabbath as such. That's not what's going on. Jesus is, I submit, describing the true intention and purpose of the Sabbath. He is the true Sabbath-keeper, and He says that His disciples are "innocent" and later says that He has not violated the law in doing good on the Sabbath (v. 5, 12). Jesus doesn't literally mean that David broke the law, any more than He means that the priests break the Sabbath by offering sacrifice (v. 5). Both are innocent, and so are the apostles.

Jesus reminds them of the incident in which David and his men ate from the showbread, normally reserved for the priests (1 Samuel 21:1-7; cf. Leviticus 24:5-9). There are some analogies between Jesus and David. Jesus' disciples are hungry, as David's men were hungry. They meet opposition, as David's men faced the opposition of Saul. And the disciples are eating on a Sabbath, as David's men did. We know that David's men ate on the Sabbath because Ahimelech the priest says that the bread has just been changed and new bread put in. What is Jesus saying in bringing this case to the fore? With regard to the Sabbath, the emphasis is on the use of the law to relieve and show mercy. David and his men came to the tabernacle famished, starving. Ahimelech had no bread but the showbread, and he's faced with a choice: Withhold the bread so David and his men have to go on searching, or relieve their hunger by offering the showbread. The question is, Did

Yahweh give the showbread to the priests so that they could ignore need? It's ours and no one else's, even if the man is starving? Is the law designed to limit kindness and compassion or to promote it? Ahimelech concludes the latter – that the law exists to promote mercy, justice, and truth; the law doesn't exist for the sake of the law. The law exists for the sake of achieving these goods.

Jesus' point is also, centrally, about Himself: He is greater than David and greater than the temple (v. 6), and as Lord of the Sabbath He can rule about what constitutes Sabbath observance (v. 8). The issue He raises with the Pharisees is not simply about this or that Sabbath observance, but about who decides whether thus and such can be done on the Sabbath. Jesus does. Because Jesus is here, because Jesus is greater than David, then He has the authority to do what David did, authority that goes beyond what the run-of-the-mill Jew would dare. David takes the showbread, and Ahimelech gives him the showbread, because he is the anointed king. He also makes a comment about His opponents: The Pharisees have aligned themselves with Doeg the Edomite and Saul, who persecuted David and his men.[21] Jesus and His disciples are like David's men engaged in a war, a war of conquest, and like David they are hungry from battle and looking for food. They need provision. Jesus' emphasis in His second Old Testament example is similar. The priests are commanded to do work on the Sabbath. In fact, they have to do extra work on the Sabbath since they have to offer more sacrifices on the Sabbath than they do on other days. Yet, this is no violation of the Sabbath, since they are commanded to do this on the Sabbath. This is the way they keep Sabbath. Jesus doesn't mean they are breaking the law; by Pharisaical lights, they might be, but they aren't in reality.

In part, Jesus points to the complexity of the law. The law commands no work on the Sabbath. The same law requires the priests to do extra labor on the Sabbath, labor that is described as "service." The temple work is in some sense higher than the Sabbath rule that tells them to stop working. More importantly,

---

21. Wright, *Jesus and the Victory of God*, p. 394.

Jesus is again saying something about Himself. The fact that the priests work in the temple on the Sabbath means they are not breaking Sabbath. If they did the same work outside the temple on the Sabbath, they would be in violation. The temple makes their labor Sabbath labor instead of Sabbath violation. Jesus says that something greater than the temple is here: Jesus Himself is that greater-than-temple Something. He is the locus of the presence of God, the place where God dwells in fullness. As long as He's there with His disciples, their work, even if it was work, is legitimate work on the Sabbath. Where Jesus is, there is the temple and presence of God, and therefore the disciples are doing what is "not lawful" and yet are "innocent" (vv. 5, 7). Jesus is assuming a connection between His work and the work of His disciples and temple labor. He and His disciples form a traveling temple and traveling priesthood. This is central to Jesus' ministry. Whatever Jews would have sought from the temple they are now to seek from Jesus. They once sought cleansing for leprosy from the temple priests; now they go to Jesus. They looked for deliverance from the death of corpse defilement, but now they go to Jesus. They look for instruction from the priests, but Jesus is the one who provides instruction. Jesus is the center of a "counter-temple" movement, and that makes His disciples' labor priestly service on the Sabbath.

Both of Jesus' Old Testament illustrations concentrate on Him. He is the greater David, and because His disciples are the retinue of a great king, they eat from the showbread in the field. Jesus is the Greater Temple, and because of that His disciples' labor is temple service, lawful on the Sabbath. Both of these illustrate Jesus' claim at the end of the story: "the Son of Man is Lord of the Sabbath."

Along the way, Jesus also quotes from Hosea 6:6. In the midst of a condemnation of Ephraim, the Northern kingdom, for attention to their sacrifices and their lack of interest in righteousness and compassion, the Lord says "I desire mercy and not sacrifice." Jesus doesn't mean that compassion cancels out the need to look at the law. He's not saying that we can safely ignore the law so long as we act compassionately. Nor is He saying that the ritual laws are unimportant and irrelevant. He's saying that the true intent of the law is mercy and justice and truth. Compassion is the intent of the law, and Sabbath regulations, like the rest of the law, need to be interpreted in the light of that goal.

This is also the point of the second Sabbath incident in verses 9-14. In the second incident, the Pharisees try to trap Jesus by asking if it's lawful to heal on the Sabbath (v. 10). This shouldn't be an issue. The Sabbath laws require that we *give* rest (Exodus 20:8-11; Deuteronomy 5:12-15), and healing is a way of giving rest. Jesus' example follows this logic (vv. 11-12). Pulling a sheep from a pit is not an *exception* to Sabbath observance; the Sabbath laws command that we give rest to animals, and a sheep in a pit is not resting. The Pharisees go out to plot to destroy Jesus, which is hardly a proper use of the Sabbath (v. 14). Jesus isn't making exceptions. Pulling the sheep from the pit is not an exception to Sabbath-keeping. It *is* Sabbath-keeping because it's giving rest, just as it is "lawful to do good" by healing a man. Jesus' point is that Sabbath is for good and not for evil. He's saying the Sabbath was designed as an institution of compassion, not an institution of harshness. He's saying that the Sabbath is about rest, giving rest, rather than oppression. Jesus is *not* saying that need trumps keeping the law. He's saying that what the law aims at is giving relief and rest, and therefore our keeping of the law should aim at and achieve that intention. He's not saying that meeting needs is an *exception* to the law; He's saying that meeting needs is the *form* of law-keeping.

Jesus never broke the Sabbath or made exceptions to the biblical Sabbath rules. As Lord of Sabbath, He shows us what Sabbath-keeping is supposed to look like. What He shows us is that Sabbath-keeping is as much about giving relief and rest as it is about taking rest for ourselves. True Sabbath keeping includes pulling sheep from pits, healing men with withered hands, feeding the hungry. If we use the Sabbath laws to justify ignoring sheep who are in need, if we use the Sabbath laws to turn away people who need healing, if we use the Sabbath laws as a rationalization for not feeding the hungry, we are using the Sabbath laws contrary to their intention. The Sabbath is an institution of mercy, and our practices on the Sabbath should aim toward that, not against it.

This is a crucial question as we are thinking through our own Sabbath practices. Jesus doesn't abolish the Sabbath, and we are still supposed to observe the Sabbath today. But we have to think through what's involved, and we have to think it through based on Jesus' Sabbath-keeping—that is, do our Sabbath practices promote healing, relief, restoration; do your Sabbath practices relieve needs or intensify needs? Do our Sabbath practices heal or kill? We can't avoid getting into details: Is it right to shop on the Lord's Day? Is it right to eat at a restaurant and engage in other sorts of commerce? Is it work to do my schoolwork on the Sabbath? As you think about what to do on the Sabbath, ask yourself not only "Am I working?" but "Am I imposing burdens on others? Am I giving others rest?"

The Pharisees react violently to Jesus' Sabbath teaching. They think He is undermining the basic institution of Jewish life. Knowing that the Pharisees want to kill Him, Jesus withdraws (cf. 14:13; 15:21), widening the gap between Jesus' new Israel and the old Israel of the Pharisees. Matthew says that this withdrawal fulfills the prophecy of Isaiah 42. Instead of responding to the Pharisees, He quietly continues His ministry of healing (v. 15). He is bringing justice, but He does it as One who is gentle and lowly in heart.

The quotation from Isaiah sums up Jesus' work, much as the quotation in 8:17 did. Jesus is the Servant of Yahweh, the One chosen and beloved by His Father. Jesus is the One in whom the Father takes pleasure. Jesus has received the Spirit, and in the Spirit He gives rest and relief, performs miracles and exorcisms. Jesus comes proclaiming the kingdom, a kingdom of justice and peace, a kingdom of compassion and rest. Jesus' method is not one of showmanship, or one of quarrelsomeness. He withdraws and yields, moving away from confrontation with the Pharisees until the right time. He also acts in a way that doesn't destroy the reed that is fragile and might break, the wick that is smoldering and might go out. He doesn't quarrel and shout because He doesn't want anyone to be crushed, to be ground up and spit out in a confusing rumble. This quiet work, this quiet compassion, is not a defeatist work, a defeatist program. He does not withdraw because He's been beaten. He is acting this way because He is bringing justice to victory, and He is acting this way as the hope of the Gentiles.

We are servants of the living God, chosen and beloved. We have received the Spirit, the very same Spirit of Jesus, the Spirit now of resurrection power, and in that Spirit we proclaim justice to the nations, the justice of God in Jesus, the justice that God is bringing through Jesus. We are to follow Jesus in His humility, in His refusal to quarrel and shout and clamor and call attention to Himself. We are to follow Jesus in His compassion for the bruised reed and smoldering wick. We are to follow Jesus, who is Lord of the Sabbath, by giving rest, offering relief, showing mercy and compassion. That is true Sabbath-keeping. That is genuine law-keeping. This is the righteousness that exceeds the righteousness of the scribes and Pharisees.

The Spirit and Satan's Kingdom
Matthew 12:22-37

Then a demon-possessed man who was blind and mute was brought to Jesus, and He healed him, so that the mute man spoke and saw. [23] All the crowds were amazed, and were saying, "This man cannot be the Son of David, can he?" [24] But when the Pharisees heard this, they said, "This man casts out demons only by Beelzebul the ruler of the demons." [25] And knowing their thoughts Jesus said to them, "Any kingdom divided against itself is laid waste; and any city or house divided against itself will not stand. [26] "If Satan casts out Satan, he is divided against himself; how then will his kingdom stand? [27] "If I by Beelzebul cast out demons, by whom do your sons cast them out? For this reason they will be your judges. [28] "But if I cast out demons by the Spirit of God, then the kingdom of God has come upon you. [29] "Or how can anyone enter the strong

man's house and carry off his property, unless he first binds the strong man? And then he will plunder his house. [30] "He who is not with Me is against Me; and he who does not gather with Me scatters. [31] "Therefore I say to you, any sin and blasphemy shall be forgiven people, but blasphemy against the Spirit shall not be forgiven. [32] "Whoever speaks a word against the Son of Man, it shall be forgiven him; but whoever speaks against the Holy Spirit, it shall not be forgiven him, either in this age or in the age to come. [33] "Either make the tree good and its fruit good, or make the tree bad and its fruit bad; for the tree is known by its fruit. [34] "You brood of vipers, how can you, being evil, speak what is good? For the mouth speaks out of that which fills the heart. [35] "The good man brings out of his good treasure what is good; and the evil man brings out of his evil treasure what is evil. [36] "But I tell you that every careless word that people speak, they shall give an accounting for it in the day of judgment. [37] "For by your words you will be justified, and by your words you will be condemned."
– Matthew 12:22-37

C.S. Lewis warns against the error of taking the devil too seriously, obsessing over the devil, thinking that the devil is behind every inconvenience that we suffer. If the car won't start, it's the carburetor demon; if a child skins his knee, it's because of some low-ranking demon that specializes in causing pain to small children; if the evangelism campaign at the local church never gets off the ground, it's not organizational incompetence but the army of demons that don't want the gospel to go out. This is almost Manichean, the ancient heresy that said that the world was divided between warring Good and Evil principles, that are just about equally powerful.

Scripture makes it plain that the devil is not anywhere equal to God in power. It's clear from Job that the Satan can only cause mischief by Yahweh's permission. And in the New Testament, we see clearly that Jesus, and the saints, overcome Satan. Jesus is the Last Adam, the Seed of the Woman who crushes the head of the serpent, and Paul says that we will crush Satan under our feet as well. On the other side, there is the error of ignoring the devil, of mocking the notion that he's real or active. This can take a secular form. Many modern secularists think the notion of a personal locus of evil is absurd, despite the Gulag, despite Auschwitz, despite the genocide in Rwanda, despite the horrors of the last century. But Christians can use their theology to ignore what the Bible teaches about Satan. Satan is bound, postmillennial Christians like to say, and therefore we can safely ignore Him.

The gospels make it clear that demon possession is real and that demons cause bizarre, self-destructive, and violent behavior. But the New Testament also indicates that demonic and Satanic activity can take a corporate form. Paul talks about our combat with "spiritual forces of wickedness in the heavenly places," and the book of Revelation makes clear that Satan affects rulers and political institutions. In Revelation 13, the dragon, Satan, who has been cast from heaven to earth, calls up two beasts—one from the sea and one from the land—and these two beasts, inspired by the dragon, carry on a vicious persecution of the saints. These represent the Roman Empire and the Jews who join Rome in persecuting the church.

If you think this doesn't happen today, read or listen to some of the accounts of the genocide in Rwanda. The people who slaughtered their neighbors with machetes and left their bodies lying along the roads talk about being caught up in a frenzy that they couldn't control. There had been tribal hostilities between Hutus and Tutsis for generations; they let many suns go down on their anger. They gave the devil a huge opportunity. Satan lurks in the dark corners where people cultivate their anger.

Nowhere in the Bible do we find as many references to Satan or demons as in the gospels. We know from elsewhere in Scripture that the serpent that tempted Eve was the devil, the accuser, Satan, the great dragon. The early chapters of Job show Satan—named here for the first time as the "adversary" or "accuser"—in the presence of God, appearing with the sons of God to bring a charge against Job. We see Satan again in a similar position in the third chapter of Zechariah, standing as an accuser at the right hand of the high priest Joshua to accuse him—a "satan" to "satan" him. According to Chronicles, Satan enticed David to take a census of the people. There are a few scattered references to evil spirits in the Old Testament. Yahweh sends an evil spirit to disrupt the relations between Abimelech and the men of Shechem. He sends a spirit of some sort to deceive the prophets of King Ahab so that they entice him to go into battle where he will be killed. That's about it. There are only a handful of references to Satan and to evil spirits. As soon as Jesus appears on the scene, Satan is unleashed.

In Revelation, John depicts the dragon, Satan, waiting for the birth of a child, Jesus, in the hopes of devouring Him at his birth. Historically, this looked like Herod slaughtering infants, but behind this is Satan trying to stop the Messiah's work from happening. And in Matthew, as soon as Jesus appears on the scene, He goes into the wilderness to be tempted by the devil. Every time Matthew summarizes Jesus' ministry, He mentions that Jesus casts out demons (cf. 4:23-24; 8:16). He casts demons out of the Gadarene demoniacs (Matthew 8:38-34), He delivers a mute man from the evil spirit that possesses him (9:32-34), He sends His apostles out to heal and cast out demons (Matthew 10:8). Later, He will cast out a demon from the daughter of a Canaanite woman (15:22), and at the foot of the mount of Transfiguration He will cast a demon from a boy whom the disciples were unable to help (17:14-18). When Jesus arrives, Satan begins an all-out assault, and this provokes the great conflict at the center of history: Satan and his demons mount their all-out assault against Jesus, and Jesus as the Divine Warrior takes on the demons, fighting Satan himself in the wilderness and casting demons out. The crowds recognize what this means. The last time a man had such power over evil spirits, it was David. When Saul was plagued by evil spirits from God, David played the harp for him and drove the demons away. Now, Jesus is driving the spirits away from Israel, from the corrupted Israel ruled by the Saul-like Herod. He is, as the crowds begin to recognize, "the son of David" (12:23).

Not everyone sees it, though. Not everyone in Israel is convinced that Jesus is casting out demons as the son of David. Jesus drives a demon from a blind man, but the Pharisees who stand by watching it happen are blinder than the blind man. Jesus casts out a demon, and Israel is again divided. The crowds wonder if Jesus is the Messiah, David's Son. But the Pharisees think the opposite. In fact, the Pharisees are responding to the opinion of the crowds as much as to Jesus' own actions. Verse 24 says that the Pharisees begin accusing Jesus when they "heard it," that is, when they heard what the crowds were saying. The Pharisees think they have to act to prevent Jesus from gaining a foothold in Israel. They need to stop Him before the crowds conclude that He is indeed the son of David. And so, not for the first time, the Pharisees accuse Jesus of casting out demons by the power of Satan, using the name "Beelzebul," Lord of the flies, a name used only a few times in the Old Testament, and there always corrupted into Baalzebub, "Lord of the flies," which probably means "Lord of the garbage heap," or worse.

The last time they leveled this accusation, Jesus didn't respond (9:34). This time He does, with a series of arguments. Even if the charge were true, He points out, Jesus would be destroying Satan's kingdom, since He would be dividing Satan's kingdom (vv. 25-26). On the one hand, Jesus is accepting the Pharisees' premise and saying that if it were true, it would still mean that Satan's kingdom is doomed. Jesus would still be undermining Satan's kingdom. On the other hand, Jesus is showing the absurdity of their charge. Why would Satan give power to Jesus that Jesus is using to deliver men from the power of Satan? Why would Satan give power to Jesus in such a self-defeating way? Jesus says that He is "laying waste" Satan's kingdom, turning it into a desert. That's the word used for the destruction of the great city, the harlot, in Revelation, and that's talking about Jerusalem. This suggests, I think, that He's talking about Israel as Satan's kingdom. The Jews have taken Satan as their father, and as Satan's kingdom is laid waste, Israel is being devastated. Besides, the Pharisees are inconsistent. They too acknowledge exorcisms, and if Jesus casts out the demons by Satan's power, what do the Pharisees say about their own disciples ("sons," v. 27)? What is the difference? How can they charge Jesus without also charging their sons and disciples?

Jesus' alternative explanation for His power over Satan is the Spirit.[22] The fact that He is able to cast out demons by the Spirit (cf. 3:16; 12:18) is a sign that God has begun His triumphant conquest (12:28). What is Jesus saying here about other exorcists? Is he saying that other exorcists also have power over demons? Is he saying that their power over demons also manifests the kingdom of God? Jesus acknowledges, it seems, that there are other exorcists who actually cast out demons. But He claims to have unique power to cast out demons. He claims to do it in a new way, a way that no one else has done. As Matthew told us at the end of the previous section, Jesus is the one who has the "Spirit upon Him" to "proclaim justice to the Gentiles" and to bring justice to victory (12:18, 20). Jesus is uniquely endowed by the Spirit, and this is what gives Him unique power to cast out demons.[23]

---

22. When Ahaziah the son of Ahab sends messengers to consult the Baal-zebub of Ekron, Elijah confronts the messages with the question, "Is there no God in Israel, that you go to inquire of Baal-zebub?" (2 Kings 1:1-4). Elijah is himself a "man of hair" (literally, a "baal" of hair), and proves that he, as the man of God, has more power than the god of Ekron. The question about Yahweh's absence from the land is a key one in the passage, and this story echoes in the background of the incident in the gospel. Jesus is the presence of Yahweh among the Jews, but the Jews think He manifests the presence of a false god.

23. How could the Pharisees have guessed that He's doing it differently from others? The answer becomes obvious when we consider accounts of Jewish exorcisms from the intertestamental period. Dennis Duling has written, "In a reinterpretation of a Genesis story in the Dead Sea Scrolls, Abraham is said to have exorcized a demon from Pharaoh by prayer, the laying on of hands, and rebuking the evil spirit (GenApoc 20:16-19). David was said to have done the same thing by playing his harp (LibAntBib 60:1-3) and Noah by medicines and herbs (Jubilees 10:10-14). Solomon was especially remembered for his wisdom-- here we note the influence of the Wisdom tradition--and that wisdom included his vast knowledge of magic and medicine" (Duling and Norman Perrin, *The New Testament: An Introduction* [Harcourt Brace Jovanovich, 1982], p.33). Josephus writes, "He put to the nose of the possessed man a ring which had under its seal one of the roots prescribed by Solomon, and then, as the man smelled it, drew out the demon through his nostrils, and, when the man at once fell down, adjured the demon never to come back into him, speaking Solomon's name and reciting the incantations which he had composed" (*Antiquities* 5:2, 5). Demons

The Pharisees should have seen the personal authority that Jesus had over demons, and should have recognized that something unique was happening. Jesus is triumphing over Satan Himself, not appealing to God, not using magic and devices. He has authority over demons because of who He is, because He is endowed by the Spirit. Again, the Pharisees don't discern the signs of the times (11:16-19). They can see that Jesus is casting out demons, and they should be able to conclude from this that Jesus' power is the power of God at work. Jesus' ministry shows the ministry promised to the Servant of Yahweh who would lead Israel out of exile and bring blessing to the nations. The Pharisees can't deny that Jesus is casting out demons. But they claim that it is not a sign of the kingdom or of the Spirit; they claim that it is the opposite. They can't see the point of what's right in front of their eyes.

Jesus explains with a brief parable alluding to the exodus. One can only defeat and plunder a strong man by binding him (v. 29). Jesus binds the strong man, Satan, and, as Israel plundered Pharaoh, so Jesus plunders the house of Satan. In Luke's account of this debate, the reference to the exodus is even more explicit. Jesus says there that He casts out demons by the "finger of God" (Luke 11:20), and this refers back to the power of God exerted in the exodus plagues (Exodus 8:19). Jesus is the greater Moses, the Son of David, who casts out demons, who comes to deliver Saul-Israel from the evil spirits that plague them. Jesus says that He comes as the Divine Warrior, in the power of the Spirit, to do battle with Satan and the evil spirits. He is the Spirit-filled Son of David, the Servant of Yahweh. This is the climactic battle of the ages, a battle for the future and control of Israel and of the creation. In

---

play a prominent role in the story of Tobit as well, and the methods of exorcism are bizarre. Jesus' exorcisms were clearly of a different order than these Jewish exorcisms. Jesus cast out demons by His own authority, by His word, without incantations or fish-based fumigants.

To the Lost Sheep

this war between the Satan and the Spirit, there is no neutrality: Whoever is not with the Spirit-filled Servant is an enemy and will be bound and plundered along with Satan.

Jesus heals a blind man, but the Pharisees are the real blind men in the story. Jesus heals a mute man, but the Pharisees are the ones who need their tongues healed, who need to have their tongues loosed to praise God. Jesus says, "Don't you see? Can't you see that I cast out demons by the Spirit? Can't you see that the kingdom of God has come?" Then He talks about their blasphemy and their evil fruit. Verses 31-32 have often been isolated from the context and interpreted as a passage about "the unforgivable sin." Many faithful Christians have worried if they have committed the unforgivable sin, worried that they might have done something that will make it impossible for them to return and be forgiven. Some have interpreted this verse as an example of hyperbole: Jesus is not actually saying that there is such a thing as a sin that God doesn't forgive. He's saying that there are sins that put people in great danger. He's saying that there are people who commit sins that get *close* to the point of no return, but He doesn't say that anyone ever actually crosses the line. But this doesn't fit with other passages of the New Testament, where it's clear that there are sins that God holds against people and that He does not forgive (cf. Hebrews 6:4-8; 12:15-17; 1 John 5:16-17). All these passages deal with people who have turned away from Christ after being brought into the life of the new covenant. They have shared in the blessings of the new covenant, and then have turned into enemies of Christ. In historical context, these passages are mainly about Judaizers, or those who return to Judaism after being converted to Jesus. They have committed an act of apostasy that will not be forgiven. Even in these cases, though, these passages are not talking about a situation where someone is remorseful for sin and returns to the love of Jesus, and yet Jesus rejects him. Esau seeks "with tears" to have the birthright back, but he found no place for repentance, and therefore didn't receive the birthright. God gives people over to their sins, but this doesn't mean that we really want to repent and can't. We harden ourselves and don't want to repent. God hardens us.

Jesus' saying should be understood redemptive-historically. Jesus distinguishes blasphemy against the Son of Man from blasphemy against the Spirit. He is the Son of Man, and He comes in humility. Those who reject Him will have a chance to repent. The Jews will put Jesus the Son of Man on the cross and kill Him, but once the Spirit comes at Pentecost, the Jews are told again and again what they've done, and many repent and are forgiven, forgiven specifically for blasphemy against the Son of Man. The Pharisees have perhaps committed the former, charging Jesus, the Son of Man, with being in league with Satan. Some of the Pharisees in Acts, after all, repent and become disciples and members of the church. But some of the Pharisees are also blaspheming against the work of the Spirit that Jesus is performing. They charge that exorcisms by the power of the Spirit were in fact empowered by Satan. They have already hardened themselves against the Spirit. And after His ministry comes the age of the Spirit, beginning at Pentecost, and the Pharisees who blasphemed the Spirit from the beginning will continue to blaspheme the Spirit.

The Pharisees' condemnation of Jesus has only one explanation: They are evil trees and bear evil fruit (v. 33). Jesus is referring specifically to their words.[24] The "good/evil" fruit is the "evil speech" of verse 34. Jesus has several points about the Pharisees' speech, points that apply quite directly to us. They are little snakes, spawn of the serpent, and the poison of asps is under their tongues (v. 34; cf. Psalm 140:3). Words can be used satanically, used for accusation and condemnation and blasphemy rather than for health.

---

24. The chiasm of these verses reinforces this point:
   A. Blasphemy
      B. Good/evil
         C. Vipers
      B'. Good/evil
   A'. Careless words

As is often the case in Scripture, Jesus points to an inherent relationship between the heart and the tongue. The mouth speaks what comes from the heart. They show their Satanic inspiration in what they speak, for what fills the mouth comes out in speech. Good men bring out good words from the treasure of their heart, and evil hearts flow with evil words. We can speak lies—cover over our real character with deceptive talk. But our lies still flow from our hearts—they come from the evil treasure of our hearts. What we need to speak rightly is a change of heart; we need to have a different treasure chest, become different sorts of trees. We need to have the demons driven from us, as Jesus drove them from the blind and mute man, so that our tongues can work properly.

Our words are thus the standard by which we will be judged. Though we are accepted before God by faith without works, we will finally be judged by our works and words (cf. Romans 2:1-16). So, be careful how you talk, because we have to give account of careless words (v. 36). Jesus condemns the Pharisees here. They are blinder than the man Jesus heals. Their mouths speak blasphemies. They need to be delivered from the power of Satan through the power of the Spirit. But we are like them. We are blind to God's work; our mouths are full of cursing and deceit, full of deadly poison. We too need to be plundered from the house of the strong man. But that's precisely what Jesus has come to do: To open the eyes of blind people, like us; to loose the tongues of blasphemers, like us; to deliver us from Satan's kingdom by the power of His Spirit.

Sign of Jonah
Matthew 12:38-50

Then some of the scribes and Pharisees said to Him, "Teacher, we want to see a sign from You." [39] But He answered and said to them, "An evil and adulterous generation craves for a sign; and yet no sign will be given to it but the sign of Jonah the prophet; [40] for just as Jonah was three days and three nights in the belly of the sea monster, so will the Son of Man be three days and three nights in the heart of the earth. ⁴¹ "The men of Nineveh will stand up with this generation at the judgment, and will condemn it because they repented at the preaching of Jonah; and behold, something greater than Jonah is here. ⁴² "The Queen of the South will rise up with this generation at the judgment and will condemn it, because she came from the ends of the earth to hear the wisdom of Solomon; and behold, something greater than Solomon is here. ⁴³ "Now when the unclean spirit goes out of a man, it passes through waterless places seeking rest, and does not find it. ⁴⁴ "Then it says, 'I will return to my house from which I came'; and when it comes, it finds it unoccupied, swept, and put in order. ⁴⁵ "Then it goes and takes along with it seven other spirits more wicked than itself, and they go in and live there; and the last state of that man becomes worse than the first. That is the way it will also be with this evil generation." ⁴⁶ While He was still speaking to the crowds, behold, His mother and brothers were standing outside, seeking to speak to Him. ⁴⁷ Someone said to Him, "Behold, Your mother and Your brothers are standing outside seeking to speak to You." ⁴⁸ But Jesus answered the one who was telling Him and said, "Who is My mother and who are My brothers?" ⁴⁹ And stretching out His hand toward His disciples, He said, "Behold My mother and My brothers! ⁵⁰ "For whoever does the will of My Father who is in heaven, he is My brother and sister and mother. – Matthew 12:38-50

Matthew presents Jesus as the true Israel, the new Israel who is living through Israel's history again, this time faithfully, without sin. Part of Matthew's depiction of Jesus is to show that He fills the roles of various Old Testament figures. In the early chapters of Matthew, Jesus is shown as the new Moses and the new Israel. He is rescued from a murderous king as a baby, just as Moses was. He goes to Egypt, recalling Moses' time in Egypt. He is baptized in the Jordan River, as Moses led Israel through the Red Sea at the exodus. Jesus stands on a mountain to deliver the law, and then He commissions His twelve apostles to conquer the land, as Moses instructed Israel on how to conquer the Canaanites in the land.

The focus is shifting in chapter 12. Jesus has been the new and greater Moses, but now the focus is shifting. When Jesus casts out a demon from a mute and blind man, the crowds don't wonder if He's Moses, but they wonder if He's the "son of David" (v. 23).

That is a good speculation, since David is the one man in the Old Testament who showed some power over evil spirits, driving away the spirit that plagued Saul by playing His lyre. Jesus is also like David in that He shows Himself a *gibbor*, a strong man, a mighty man, confronting Satan's kingdom, binding the strong man in order to plunder his house. By the end of chapter 12, Jesus is comparing Himself to Solomon (v. 42). And in the following chapter, He takes the role of Solomon in teaching about the kingdom of God in parables. But there's not a clean break. The Scriptures are too rich to be cleanly boxed into one or another category. The focus is shifting to Jesus as the son of David, the greater Solomon, but this chapter also includes some references to the generation of the exodus as well, and to other periods of Israel's history.

Jesus has made claims, and the Pharisees want to see them backed up. They are looking for a sign from heaven, a sign from God that proves Jesus' claims to cast out Satan by the power of the Spirit. They want God to authenticate this, to demonstrate by some sign that it's all true. Jesus treats the demand for a sign as itself a sign of evil and faithlessness. Satan demanded signs from Jesus to show that He was Son of God (Matthew 4:1-11). If you are the Son of God, Satan said, make these stones into bread, cast yourself from the top of the temple. If you are the Son of God, prove it by some sign, some miracle. The Pharisees make the same demand. Despite the many signs Jesus has done, the scribes and Pharisees make the same demand (12:38), thus proving they are spawn of vipers (12:34). They show that they are children of their father the devil.

Jesus declares this generation an "evil and adulterous generation" (v. 39). He is making a specific allusion to the generation of Israel that came out of Egypt. The only time the Old Testament uses the phrase "evil generation," it is in reference to the generation that rebelled against Yahweh in the wilderness. That generation had witnessed the plagues; they had seen the sea divided in two; they had seen water gush from the rock and found manna all over the ground. They had heard the voice of Yahweh from the mountain and caught a glimpse of the glory of the Lord in the face of Moses. Despite it all, they still asked "Is God among us or no?" In spite of all these assurances of Yahweh's favor to Israel, they turned from Him and rebelled again and again. An "adulterous" generation is comparable to Israel in the wilderness (cf. Matthew 16:4; Mark 8:38; Isaiah 57:3). Jesus is leading Israel out of an Egypt of oppression, but Israel grumbles. He is calling Israel to repentance, but they wonder if Yahweh is really with them. Despite all his miracles and signs, they still ask for a sign.

But what makes this generation "adulterous"? Why add that epithet? The idea in the background is that Israel is the bride of Yahweh, called to be faithful to her husband. More specifically, Jesus seems to be alluding to Hosea 3. John Nolland points out that the combination "evil and adulterous" is found in the Septuagint of Hosea 3:1, applied to Gomer. He suggests that by using this phrase, Jesus is echoing Hosea and implicitly comparing the Jews to the generation of the exile.[25] This makes sense of the following verses in Matthew 12, where Jesus moves from condemning the adulterous generation to saying that He will give the sign of Jonah. Jonah, of course, was the prophet who delivered Nineveh from destruction, so that the Assyrians survived to destroy the Northern kingdom. Hosea's "evil and adulterous" bride/generation was, in fact, the same generation as Jonah's (both during the days of Jeroboam II, Hosea 1:1; 2 Kings 14:23-25).

This reference helps to specify the nature of the adultery of the scribes and Pharisees. Hosea 3:1 explicitly compares the adulteress to Israel: "Go again, love a woman who is loved by her husband, yet an adulteress, even as Yahweh loves the sons of Israel, though they turn to other gods and love raisin cakes." By asking for a sign, Jesus implies, the scribes and Pharisees are betraying their love for other gods. Jesus is the bridegroom (9:15), but their demand for a sign veils the bride's preference for

---

25. Nolland, *The Gospel of Matthew: A Commentary on the Greek Text* (NIGTC; Grand Rapids: Eerdmans, 2005), p. 510.

another. Behind their apparently innocent request for a sign is lust for another husband. If the generation is adulterous, then it's not surprising if she receives divorce papers, which is what Jesus will later warn. The city will be burned, like the daughter of the priest who commits harlotry.

Jesus promises only one sign, the sign of Jonah (v. 39). The sign of Jonah is a complex sign. It's not just one thing. The explicit comparison that Jesus makes is between Himself and Jonah, between Himself dying and going into the earth and Jonah being swallowed by a fish. Jesus will be in the "heart of the earth" (or "land") for three days and nights, just as Jonah was in the heart of the sea.[26] Then Jesus will be raised up, just as Jonah was vomited back from the great fish. But to see the full scope of the sign of Jonah, we need to remember the whole story of Jonah, not merely the most famous part about Jonah being swallowed by a fish. Jonah was sent by Yahweh to preach to the city of Nineveh, and he initially refused to go. Why? Jonah was not a coward. He was not faithless. He was not even, in any simple sense, opposed to the conversion of Gentiles. He was a true prophet of Yahweh, and as such He believed in the Abrahamic promise that the Lord would

---

26. James Jordan has handled the problems surrounding Jesus' "three days and three nights in the heart of the earth" (Matthew 12:40) not by pushing Jesus' death back from Friday to mid-week but by reinterpreting what "heart of the earth" means. Earth often signifies land, the land of Israel, and being at the "heart of the earth" means being thrust into the central power structures of Judaism, swallowed like Jonah into the "belly of the beast." Matthew's chronology of Jesus' final days fits that supposition in certain respects. Assuming that Matthew is indicating the days in sequence, without any gaps, we have this result:

Evening #1: Jesus has a meal with His disciples, prays and is betrayed in Gethsemane, is tried by the Sanhedrin, 26:20-75

Day #1: Jesus is tried before Pilate and is crucified, 27:1-56

Evening #2: Jesus is buried, 27:57-61

Day #2: Day of preparation, 27:62

Evening #3: Guard set at Jesus' tomb, 27:62-66

Day #3: First day of the week, Jesus rises, 28:1

This leaves us with a very partial "Day #3," since the women discover that Jesus' tomb is empty "as it began to dawn toward the first of the week" (28:1). But Matthew does begin enumerating the days, which appear to fulfill Jesus' prediction, not from the time of His death but from the time of His arrest and trial.

bring the Gentiles to faith. Jonah also knew the song of Moses, in Deuteronomy 32, the song that Moses was to teach Israel as a reminder to them to keep the law. In that song, the Lord said that He would abandon Israel for other nations if she abandoned Him for other gods. If Israel provoked Yahweh to jealousy with what were not gods, Yahweh would provoke Israel with people that were not a people: "They have made Me jealous with what is not God; they have provoked Me to anger with their idols so I will make them jealous with those who are not a people; I will provoke them to anger with a foolish nation" (v. 21). Jonah knew that Israel was faithless, and that the Lord was sending him to a foolish nation to provoke Israel to jealousy. Jonah knew that when Yahweh sent His prophet to another nation, then the Lord was judging Israel. Jonah's generation was also an "evil and adulterous generation," and the Lord provoked His faithless bride to jealousy by turning to Nineveh. So, part of the message of the sign of Jonah is that the Lord is going to turn to another nation and will provoke Israel to jealousy. Jonah was a preacher to the Gentiles, and part of the sign of Jonah is the fact that Jesus' disciples will take the gospel to Gentiles (vv. 41-43). The Ninevites received Jonah's preaching, though he preached without showing signs, and thus showed they were more worthy of the kingdom than Israel.

Beyond this, the sign of Jonah includes hope for the success of a mission to the Gentiles. Nineveh repented, and the Gentiles of the first century will do the same, responding to the preaching of the apostles when the Jews refuse. Jonah preached to Nineveh, and Nineveh repented, was spared, and later turned on Israel and took the Northern kingdom of Israel into captivity. This too is part of Jesus' warning to the Jews—they will face a Gentile power that will take away their temple and their kingdom and scatter them.

The sign of Jonah is also, ultimately, a sign of the rescue and salvation of Israel. Jonah represents Israel as a whole, the people who worships the God of heaven and earth and sea. And as the representative Israelite, he is cast into the sea. The sea is a common image of the Gentile nations, and Jonah cast into the sea is a symbol of exile. The grave that Jonah goes to is the grave of exile, and this means that when the great sea creature vomits Jonah back to land, he is being restored from the sea of the nations, restored from exile. The story of Jonah is the story of Yahweh provoking Israel to jealousy; it's the story of Yahweh showing mercy to a nation other than Israel; it's a story about the Lord's raising up a Gentile nation that will be His axe against Israel; but it's also a story about exile and return, about death and resurrection. When Jesus says He fulfills the sign of Jonah, He is talking about this entire story line. That is the one sign that He will give the generation.

The sign of Jonah is not just the resurrection, but the fact that Gentiles will rise up to condemn the generation of Israel that saw something greater than Jonah. Likewise, the Queen of Sheba (cf. 1 Kings 10) sought the wisdom of Solomon, while the scribes and Pharisees refuse to accept Wisdom Incarnate.

Solomon gained an international reputation due to the wise organization of his kingdom, and the wealth and success that he had. People came from all over the world to learn of the wisdom of Solomon. But the exemplar of Gentile interest in the kingdom of Solomon is the Queen of Sheba, who came to ask Solomon questions and to see his kingdom. Sheba came as a skeptic. She tells Solomon she didn't believe the reports that she heard about Solomon's kingdom. But when she asked Solomon questions, and saw the organization of his kingdom, she said that the truth was even greater than Solomon's reputation. She was breathless and confessed that the God of Solomon was a great God. Jesus is greater than Solomon. He is the Wisdom of God in human flesh. And yet, though He is greater than Solomon, the scribes and Pharisees don't respond. Sheba had to travel across the world to hear Solomon's wisdom; Jesus comes directly to the scribes and Pharisees, but they refuse to hear His wisdom, and instead of confessing the wisdom of God they stand in judgment over that wisdom.

Jesus' parable about the demon is also about "this evil generation" (v. 45). This parable seems to come up abruptly, but it's on topic. Jesus is talking about the generation of Jews to whom He has ministered. It is a summary of Jesus' ministry and the consequences of the rejection by Israel's leaders. Jesus drives demons from Israel. They are driven out of the fruitful Edenic land of Israel into the wilderness areas. They are driven from the well-watered garden into the dry places. The Old Testament frequently associates various kinds of predators and scavengers with the wilderness, and demons are associated with these predators. Jesus comes to drive them out and to restore the land to His people. Jesus has been doing that. He has been driving out demons by the power of the Spirit so that the land can be restored and flourish by that Spirit. Though Jesus has driven out the demons, Israel has not accepted Jesus. They have been resisting and blaspheming the Spirit. And the result will be that those who have been cleansed of unclean demons will find the demons coming back. The demons will return in force because Israel has not received the Spirit that Jesus brings. Nature abhors a vacuum, and so does the human soul. If the demons are driven out and nothing takes its place, the last state will be worse than the first. The story Jesus tells here has very concrete, political implications. By the end of the generation, the Jews had lathered themselves into a frenzy of rebellion against Rome, which led to the destruction of Jerusalem and its temple.

As Jesus had said before, Whoever is not with me scatters abroad. If Jesus drives out a devil, and yet the person from whom it is driven does not attach to Jesus and follow Him, then that person is going to be against Jesus. The victory of Jesus over Satan is only a temporary victory, an interlude (Harrington) because the generation is adulterous. Because the generation is evil and looks for another husband, she will eventually be infested with more demons than ever. Jesus has been defining His disciples over against the generation of Jews, who in their lust for another husband, another god, have sought for a sign. The family has been disrupted. The bride has been adulterous, and this means that the family is topsy turvy.

This comes out in Jesus' response to someone who tells him that His brothers and mother are waiting to see Him. Jesus has apparently been teaching in a house, or at least there's a large enough crowd to create an "inside" and an "outside." Significantly,

Jesus' mother and brothers are standing outside wanting to come in. This doesn't necessarily mean that they are outside the circle of Jesus' disciples and followers. Jesus' brothers are named in 13:55, and 13:56 mentions that Jesus has sisters as well. And some of the members of Jesus' family became believers, followers of Jesus. Mary shows great faith in her response to the angel's announcement that she will become the mother of the Messiah, and later she's among the disciples as they wait for the gift of the Spirit at Pentecost. James the brother of Jesus was also a believer, as Paul says (Acts 1:14; Galatians 1:19). But their blood kinship with Jesus is not what makes them part of the "inside group." What Jesus says is pretty shocking to our ears, and it would be even more to Jewish ears in the first century. He is not disowning His mother, but He almost sounds as if He is disowning her. He is saying that His disciples are as much His mother as Mary is. As He often does, Jesus relativizes family bonds. James and Mary and the others are not part of Jesus' family simply by being related to Him by blood. What makes someone a mother or brother of Jesus is not blood but doing "the will of My Father who is in heaven" (Matthew 12:50).

Christians have sometimes exalted blood kinship, going against Jesus' repeated teaching about blood kinship. This happens when Christians adopt a kind of familialism that makes the blood family equal to, even greater than, the spiritual family of the church. The Jews had made an idol of blood kinship. To be a true member of the people of God meant sharing the blood of Abraham. As a result, they despised Gentiles, even God-fearing Gentiles, as lesser humans. Christians have sometimes exalted blood kinship with Jesus in a way that doesn't fit with Jesus' own teaching. This happens more traditionally when, because of Mary's blood kinship with Jesus, her role in redemption is exaggerated and distorted. Mary was a faithful believer; she is to be honored above all women; she is a model for the Christian and the church. But according to Jesus, she is truly mother of Jesus because of her faith, not because she carried Him in her womb.

Jesus doesn't endorse either of these. Jesus radically relativizes blood relations. What matters for being a family member in Jesus' house is not blood but behavior. This passage is about "this generation," but it is also about the definition of the people of God. What defines the disciples of Jesus, His family, His "inner circle"? Jesus defines His disciples by distinguishing them from the "evil and adulterous generation" of Jews who oppose Him. Jesus also defines His disciples by distinguishing them from the blood family, from the fleshly relations. His family is not defined by Jewishness; the Jewish leaders have become adulterers. His family is not defined by blood. Positively, Jesus says that His family is those who do the will of the Father who is in heaven. Who is the mother of Jesus? You are if you do His Father's commandments. Who are His brothers and sisters? All who do His will. Are you a brother of Jesus? Are you His mother? That is to say, are you doing the will of His Father? Are you doing righteousness that surpasses that of the scribes?

www.ingramcontent.com/pod-product-compliance
Lightning Source LLC
Chambersburg PA
CBHW050628300426
44112CB00012B/1703